EXCEPTIONAL LEARNERS

ABOUT THE AUTHOR

Ivan Z. Holowinsky is a professor of educational psychology, Graduate School of Education and a member of Graduate Faculty in Psychology at Rutgers University. He is a fellow of the American Psychological Association, American Psychological Society, the American Association on Mental Retardation, and American Academy of School Psychology. Holowinsky was a Fulbright scholar to Ukraine in 1995. His research interests include mental retardation, developmental disabilities, East European psychology, and special education. He is author of *Psychology of Exceptional Children and Adolescents: U.S. and International Developments* (1983) and co-editor of *Teacher Education in Industrialized Nations* (with N. Ken Shimahara, 1995).

EXCEPTIONAL LEARNERS

Education and Research from a Global Perspective

By

IVAN Z. HOLOWINSKY

Rutgers University

Charles C Thomas

P U B L I S H E R • L T D.

SPRINGFIELD • ILLINOIS • U.S.A.

Published and Distributed Throughout the World by

CHARLES C THOMAS • PUBLISHER, LTD.
2600 South First Street
Springfield, Illinois 62704

©2001 by CHARLES C THOMAS • PUBLISHER, LTD.

ISBN 0-398-07163-2 (cloth)
ISBN 0-398-07164-0 (paper)

Library of Congress Catalog Card Number: 00-050950

Printed in the United States of America
SR-R-3

Library of Congress Cataloging-in-Publication Data

Holowinsky, Ivan Z.
Exceptional learners : education and research from a global perspective / Ivan Z.
Holowinsky.
p. cm.
Includes bibliographical references and index.
ISBN 0-398-07163-2 (cloth) – ISBN 0-398-07164-0 (pbk.)
1. Special education. I. Title.

LC3965 .H63 2001
371.9–dc21

00-050950

This book is dedicated to the loving memory of my parents and to my wife, children, and grandchildren, whose support, understanding, and patience made easier the accomplishment of this task.

FOREWORD

The task of establishing and extending the provision of the education of exceptional learners and those with special needs is indeed challenging. More basically, much can be done to assure that special needs populations receive the best programs and services possible, informed by sound research practices and evaluation results. This has been the case in the past, currently, and no doubt into the foreseeable future.

In addition, the above challenge and task, now more than ever, has taken on global proportions. As we enter the new millennium and as advances in electronic communications occur on almost a daily basis, there is need for comprehensive and substantive information about research and education in special education, especially in relation to issues and trends from around the world.

Information of this nature and scope can help a range of people to become more informed about, aware of, and motivated toward the design, implementation, and evaluation of effective and efficient programs and services for the exceptional learners within relevant cultures and linguistic contexts. These people include policy makers, educational administrators, psychologists, teachers, parents and, indeed, exceptional learners themselves.

Professor Ivan Holowinsky's academic career has been highlighted by unswerving dedication to better understanding issues and trends in special education and related services. In particular, Professor Holowinsky's scholarly work has focused, in a stellar manner, on the education of the exceptional learner not only in the United States but also in many other countries. This concern has included attention to both established and developing countries alike.

This book, authored by Professor Holowinsky, is a creative effort on his part. Herein, he has analyzed and synthesized a range of forces and factors that have shaped the education of the exceptional learner down through the ages. In addition, he had melded this information into ten carefully sequenced chapters that take the reader on a journey through important origins of special education, actually from ancient Greek times, and then up to and including the present. As such, he has done so with due references to important developments in all parts of the world.

Chapter 1 of this volume provides a clear, concise, and cogent rationale for the relevance of taking a global perspective on the education of exceptional populations.

Chapter 2 offers an account of special education from its historical roots and shows how culture has played a big part in special education, albeit always not as people had expected.

Chapters 3 and 4 discuss the various ways that exceptionalities can be considered including normative, physical, psychological, educational, sociological, and anthropological viewpoints.

In Chapter 5, the notion of general education is examined from various geographical points of contact including international agencies such as UNESCO.

Chapters 6 and 7 focus on particular programs and services from around the world for exceptional individuals. Relatedly, Chapter 8 considers teacher training and other programs of professional preparation for those who desire to work with exceptional learners.

Chapter 9 attends to research with exceptional learners over the course of the last century. Finally, and most importantly, Chapter 10 discusses trends in the education of the exceptional, worldwide.

For about twenty years, I have had the good fortune to have provided program planning and evaluation assistance to agencies serving the exceptional learner in many of the countries that are referred to by Professor Holowinsky. From my experiences in such settings, coupled with those of colleagues, this book provides valid, practical, yet scholarly context-based information.

The insights, opinions, and directions provided by Professor Holowinsky herein comprise nourishing and refreshing food for thought–and then some–for policy makers, researchers, administrators, psychologists, educational consultants, teachers, parents, and students of the education of the exceptional learners.

Charles A. Maher, PsyD, ABPDC
Professor of Psychology
(Former Director, Rutgers School Psychology Program)
Graduate School of Applied and Professional Psychology
Rutgers University
152 Frelinghuysen Road
Piscataway, NJ 08854-8085

PREFACE

For thousands of years humans have been both intellectual and social creatures. Their intellectual faculties enabled humans to reflect upon the past, to understand the present, and to project into the future. With the emergence of the written systems thousands of years ago in Egypt and Central Africa, it became possible for the ancient civilizations to preserve and transmit existing knowledge to future generations. Approximately at that time the first book depositories of "libraries" were established in Egypt and Africa.

Throughout history knowledge dissemination and utilization in short education became a crucial factor in socio-cultural evolution. This position has been accepted especially by social reformers and fundamentalists alike. An extreme example of this emphasis can be found in Marxist-Leninist education (Holowinsky, 1999). Within the field of education, however, a subgroup emerged in the nineteenth century commonly known at the present as education of exceptional learners or special education.

Initially the roots of special education or child study in Europe can be traced to the philosophical influence of empiricism. It is evident that empiricism was very strong in Europe in the nineteenth century and it did influence the thinking of Itard and Seguin, pioneers in the education and training of handicapped and mentally retarded children (Spitz, 1986). Toward the end of the nineteenth century and the beginning of the twentieth, the strong movement known as pedology emerged in Europe. It was defined as the study of the child from all facets (Depaepe, 1985). In the Fall of 1909, with the help of a group of teachers in Lviv (at that time in Austro-Hungary) Professor Twardowski organized a pedological society. The next year, a similar society was organized in Cracow (Grudzinska, 1912).

It is a generally accepted premise that Special Education evolved from general education in order to provide training and education for exceptional learners. As a discipline within the field of education its foundations include three emphases: research, teaching and service. Earlier emphasis upon child study in order to identify children in need of special services promoted the development of such fields as pedology and individual intelligence testing (Binet-Simon). However, equally or even more important for special education is the development of methodologies that will enable an exceptional learner to develop his/her maximum potential. Unfortunately, over reliance upon methodologies is not sufficient and could be misleading. We should not forget that very important is the human element or personality qualities of a teacher. As the history of the field reveals, pioneers in special education were idealistic individuals, dedicated to the education of exceptional learners.

The direction of special education in the near future will also be based upon the resolution of many of the unsolved issues. Some of those issues have to do with the nature of the relationship between maturation, learning and training; the relationship between cognitive levels and direct training; quantitative and/or qualitative differences between retarded and nonretarded populations; and teaching skills and strategies for exceptional children. In the long run, issues and problems in special education can only be viewed in the context of past practices, current needs and future discoveries.

A global view of education of exceptional learners reveals a complex tapestry of interrelative factors. Historically, cultural, traditional, socio-economic, as well as political realities should be kept in mind in order to understand special education in various regions and countries.

Apart from the differences, there are unique factors in special education that make it a separate discipline. In my judgment the three most important factors are:

a) Pedagogical methodology to maximize cognitive development and emotional adjustment of exceptional learners.

b) Personality qualities, attitudes and skills to deal with individual differences of exceptional learners.

c) Ability to appreciate and recognize individual differences and to conduct instruction accordingly.

The purpose of this book is to provide as much as possible an overview of special education from a global perspective and to help the reader in his/her search for more information. It is apparent that the education of exceptional learners worldwide presents a very complex picture. It is obvious that the development of programs did not occur at the same time. As recently as the 1970s only eighteen countries provided services for the communication disabled, four for the gifted, and three for the learning disabled. There is also a wide discrepancy per country in the percentage of elementary or secondary pupils receiving special education services. The range is one in twenty in the United States to one in five thousand in less developed countries.

The enormity of the problems in developing countries has been recently emphasized by Rampaul et al. (1992), who estimated that more than two hundred million children with special needs are experiencing learning difficulties. The twenty-first century will present new challenges and new opportunities for education of exceptional learners. New educational technologies will facilitate rapid knowledge dissemination. At the same time information overload will create a need for careful analysis of available data. In spite of technological advances human factor will always be crucial in the education of exceptional learners. To make a global impact in the areas of greatest need, special education, will require commitment of caring teachers like the pioneers: Helen Keller, Maria Grzegorzewska, Janush Korczak or Ivan Sokolansky and the willingness of advanced societies to share their technologies and resources with those in greatest need.

Ivan Z. Holowinsky
Rutgers

ACKNOWLEDGMENTS

I would like to acknowledge the support, advice, and encouragement of many professional colleagues who made this work possible. I would like to express sincere thanks to Louise C. Wilkinson, the dean of the Graduate School of Education, whose interest in international education provided encouragement. I am indebted to my professional colleagues Nobuo K. Shimahara, Stanley Vitello, Petro P. Kononenko, and Anatoliy Pohribny for their helpful suggestions. Many sincere thanks to Sandra Chubrick who provided expert typing and preparation of the manuscript, as well as suggestions concerning the style and English grammar.

CONTENTS

CONTENTS

EXCEPTIONAL LEARNERS

Chapter 1

RATIONALE FOR THE BOOK AND
OVERVIEW OF THE CONTENT

We are into the twenty-first century, and our time is characterized by changes in education brought about by new technologies, mass media, distance learning, electronic communication, and emphasis on exchanges of ideas and cross-cultural cooperation. Interest in international issues and trends has become obvious in the past twenty years. It is conceivable that a future reader may refer to the 1990s as the decade of international efforts in education. *International* became a popular word, with some journals emphasizing "international" in their titles. One example of this group is the *International Journal of Special Education,* published in Canada since 1986.

Clearly, an information explosion has occurred in the field of education of exceptional learners. However, the need exists to present this information from a global perspective in a single volume for easy, comprehensive overview. It is expected that this book will be used as a source of information for teacher educators and psychologists interested in developments in the field of education of exceptional learners.

The material in this book is organized into ten chapters. Chapter 1 will present a rationale for the book and a brief overview of the content. Chapter 2 will discuss, within a historical context, the influence of culture as well as sociopolitical, ideological, and moral-ethical issues in the development of the field of special education.

The ability to make comparisons, to notice similarities and differences, and to group observable phenomena has been at the root of human cognitive development and sociocultural evolution. Anthropological discoveries and recorded history suggest that differences in behavior among individuals have been noticed very early in the history of sociocultural development. Societies tended to attach verbal labels to those differences, creating categories based on observable phenomena. However, at various times in the history of the human race, societies exhibited various attitudes toward those perceived as being different. Different attitudes, in turn, have been influenced by complex cultural, social, philosophical, and ideological interactions.

In ancient and medieval times, only general concepts were employed as labeling "idiot" or "insane." Since only aristocrats and nobility were expected to be able to read and write, only severely handicapping conditions were noticed. It was not until the nineteenth century that the labels became more detailed and "scientific."

Concepts and labels became increasingly differentiated with the progress of sociocultural evolution. The ancient Greek concept of idiot, which initially meant any behavior associated with inadequate social functioning, eventually was differentiated into several concepts describing cognitive, affective, and social exceptionalities. With the growth of the behavioral sciences and increased influence of professional and parent organizations, the common sense approach to labeling has been replaced by elaborate classification systems.

Education of exceptional children, as we now know it, evolved gradually over the past few centuries. Prior to the nineteenth century, education of exceptional children was sporadic, conducted by private individuals or private institutions. First efforts were with children who manifested obvious physical disabilities, such as deafness or blindness.

Concern with the education of the mentally retarded began in earnest around the turn of the twentieth century. It should be pointed out that education of emotionally disturbed children is clearly a twentieth century development. In all probability this late interest in childhood emotional disturbance can be associated with the long-lasting belief that emotional illness results from the "stress of life." Since children did not yet live long enough, it was erroneously concluded that they could not be emotionally disturbed.

Chapter 3 discusses the interpretation of exceptionalities from normative, physical, psychological, educational, and social points of view, as well as etiological variables. It should be noticed that the degree of consensus about the nature of exceptionalities diminishes as we discuss normative perspective in comparison with others. Briefly understood, normative perspective, related to the nomothetic theory of assessment, views exceptionalities as deviations from the most frequently occurring characteristics in either direction from the average value. Simply stated, *exceptional* is a characteristic least frequently occurring.

From a physical perspective, exceptionalities are perceived on the healthy–unhealthy continuum. *Healthy* is interpreted as normal. *Unhealthy* is interpreted as exceptional, atypical, abnormal. The medical model is most evident in physical, sensory, and biological dysfunctions; less in cognitive and affective disabilities.

From a psychological perspective, normal behavior is a "well-balanced," "well-adjusted" behavior, which enables the individual to cope adequately with the environment. Behaviors characterized by high levels of anxiety, ambiguity, and disruption of interpersonal relationships are usually classified as exceptionalities.

Educationally, exceptional behavior is characterized by the lack of learning, as is the case in cognitive disabilities (intellectual subnormality, mental retardation, mental deficiency, oligophrenia), or by enriched learning experiences, as is the case with talented and gifted individuals. Basic to these comparisons is a rationale that there is a high correlation between overall development and learning potential.

Social perspective views maladaptive behaviors and exceptionalities within a context of interpersonal interaction (individual in group, class, society, etc.). Since by definition socially maladaptive behaviors can be defined only in terms of social and cultural norms, what is termed an *exceptional social behavior* can be determined only within a given society. Furthermore, two important considerations influence the definition of socially maladaptive behaviors: ideological-political reality, which defines the nature of interpersonal relationship; and the level of sociocultural development of a given society.

Chapter 4 will discuss current classification of exceptionalities. For an easy overview, exceptionalities will be divided into the following larger areas or clusters: physical disabilities, sensory-motor disabilities, cognitive disabilities, learning disabilities, affective and emotional disturbances, socially maladaptive behaviors, and gifted and talented learners.

Currently, there are numerous classification systems, which reflect professional consensus, scientific evidence, and sociocultural influences.

From a historical perspective, classifications have been influenced by level of scientific knowledge, cultural factors, and even sociopolitical considerations. Although such conditions as blindness, deafness, and mental retardation have been identified in ancient and medieval times, some conditions have not been described until the twentieth century. For example, demential infantalis was identified by Heller in the 1920s, childhood schizophrenia by Kasanin and Kaufman in 1929, and infantile autism by Kanner in 1943. The most recent development in the field of education of exceptional children is the emergence of the concept of learning disabilities.

Chapter 5 will discuss general education context from a geographical perspective. The complexity of the world we live in requires more comprehensive and in-depth preparation for the students of today and the leaders of tomorrow. Currently, we are witnessing a movement toward partnership in education. Such effort from an international perspective involves many issues of a sociopolitical, economic, and philosophical nature. In spite of the many efforts by international and national agencies, such as the United Nations Educational, Scientific, and Cultural Organization (UNESCO) and the United States Information Agency (USIA), individual nations are very protective of their educational goals and policies. The socioeconomic development of a nation almost always determines the extent to which educational programs serve the needs of children and adolescents. Strange as it seems, there are even a few countries in the world without compulsory attendance laws. In some countries, formal education ends at 14 years of age, and in a number of countries, services for exceptional learners are limited to those with the most severe handicapping conditions. Cates and Kinnison (1993) reported that, as interactions among nations increase, it is nearly impossible to ignore conditions in the rest of the world, especially among developing nations.

Chapter 6 will describe special education programs, and Chapter 7 will focus on community adjustment of exceptional individuals.

Despite increased international communication, significant differences exist in educational practices and service-delivery systems for exceptional children. Some countries did not have any programs for exceptional children as recently as 1983 (Holowinsky, 1983a). Most provide service to traditional categories, while few have elaborate systems of service delivery.

Putnam (1979) reported on special education services, by categories, in 110 countries. It is obvious that most provide services for the blind, deaf, physically disabled, and mentally retarded. However, only eighteen countries provided services for the communication disabled, four for the gifted, and three for the learning disabled. Putnam also noticed a wide discrepancy per country in the percentage of elementary or secondary pupils receiving special education services. The range is one in twenty in the United States to one in five thousand in less developed countries.

Because of hunger and poverty, a new international institute is needed to help prepare for the growing number of children who will be severely disabled. The enormity of the problem has been highlighted by Rampaul et al. (1992), who estimated that more than two hundred million children with special needs are experiencing learning difficulties in developing countries. They suggested that one problem with international efforts is their reliance on scholarship programs that involve few individuals. This important issue has been further commented on by Malapka (1992), who emphasized that developing nations regarded education as a powerful tool for nation building. If education planning is to be effective, it must be all-inclusive. It is generally recognized that, in the developing countries, services for the handicapped are either nonexistent or inadequate. Malapka pointed out that surveys show approximately thirty developing countries indicated that their governments do not attach high priorities to disabilities. Malapka thinks that lack of knowledge about educability, trainability, and potential economic productivity of persons with disabilities is a major reason for governments' default in this area. Unfortunately, individuals with disabilities are generally excluded from educational plans in most developing countries.

Sociocultural factors play a very important role in educational services. For example, in Tanzania, stigma and overprotection of children with disabilities account for the fact that parents are hiding children and refusing to send them to hospitals and schools (Possi, 1994). In the 1960s, schools for the blind, deaf, and physically handicapped were organized by missionaries. By the 1950s, there was only one school for students with disabilities in Tanzania. As recently as 1990, a very small percentage of handicapped children in Iran were receiving schooling (Afrooz, 1990). For centuries, mosques have served Iranians not only as places of worship but also as centers of learning. In rural areas the handicapped and mildly and moderately retarded work on routine jobs and are mainstreamed in their local communities without considerable social and vocational problems.

Chapter 8 will discuss teacher training and professional personnel preparation from an international perspective. Apart from common problems found across cultures, a unique situation exists in central and eastern Europe. The field of education in that region can clearly be described as being in transition from centralized, one-ideology-oriented teacher training to democracy and pluralism.

Chapter 9 will discuss research with exceptional learners in such areas as etiology and learning potential, special intervention, and curriculum development.

Research with exceptional children originated with the work of Itard, Seguin, S. Hall, and Binet. An interesting development in the early research efforts was the European movement of pedology, defined as "total child study" (Depaepe, 1985). The first world congress of pedology, held in Brussels in 1911, attracted nearly three hundred participants from twenty-two countries. The congress provided initiative for the establishment of the Faculte Internationale de Pedologie. Throughout the early part of the twentieth century, the contributions of Binet, Piaget, Vygotsky, and Luria became internationally recognized.

Current research efforts with exceptional individuals are concentrated at numerous universities and research centers. Findings are disseminated through hundreds of journals. Indeed, we are witnessing a true information explosion, which some scholars suggested is an "ignorance explosion" (Lukasiewich, 1972). An inordinate amount of information available in print suggested new ways of evaluating it. This led to the emergence of the field of meta-analysis (Kavale, 1982).

The book will conclude with a chapter on future trends and issues.

Recent innovations and technologies will enhance the achievements of many exceptional learners. Multiethnic and multicultural societies will focus more on precise definitions of learning difficulties and learning disabilities that can be related to cultural complexities. As societies become more technological and complex, the at-risk population will create more challenges in the areas of full employment and economic competition. Finally, full inclusion of exceptional learners within the educational mainstream will be implemented.

Chapter 2

HISTORICAL BACKGROUND

The emergence of labels and concepts of exceptionalities has been intrinsically related to the whole complex process of cognitive and sociocultural evolution. Cognitive functioning, which is species specific for humans, enabled our ancestors to observe similarities and differences in appearance and behavior. This led to the first attempt at labeling and categorization. Gross deviations from perceived norms were obviously recognized early in the history, and references to physical and communication disorders were found in ancient times. The earlier focus on gross physical and sensory deviations (for example, blindness and deafness) is understandable when we consider that until relatively recent history, only a small percentage of the population was expected to know how to read or write. Lack of abstract, symbolic learning skills was not an issue, and as a result, societies were not concerned with the population currently described as mildly retarded or learning disabled.

Prior to the nineteenth century, only isolated historical accounts of treatment or training of the physically handicapped were recorded. Seizures, as a physical disability, were recognized by ancient Greeks (Hippocrates), and mention of deaf people is found in the writings of Aristotle. Before the fifth century B.C., people with a history of seizures were assumed to be possessed by supernatural forces. Hippocrates, who is referred to as the father of medicine, introduced in the fifth century B.C. an attempt to describe and systematically evaluate seizures. For many centuries, until approximately the nineteenth century, medical thinking in reference to seizures was influenced by these ideas. Most of the earliest recorded attempts to provide services to the handicapped have been associated with church institutions. Yarmachenko (1968) reports that in the eleventh century, a home was established for blind, deaf, physically disabled, and orphaned children at the Kyiv-Pechersk monastery in Ukraine.

Earlier efforts to educate physically handicapped and exceptional children in China, Japan, and Korea were initiated by missionaries from the United States. Pearl S. Buck, noted writer and a daughter of an American missionary in China, introduced special education to Japan at the turn of this century.

Kyoto Institute for the Blind was established in 1878. A second school for the blind was established in Tokyo in 1880. By 1907, there were 38 schools for blind and deaf individuals. In 1896, Nagano Elementary School organized special classes for slow-learning children. In Shanghai, China, a school for deaf-mute children was established in 1926 by an American missionary.

Services for the physically handicapped expanded considerably from the sixteenth to the nineteenth century.

Ponce de Leon (1508–1584) pioneered the education of the deaf-mute in Spain. He established a school for deaf children at the monastery of San Salvador (Irwin, 1977). Another noted pioneer in the education of the deaf was de Carrion (1579–1652). In the early seventeenth century, some works appeared that dealt with the training and education of the deaf-mute. In 1644, John Bulwer published the first book in English on the education of the deaf. In 1692, a book was published in Amsterdam by Amman (1669–1724) entitled *Speaking Deaf-Mute; or, A Method of Teaching Congenitally Deaf-Mute How to Talk* (Dziedzic, S., 1977). This book had a very important influence on language training for the deaf. Isolated efforts continued until the eighteenth century, when the first public school devoted to the education of the deaf was established in Leipzig, Germany, by Heinicke in 1778 (Irwin, 1977). The first school for the deaf in Great Britain was established in Edinburgh in 1767.

In the field of education of the blind, Hay, a French philanthropist, is recognized as a pioneer. In 1784, he established the first school for the blind, known as the National Institution for the Young Blind. The institution provided instruction in academic subjects as well as vocational training. Before the turn of the nineteenth century, four schools for the blind opened in England and, by 1810, similar schools were established in other European countries (Irwin, 1974).

Throughout the nineteenth century, significant developments occurred in services for the blind and deaf, both in eastern Europe and the United States. In 1817, the Institute of Deaf-Mute and Blind was established in Warsaw, Poland, and in Estonia. The first school for the deaf was organized in 1867 and for the blind in 1883 (Korgessar, 1988). In Ukraine, systematic instruction of blind children began in the nineteenth century, with seven schools being organized between 1840 and 1894 (Holowinsky, 1987).

In the United States, Howe (1801–1876), a pioneer in the education and training of the blind, is credited with organizing the first school for the blind, known as the Perkins School for the Blind, in Watertown, Massachusetts.

Howe's interest in handicapped children eventually expanded into an interest in mental retardation, which led to the establishment of a school for the mentally retarded in Massachusetts, known as the Fernald State School.

An American medical missionary, Rosetta Sherwood Hall, began to teach blind children in Korea in 1894. In 1913, an institution was set up by the Japanese military government in Korea to accommodate the homeless, including the handicapped. The first Oriental Conference of Special Education was held in 1914 in Pyongyang, presently the capital of North Korea.

With the growth of the basic sciences during the nineteenth century, the emphasis shifted toward neurological and physiological interpretation of seizures. The American neurologist Jackson, whose writings appeared in the 1870s, contributed considerably to the understanding of convulsive disorders (Kram, 1963). The understanding of brain-injured, cerebral-palsied children has also been enriched by the contributions of Phelps and Carlson (Hewett & Forness, 1977). Earlier understanding of handicapping conditions, however, was not necessarily followed by the development of appropriate treatment and training facilities.

From the earliest days of human civilization, communication disorders were considered deviant behavior. References to them are found among the hieroglyphics of ancient Egypt, which describe stammering and cleft palate (Eldridge, 1968). The story of Demosthenes, who was a stammerer but became a leading orator and statesman of his time, is well known. It is said that he apparently trained himself in breath control, articulation, and voice production by putting pebbles under his tongue. In all probability, there were individual and sporadic efforts throughout recorded human history to help people with communication and speech disorders.

Scientific investigations into speech disorders began with the work of Amman in 1700 (Eldridge, 1968). Herries, who published in 1773 one of the most important books on speech, gives the following credit to Amman: "Dr. Amman from Amsterdam was the first who emerged from the obscurity of scholastic definition and described the formation of the voice from nature and experiment alone" (Herries, 1968, p. 29). At the turn of the twentieth century, one of the better known centers for speech pathology and therapy in the United States was located at Columbia University in New York City.

In the area of cognitive disorders, the first reported evidence of exceptionality dates to Talmudic times, where a reference is found to imbecility: "All my slaughter and their slaughtering is valid except by a deaf-mute, an imbecile or a moron" (Talmud Hulin, Sancino translation, 1948, p. 1, as reported by Novick, 1987).

In the sixteenth and seventeenth centuries, there were attempts to describe mental retardation functionally and legally. It was not until the end of the eighteenth century that the first attempts were made at treatment and research in the field of mental retardation (Kanner, 1960).

For the purpose of our discussion, the prescientific era extends to the end of the eighteenth century, specifically 1799, when Itard's study of the "Wild Boy of Aveyron" commenced. There is a scarcity of references in ancient or medieval sources to retarded individuals. Several factors account for this. It is conceivable that, in primitive conditions, most physically defective infants simply did not survive into adulthood. Furthermore, the society itself did not require complex cognitive skills for its functioning; consequently those now labeled "mildly retarded" or "borderline" were simply unrecognizable. In any case, there were not too many written accounts.

The label "idiot" appears first in ancient Greek sources and had a very broad generic meaning: a person who was ignorant or unfit for public office. The first use of the word *idiot* in English literature to describe someone who is intellectually deficient appears at the beginning of the fourteenth century. The first colony for the retarded was established in Europe at approximately that time. The attitudes toward the retarded person ranged widely from amusement and tolerance to hostility and persecution.

Many less severely retarded persons, in order to survive, became jesters or court fools. Their behavior became rather commonplace at the courts of kings and princes. As a result, the concept of fool in the English language implies a lack of cognitive abilities or low intelligence.

The end of the eighteenth century and the beginning of the nineteenth century were times conducive to pioneering; indeed, revolutionary developments occurred in the field of mental retardation. Under the influence of the philosophical ideas of Voltaire, Montesquieu, and Rousseau, the "temper of the time" was such that nothing appeared impossible. For the first time, the blind were trained to see, and Pinel removed chains from the insane (Kraepelin, 1962).

In the context of this pioneering time, the French physician Itard attempted to educate a "wild" boy found in the woods of southern France in 1799, whom he subsequently named Victor. It is interesting to observe that Pinel did not believe that Itard would succeed with his training, and he labeled Victor an "incurable idiot." Yet Itard persisted with the training and provided an example of commitment for future generations of special educators. Although Itard did not completely succeed in his training of Victor, he nevertheless achieved considerable relative success. When found in the forest of Aveyron, the boy presented a classic picture of complete lack of social skills and most severe deprivation. He could not talk, nor was he able to climb on a chair. A pistol fired near him hardly provoked any response, but he turned around when he heard a nut cracking. Victor did not know how to clear his nostrils, and he pulled potatoes with his bare hands from boiling water.

Itard set up a training schedule for Victor that included several objectives. He attempted to interest the boy in socially appropriate behavior by making it pleasant for him. He employed energetic stimulation and occasionally intense emotions to stimulate Victor's nervous sensibility. Itard also developed a set of ingenious visual-motor exercises in order to stimulate perceptual development. As a result of Itard's training, Victor became more socialized, was able to say a few words, and understood the meaning of simple directions.

It is interesting to note that Itard's notion of the increasing complexity of functions and their integration into a schematic pattern of cognitive training has been basically accurate from the position of our present-day neuropsychological knowledge. It has been generally accepted by Luria, Piaget, and Vygotsky that development and maturation of cognitive skills rests on prior development of sensory-motor and communication skills. In an applied sense, a similar idea has been incorporated into a patterning exercise, also known in the 1960s as the Doman-Delacato treatment method.

In addition to Itard, Seguin became a pioneering figure in the field of mental retardation during the nineteenth century. However, unlike Itard, whose efforts were exclusively in France, Seguin's work can be claimed by both the United States and France. At the suggestion of Itard, Seguin began to teach mentally retarded children at a private school in Paris in 1837 and in 1842 became the director of the school. In 1850, he arrived in the United States. Seguin's work, *Idiocy and Its Diagnoses and Treatment by the Physiological Method,* was published originally in French and subsequently translated into English (Sloan & Stevens, 1976). He was one of the founding members of the Association of Medical Officers of the American Institutions for Idiots and Feeble-Minded Persons, which in 1907 was renamed the American Association for the Study of the Feebleminded, and again in 1933, the American Association of Mental Deficiency (AAMD) (Sloan & Stevens, 1976).

The AAMD changed its name again in 1987 to the American Association on Mental Retardation (AAMR). In 1919, the then American Association for the Study of the Feebleminded appointed a committee on classification. The AAMD published its first manual, the *Manual on Terminology and Classification in Mental Retardation,* in 1921. The AAMD and the National Committee for Mental Hygiene cooperated on the second edition in 1933 and on the third edition in 1941.

Seguin maintained that the etiology of severe mental retardation is associated with an organic defect of the craniospinal axis that may occur in utero or in the neonatal period. Such a defect incapacitates those functions that are related both to reflex and the conscious aspects of life. He suggested that the goal of training and education should be to improve activity, intelligence, and will. Seguin believed that exercise conducted in the fresh air, along with positive attitudes, contributes greatly to success in education. He recognized that happiness and contentment are important for everybody, especially mentally retarded children, and he emphasized to his students that children will not be ill if they have the opportunity to laugh.

During the nineteenth century, efforts on educating the mentally retarded were generally associated with the establishment of state schools. Between 1848 and 1900, twenty-one states had established twenty-nine institutions for the training and education of the handicapped (Braddock & Heller, 1985a).

In 1897, the University of Pennsylvania offered a sequence of three courses in the education of the mentally retarded (Lilly, 1979). Prior to 1910, the Training School at Vineland conducted summer workshops for teachers of the mentally retarded. One of the earliest state certification requirements for teachers of the mentally retarded was enacted in New Jersey in 1911. Certification to teach the mentally retarded in New Jersey required elementary or secondary permanent certification, "competency" in psychology, familiarity with manual training for boys and girls, and ability to conduct physical training.

During the 1920s and 1930s, significant developments occurred in the United States in research and education of mentally retarded, emotionally disturbed, and gifted children. Influenced by the seminal work of A. Binet, B. Goddard, and E. Doll, many made their pioneering contributions to the field of mental retardation. Goddard established at the Training School at Vineland the first laboratory in the United States devoted to the study of mental retardation. He translated the Binet-Simon test into English and introduced it to the United States. The test was subsequently standardized at Stanford University and became known as Stanford-Binet. Goddard became widely known for his controversial book, *The Kalikak Family: A Study in the Heredity of Feeblemindedness* (1912). For many years, this book was a source of the hereditary interpretation of the etiology of mental retardation. Doll became director of research at the Training School at Vineland following Goddard's retirement. His most noteworthy contributions were in the area of research on birth injuries as they relate to the etiology of mental retardation.

In prerevolutionary Russia, the oldest Moscow special school for exceptional children was established in 1907. At the time of the Bolshevik revolution, there were in Moscow twelve auxiliary elementary schools and six classes attached to the middle schools. Kaschenko and Rossolimo are considered among the first pioneers in special education.

In ancient times, the bizarre, peculiar, and at times frightening behavior of the emotionally disturbed, not readily understood by those in their environment, was attributed to mysterious supernatural sources.

An ancient Indian system of medicine (sixth century B.C. to second century A.D.), known as Ayurveda, classified human illness into three categories:

exogenous, endogenous, and psychic (Vankoba Rao, 1975). Mahabharata recognized three character types: "*Yudhistira*–a keen intellectual, physically lean, sensitive to wrong actions, an upholder of righteousness; the corpulent *Bhima*–a man of action emotionally unstable; and the muscular *Arguna*–a warrior whose instinct is to fight" (Vankoba Rao, p. 641).

Ayurveda classified personality into three types: pure (sattric) with seven subgroups, passionate (rajas) with six subgroups, and ignorant (tamas) with three subgroups.

In ancient Greece in the seventh century B.C., a concept evolved that viewed sanity and insanity as associated with the opposite dimensions of personality. Sanity was equated with the dominance of rational, abstracting, and categorizing functions of mind, while insanity was associated with the dominance of impulsive and appetitive functions.

In the first century A.D., Aretaeus of Cappadocia described forms of melancholia, which had a tendency to change into a mania. About a hundred years earlier (106–43 B.C.), Cicero had described our main passions as discomfort, fear, joy, and violent desire (Mora, 1975).

In medieval times, the emotionally disturbed were chained or locked in dungeons; those suspected of communication with the devil were burned as witches. It is reported that in Switzerland alone, five hundred persons were accused and burned as witches in 1515; the last execution of an accused witch in the United States took place in 1782 (White, 1964). It is not surprising that throughout medieval times and well into the seventeenth and the beginning of the eighteenth centuries, the emotionally disturbed were treated as animals, as described vividly by White: "Some of the less troublesome wandered about the countryside begging and stealing their food and finding shelter in barns and pigsties. Others were thrown into prison where side by side with criminals they lived amid revolting filth, often chained, always at the mercy of their keepers" (p. 6).

Significant changes in attitudes toward the emotionally ill occurred around the turn of the nineteenth century. Reforms instituted by French physician Pinel (1745–1826) are generally credited with bringing about changing attitudes toward the mentally ill. An eloquent plea for the emotionally disturbed is attributed to him: "The mentally sick, far from being guilty people deserving of punishment, are sick people whose miserable state deserves all the consideration that is due to suffering humanity. One should try with the most simple methods to restore their reason" (White, 1964, p. 8).

Concomitant with the change in attitude were other important developments during the nineteenth century. The first modern work on mental disorders was published by the French physician Esquirol (1772–1840) in 1838. He classified mental illness into four major groups: monomania, mania, dementia, and idiocy (Pelicier, 1975). Monomania was further subdivided into three categories: intellectual, such as systematic delirium; affective-perversions; and instinctual, such as homicide, pyromania, and so forth.

During the same century, many leading institutions for the treatment of the mentally ill were established. In the United States, pioneering work in the field of emotional disorders is associated with Benjamin Rush, who, in 1812 published a classical work entitled *Medical Inquiries and Observations upon the Diseases of the Mind*. Labels such as "mania," "melancholia," "dementia," and "idiocy" were widely used in the nineteenth century. Diagnoses of mania or melancholia were utilized most frequently. Goldhamer and Marshall (1953) informed us that in 1840, the superintendent of the Worcester Hospital summarized the first thousand admissions to the hospital as follows: 54 percent were classified as mania, 31 percent melancholia, 15 percent dementia, and less than 1 percent idiocy.

In 1844, the Association of Medical Superintendents of American Institutions for the Insane was formed, later changing its name to the American Psychiatric Association. But there was still considerable confusion and inconsistency about the reasons for adolescent insanity and its etiology. Even Esquirol believed that the "acquired idiocy" of childhood and adolescence developed as a result of such experiences as masturbation and head injury. Throughout the long history of concern for the emotionally disturbed, there was no recognition of childhood emotional disturbances. It was simply assumed that emotional disturbance is directly associated with the "stress of life" and, since children were young, that it was not possible for them to be emotionally disturbed.

At first, attention was directed to adolescents who were emotionally disturbed. In 1863, Kahlbaum described mental deterioration in adolescence as "paraphrenic hebephrenia" (Wolman, 1972). At approximately the same time, the label "dementia praecox" was used by Morel and Pick (Arieti, 1974). Morel described the case of a 14-year-old boy who apparently was psychotic. For Morel, the word *praecox* meant that dementia started early or precociously in life, in contrast to senile dementia, which occurred in old age. In England, Thomas Clauston, in an address delivered in 1888 as president of the Medico-Psychological Association, spoke of "adolescent insanities" (Arieti, 1974).

Henry Maudsley is regarded as the first psychiatrist to pay serious attention to childhood psychoses. In 1867, in his *Pathology of Mind,* he included a chapter titled "Insanity of Early Life" (Kanner, 1976).

In conclusion, it should be pointed out that even a very brief review of international efforts on behalf of the handicapped from a historical perspective suggests a very uneven sequence of developments. It would appear that societies less well developed economically were the ones with the most recent initial efforts on behalf of exceptional children.

Chapter 3

ETIOLOGY AND THE EMPHASES ON EXCEPTIONALITIES

Complex historical, cultural, social, and scientific conditions and variables influenced how societies consider the nature of exceptionalities, how they view exceptionality as a condition, and an exceptional individual as a person.

Historically, the concept of exceptionalities emerged from observation of existing or perceived similarities and differences among individuals. Not surprisingly, physical disabilities and sensory disorders such as blindness and deafness were noticed and described first.

With the development of empirical scientific knowledge about human behavior, a number of emphases in exceptionalities emerged. Currently, those emphases could be referred to as: normative, medical, psychological, and sociological. They will be described briefly in this chapter.

NORMATIVE EMPHASIS

Normative, or as it is commonly referred to, a statistical emphasis, considers as a normal phenomenon that which most frequently occurs. Conversely, an abnormal or exceptional phenomenon, or behavior, is one that occurs less frequently. This basic assumption became the crux of the development of assessment procedures for all phenomena. In the field of psychology and education, normative emphasis has been historically at the root of cognitive and educational assessment. Prior to our discussion of the complex issues in the assessment of cognitive and educational skills, a brief review of basic concepts is in order. The most important basic concepts are associated with the measures of central tendencies and variability.

The concept of average value, known as the measure of central tendency, is usually expressed as the arithmetical mean, the mode, or the median. The mean can be expressed as the total of all of the values observed divided by the number of observations. The mode is the value that occurs most frequently in the distribution. The median, or midpoint, is a value that has both below and above it 50 concept of the total number of cases.

The concept that describes how scores are grouped around the mean is referred to as the measure of spread or variability. More widely known measures of variability are the range, the mean deviation, and the standard deviation. The range simply means the distance between the lowest and the highest scores in the sample. The mean deviation is the arithmetic mean of the sum of deviations of the scores in the distribution from the mean of the distribution. The standard deviation is the square root of the mean of the sum of the deviations squared. Standard deviation is a useful measure that indicates the proportion of the normal distribution of scores or values with a given distance from the mean.

The concepts of normal distribution (which maintains that the number of observable phenomena, scores, items, values, decreases significantly in both directions from the mean) and standard deviation became essential in the development of a variety of intelligence tests. The most widely used intelligence tests (for example, Wechsler Adult Intelligence Scales, Wechsler Intelligence Scales for Children) employ the concept of deviational intelligence quotient. The concept of intelligence quotient (IQ) has been widely accepted in the field of intellectual or mental measurement as an indicator of a deviation of exceptionality from the average intelligence. IQ expresses the relationship between mental age (MA) and chronological age (CA) assuming that in an individual of average intelligence, MA and CA are identical. This relationship when expressed mathematically as IQ will yield a value of 1. In order to avoid using decimal numbers, the obtained value is multiplied by a constant 100. Therefore, the average IQ is 100. Table 3.1 illustrates some MA/CA relationships and their corresponding IQ values (Holowinsky, 1983a).

Table 3.2 illustrates approximate IQ ranges as they relate to operational definitions of intellectual levels.

Normal theory of assessment provided the basis for the development of tests of cognitive skills, also commonly referred to as tests of intelligence.

The purpose of these tests is to assess cognitive skills, such as memory, thought process, and problem-solving ability. According to the emphasis, such tests can be divided into verbal or performance as well as both verbal and performance. With regard to the mode of administration, the tests can be divided into those administered to individuals or to a group. Group tests are sometimes referred to as paper-and-pencil tests. The most frequently used

Table 3.1

Level	Subnormal	Average	Gifted
MA	5	10	15
CA	10	10	10
IQ	50	100	150

Table 3.2

IQ	Subnormality	IQ	Average Intelligence	IQ	Gifted Intelligence
55–69	Mild	90–109	Average	130	Gifted (Talented)
40–54	Moderate	80–89	Low average	120–129	Bright
0–39	Severe/ profound	70–79	Dull normal	110–119	Above average

tests of cognitive skills (intelligence tests) are the Stanford-Binet Form L-M; Wechsler Pre-School Scale; Wechsler Intelligence Scale for Children, Revised (WISC-R); Wechsler Adult Intelligence Scale; Leiter Performance Scale; Cornell-Cox Performance Scale; and the Peabody Picture Vocabulary Test.

Although the Stanford-Binet correlates well with educational achievement, it tends to discriminate against children who have language difficulties. On the other hand, WISC-R, by providing an opportunity to compare between various subtests, lends itself better to clinical interpretation. There are some limitations in the use of cognitive tests with exceptional children, which are related to standardization properties, emphasis on verbal skills, emphasis on quantitative concepts, and discriminatory use in the past.

Most of the tests of intelligence (cognitive skills) are not standardized on the mentally retarded population. The intellectual functioning of the retarded is simply viewed as a deviation from "normal" functioning. Such an approach presents problems in the interpretation of scores for the mentally retarded population because most scores fall below the optimum level of the power of the test. Furthermore, scores obtained below two standard deviations from the mean are not very reliable. This suggests that IQs obtained within ranges of profound, severe, and moderate retardation are highly questionable unless administered by an expert examiner. For example, it is possible for a retarded adult to obtain a Full Scale IQ of 46 on the Wechsler Adult Intelligence Scale simply by passing one item on each of the subtests.

Most intelligence tests emphasize verbal skills, precisely the kind of ability in which the mentally retarded population is deficient. This is one of the reasons that the estimated prevalence of the mentally retarded population reaches its peak during early adolescence. It is the time in life for most individuals when adjustment to the school environment requires heavy emphasis on verbal skills.

Individual intelligence tests have been increasingly criticized because of their quantitative nature. This means that the performance of an individual on a test is compared with the average performance of the sample corresponding to the individual's chronological age. In order to counterbalance the proliferation of tests based on group comparison, Underwood (1975) suggested that cognitive theory should be formulated in such a way as to allow for individual difference tests.

A misapplication of quantitative assessment methods for the purpose of placement and programming creates a situation in which some children are placed into self-contained special classes because they are educationally or culturally deprived rather than intellectually inferior. The rationale for making such an assumption is easily seen when we examine statistical data available on the number of individuals classified as intellectually inferior in the United States and relate this information to etiological factors. In the majority of retarded individuals, etiology is listed as psychogenic, sociogenic, or simply unknown.

Specialized Tests

Specialized tests were developed for the purpose of assessing either cognitive skills of the handicapped (for example, the Hayes-Binet for the blind) or special skills (for example, the Oseretsky Scales of Motor Proficiency). One may also mention Eisenshohn's Test for Aphasia and the Nebraska Test of Learning Aptitude. The latter, which has been standardized on the deaf population, is also a useful tool with nonverbal retarded children or adolescents. Since the subject does not hear the examiner, the administration of the test has to be conducted through gestures. In specialized tests, adaptive behavior measures should be listed. The better-known adaptive measures in use today are the AAMD Adaptive Behavior Scales, Vineland Social Maturity Scale, and the Denver Developmental Screening Test.

In addition to the assessment of cognitive skills, a separate field emerged devoted to the assessment of educational achievement. Detailed discussion of the educational assessment is beyond the scope of this chapter. In the context of our discussion here, only some major trends will be mentioned. Curriculum-based assessment was discussed by Fuchs and Fuchs (1986). For their review, they employed meta-analysis to investigate how well measurement of progress toward long-term versus short-term goals relates to the outcome measures of student achievement. Their review suggested that teachers prefer short-term goal measurement because it is easier to understand, and it guides instruction more directly by providing information about when to progress from one skill to another. In the opinion of Fuchs and Fuchs, the short-term goal measurement may be misleading. They suggested that curriculum-based assessment of long-term goals may represent a necessary additional strategy for validly assessing pupil progress. In another study, the same authors (Fuchs & Fuchs, 1984) questioned the accuracy of teachers' observations, one of the educational measures frequently utilized. Their research indicates that teachers do not use systematic procedures to measure children's progress. Some studies, for example, Condon, Yates-Peters, and Sueiro-Ross (1979), Figueroa (1983), and Helge (1987), discussed unique issues of the assessment of special populations. Earlier suggestions by Condon et al., and more recent findings by Figueroa, are especially helpful for planning assessment and evaluation of the educational achievement of Hispanic children. Helge's (1987) article described strategies for improving rural special education program evaluation. The writer identified three major priorities for rural special education program evaluation: assessment of student achievement, program achievement, and cost effectiveness.

In view of the needs of special populations, considerable attention has been directed recently toward the development and use of local norms, pluralistic norms, and subgroup norms. Norms provide a point of reference that makes a raw score valuable and meaningful in terms of the characteristics of the normative group (Brown & Bryant, 1984). Fuchs et al. (1985) suggested that one source of assessment bias is an examiner's familiarity or unfamiliarity with the subjects. In their study, handicapped children performed differentially with familiar and unfamiliar examiners. Nonhandicapped children did not. This suggests that examiner unfamiliarity is a source of systematic error or bias in the assessment of handicapped children.

Recently the minimum competency testing (MCT) movement became rather popular. Vitello (1988), however, suggested that standardized MCT may be contrary to the intent of Public Law 94-142, which requires that instruction for handicapped students be individualized. He expressed concern that "an appropriate education for many handicapped students may be compromised if instruction is geared to passing the MCT so that a diploma can be awarded." Some states attempt to resolve this apparent paradox by granting a waiver to the handicapped students.

Historically, assessment of exceptional children has focused on an individual child. "The science of child study" in the early 1920s (Holowinsky, 1988), development of individual intelligence testing, and the establishment of "child study" teams are examples of this tradition. More recently, however, the emphasis has shifted from the assessment of an individual child to the assessment of educational environments. The importance of this research has been underscored by Bender (1988), who pointed out that "measurement instruments that assess the learning environment from the perspective of both research on teaching effectiveness and research on specialized strategies for mainstreaming need to be developed." There is also a need to train evaluators who not only know how to conduct assessment but also understand its importance for mainstreaming. Finally, Bender suggests that "teachers should be encouraged to see this assessment as an opportunity to participate in formative self-evaluation for professional improvement."

MEDICAL EMPHASIS

From a normative perspective, a normal phenomena is that which most frequently occurs, but from a medical perspective, normality implies healthy functioning of the organism. However, healthy or unhealthy states cannot be viewed as discrete concepts.

Korchin (1976) suggests four views of medical normality: normality as health, normality as ideal (Utopia), normality as average, and normality as socially acceptable.

As a discipline, medicine has a long history. Greek medical schools were established in approximately 600 B.C. (Grey, 1978), and as early as 400 B.C., Hippocrates proposed a first medical classification. The medical model is generally considered a process that starts with the recognition of symptoms, moves to a specific syndrome, then progresses to become a disease model with known etiology, course, and prognosis. In the field of the treatment of emotional disturbance as a medical illness, the pioneering contributions of Emil Kraepelin (1855–1926), Adolf Meyer (1886–1950), and Eugene Bleuler (1856–1935) are universally recognized. Kraepelin was the first physician who named and described the two most common forms of severe mental illness: dementia praecox and manic-depressive psychosis. Meyer shifted the focus from disease entity on complex "psychobiological reactions" to life situation. Eugene Bleuler emphasized disharmony between cognitive and affective domain and suggested that the term *schizophrenia* should replace the traditional term *dementia praecox* as a label for serious emotional disturbance.

The American Psychiatric Association published in 1952 its *Diagnostic and Statistical Manual (DSM-1)*. The manual was revised in 1968 in order to bring American terminology more in agreement with the *International Classification of Diseases* published by the World Health Organization. The manual was known as *DSM-2*. Current interpretation of serious emotional disturbances involves the comprehensive multiaxial approach that takes under consideration the simultaneous interaction of such factors as heredity and constitution, physical, psychological, and the effects of stress. *DSM-3,* published in 1980, arranges classification along five axes: axes 1 and 2 include all mental disorders; axis 3, physical disorders and conditions; axis 4, severity of psychological stressors; and axis 5, highest level of adaptive functioning in the past year. *DSM-3* describes each disorder in terms of current knowledge in the following areas: essential features, associated features, age at onset, course, impairment, complications, predisposing factors, prevalence, sex ratio, familial pattern and differential pattern, and differential diagnosis. *DSM-3* was revised in 1987.

In the field of cognitive disabilities (mental deficiency, mental retardation, intellectual subnormality), medical etiologies have been presented in the AAMR classification manuals, of which there have been several editions since 1933. For the purpose of the brief review in this chapter, the 1983 edition (Grossman, 1983) will be utilized. The controversy that surrounds the most recent manual (Lucasson, 1992) will be discussed in Chapter 4.

Etiology of Cognitive and Emotional Disabilities

It should be recognized that a variety of structural, neurological, physiological, and/or biochemical abnormalities or dysfunctions are related to the etiologies (reasons associated with) cognitive and emotional disabilities. The degree of severity of those conditions is also associated with the time of onset (prenatal, neonatal, postnatal), location within the central nervous system, and other developmental complications.

Cognitive Disabilities

Mental retardation is frequently associated with prenatal and postnatal infections of the cerebrospinal column. Conditions such as maternal rubella, toxoplasmosis, maternal syphilis, alcoholism, substance abuse, and excessive tobacco smoking are usually associated with mental retardation in the offspring.

The idea that maternal rubella may cause malformations of the fetus was first set forth in Australia by Gregg in 1941 (Crome & Stern, 1967). Rubella infection is most dangerous to the fetus if it occurs during the first three months of pregnancy, but there is also evidence that deafness may occur in the child with later maternal infection. As reported in Crome and Stern (1967), Jackson's 1963 publication summarized the results of a hundred pregnancies in which maternal rubella occurred before the twelfth week of gestation. Jackson indicated that 29.4 percent had developmental disabilities as well as mental retardation.

Toxoplasmosis is a fetal infection caused by a parasite. The most dangerous period for maternal infections to occur is between the second and sixth months of pregnancy. Surviving infants may develop mental retardation as well as paralysis, blindness, and epilepsy. However, not every instance of toxoplasmosis acquired during pregnancy results in fetal infection. Maternal syphilis, which is easily transmitted through the placenta, has accounted for spontaneous abortions, stillbirths, and mental retardation. In current research, we notice an increased interest in the relationship between maternal alcoholism, tobacco smoking, and mental retardation in offspring. There is also preliminary research data available that suggests a relationship between maternal drug addiction and the child's mental retardation.

Since 1984, a tragic new etiological group emerged–infants and children with AIDS (Acquired Immune Deficiency Syndrome). As reported by Byers (1989), a total of 1,054 pediatric cases had been reported, and 502 cases were children under 13 years of age. A number of neurological problems are evident in children with AIDS, such as failure to attain developmental milestones or loss of developmental milestones. With the increasing survival rate of such children, the implications for mental retardation have to be considered.

A recent area of concern for the field of special education is the spread of HIV (human immunodeficiency virus) (Prater, Serna, Silver & Ketz, 1995). This is a worldwide concern that influences preventive curricula and teacher-training needs. The HIV infection is currently the second-leading cause of death among all persons between 25 and 44 years of age, and the number one cause of death in males in this age group. Students with disabilities, who are more vulnerable to substance abuse than their peers, are also more vulnerable to contracting HIV. This problem is compounded by the fact that special educators are inadequately trained to deal with the problem of HIV infection.

Postnatal infections in infancy or early childhood, such as meningitis or encephalitis, have also been associated with a high-risk potential for mental retardation. Whether a child acquires mental retardation, and to what degree of severity, is related to the age of the child and the quality of medical treatment. A more serious form of meningitis that affects the brain is known as meningoencephalitis. Encephalitis, the infection of the brain itself, is also associated with mental retardation.

Trauma or Physical Agent

Excessive prenatal irradiation, birth injuries, and anoxia and asphyxia at birth are associated with mental retardation.

Animal research by Cowen and Geller (Crone & Stern, 1967) reveals that microcephaly resulted in rats irradiated during the intrauterine stage.

Studies of human subjects (Murphy, 1947) also point to the association between irradiation, especially during the first trimester of pregnancy, and mental retardation. Most of the information relating irradiation to various defects in humans comes from data collected in Japan after World War II. Miller (1956) reported that Japanese women exposed to atomic irradiation had offspring with a high incidence of neonatal death, microcephaly, and mental retardation. His study shows that the amount of irradiation, the distance from the atomic explosion, and the stage of the pregnancy were the factors most highly associated with subsequent defects. More recent evidence is available from the Chernobyl nuclear catastrophe in Ukraine (Holowinsky, 1993, 1996).

It has been well established that brain injury in the neonate, as, for example, in anoxia at birth, is associated with the potential for mental retardation. Pioneering work by Doll (1933), Birch (1964), and others has been widely recognized in this field. In the former Soviet Union, Lebedev and Barashnev (1963) studied 298 neonates born in a state of asphyxia. Of that number, 29 died soon after birth, 13 were premature, 30 had neurological abnormalities, and 27 were mentally retarded. Seizures are frequently found among the mentally retarded, although seizures as such are not frequent causes of mental retardation.

Disorders of Metabolism

The most prominent metabolic disorders associated with mental retardation are carbohydrate metabolism disorders and amino-acid metabolism disorders.

Disorders involving carbohydrate metabolism interfere with the adequate supply of glucose and with brain metabolism. Prominent in this group are galactosemia, fructosemia, and hypoglycemia.

Galactosemia results from an inborn error of metabolism associated with a specific enzyme defect. Galactose is formed when lactose, the primary sugar in the milk, is divided into galactose and glucose. Infants who cannot metabolize galactose may develop jaundice, vomiting, cataracts, malnutrition, and mental retardation. Treatment with a lactose-free diet drastically improves the prognosis. Galactosemia is a rare condition. Current estimates place the incidence from one to forty thousand to one in one hundred thousand live births.

Fructosemia is a disorder of fructose metabolism. Part of the normal carbohydrate intake is provided by fructose, an ingredient in fruits and vegetables. Hereditary fructose intolerance is transmitted by an autosomal recessive gene. Somatic symptoms include vomiting, convulsions, and jaundice. Fructosemia in some cases is associated with mild mental retardation.

Hypoglycemia in infants can result in cerebral complications and possible retardation. The initial symptoms are similar to those found in anoxia. However, cerebral complications can be prevented if the condition is treated in time.

The most prominent disorder of amino-acid metabolism is phenylketonuria, known generally as PKU. This condition was first identified by Fölling in 1935 as phenylpyruvic oligophrenia, a metabolic error associated with mental retardation. The condition has been described subsequently by Jervis (1939). The metabolic error is traced to the deficiency of phenylalanine hydroxylase, an enzyme that normally converts phenylalanine to tyrosine. In the absence of this process, phenylpyruvic acid is formed. Because it is not specifically known what level of phenylalanine concentration is associated with mental retardation, Mautner (1959) suggests that treatment is indicated when the phenylalanine level is persistently elevated.

Estimates of the incidence of PKU range from 1 in 4,000 to 1 in 60,000 live births. There is a wide range of IQs in individual cases of PKU children, but more than 90 percent of patients with untreated phenylketonuria have IQs below 50 and may require institutionalization. The onset of treatment is directly related to the prognosis, and the earlier the treatment begins the higher the expectancy for mental development can be anticipated, especially if the treatment begins prior to the first year of life.

Baumeister (1967) reports that the IQ of 90 or above was reached by 45 percent of those for whom treatment began at fifteen weeks of life, 14 percent when treatment began prior to one year of life, and only 6 percent when treatment began after one year of life. Mautner (1959) indicated that a phenylalanine-free diet is suggested for children younger than four years of age. Good results are reported when treatment begins in infancy. However, the initiation of treatment after age five brings questionable results.

The first clinical effect of PKU conditions in infants is the tendency to lose weight and vomit. Untreated youngsters may also develop pathological EEGs, muscle hypertension, and eczema.

Postnatal Brain Disease

An example of such a condition is tuberous sclerosis, also known as epiloia or butterfly rash because of reddish-yellowish tumors of the face. Similar tumors may also be found in the brain tissue, heart, and kidney. Face tumors usually develop in late infancy or early childhood. Most of the children affected by this condition are severely retarded. The condition is transmitted by a dominant gene and occurs very infrequently.

Condition of Unknown Prenatal Origin

Listed in the AAMR manual as conditions of unknown prenatal origins are microcephaly and hydrocephaly. The essential feature of microcephaly is a small brain within a small skull. Mautner (1959) suggests that microcephaly can be suspected when the circumference of the head is two inches smaller than the average for the age. Recent criteria suggest microcephaly in those individuals whose head circumference is smaller than three standard deviations below the mean for a given age and sex. One should be careful not to infer mental retardation from the measurement of the head alone, although usually there is a relationship in microcephalics between the skull size and the level of intelligence. The estimated incidence of microcephaly varies from 1 in 6,200 to 1 in 8,500 live births. Penrose (1963) distinguishes between so-called true or genetic microcephaly and acquired microcephaly. The incidence of genetic microcephaly has been estimated at 1 in 25,000 live births. Possible causes of acquired microcephaly have been associated with trisomy of chromosome 13, deletion of chromosome 5, PKU, Tay-Sachs, encephalitis, and excessive X-ray irradiation. The behavior of microcephalics has been described as euphoric with rapidly shifting interests. Occasionally, they tend to engage in echolalia and echopraxia.

Hydrocephaly is related to an abnormally large head associated with excessive accumulation of cerebrospinal fluid. Although there is a correlation between this condition and mental retardation, not all hydrocephalic children are mentally retarded. Some hydrocephalics, especially of the acquired type, show insignificant intellectual deficit (Laurence, 1969).

Congenital hydrocephalus is, in most cases, of unknown origin, but such factors as congenital syphilis, spina bifida, and imperfect development of subarachnoid space in the embryonic period are thought to be contributing factors. Acquired hydrocephalus is usually less traumatic than congenital. It may be caused by untreated encephalitis or meningitis.

Chromosomal Aberrations

Chromosomal aberrations occur at the stage of cell division. Cells divide in two ways depending on whether they are sex or body cells. Sex cells divide by a process known as meiosis and somatic cells by a process known as mitosis. During this process, various types of aberrations can occur, such as trisomy (a surplus of one chromosome over the normal pair), aneuploidy (the excess or lack of one or more chromosomes in the diploid cell), mosaicism (a mixture of normal and aneuploid cell), mosaicism (a mixture of normal and aneuploid cells), and translocation (breakage of two chromosomes with the subsequent reciprocal exchange and reunion of the fragments).

Chromosomal aberrations can be associated with changes in sex chromosomes, as in Turner's and Kleinfelter's syndrome, or somatic chromosomes, as in Down's syndrome. Down's syndrome, also referred to as mongolism, acromicria, and trisomy G21, is the most common genetic disorder associated with mental retardation. Prevalence in the United States is estimated between 35,000 and 50,000. While 87 percent of Down's syndrome individuals show sexual infantilism, it is estimated that 13 percent reach normal sexual development. Considerable numbers of this group suffer from congenital heart malformations, and speech defects are common. The average IQ of Down's syndrome individuals is approximately 50, although some questionable cases of borderline intelligence were reported. The majority of Down's syndrome cases occur as a genetic accident in otherwise normal families. Twin studies reveal concordance between identical twins, and discordance between fraternal twins. Three types of chromosomal variations in Down's syndrome are reported: trisomy G21, translocation, and mosaicism. Trisomy is the most common of all Down's syndrome cases (Baroff, 1974). A study done in Poland (Kostrzewski, 1970) suggests that Down's syndrome children whose etiology is associated with mosaicism usually have a higher IQ than those whose etiology is associated with trisomy G21.

No constant biochemical and endocrinological variables have been discovered in Down's syndrome. Some investigators, however, suggest a high incidence of thyroid dysfunction in mothers of Down's syndrome. Findings of changes in the central nervous system of Down's syndrome subjects are inconsistent, although reduction in size of the brainstem and cerebellum has been observed, and there is some evidence of abnormal sleep rhythm and a low level of rapid eye movement (REM) sleep in infants with Down's syndrome.

Smith (1993) reported that Fragile X syndrome is believed to be second only to Down's syndrome as an etiology of mental retardation in males. Males with Fragile X syndrome usually display moderately to severely impaired cognitive functioning level. Awareness and knowledge of Fragile X syndrome among special educators has been reported by Wilson and Mazzoco (1993). For their study, they surveyed elementary special education teachers in Colorado. Results revealed that significantly more respondents had knowledge of Down's syndrome than of fetal alcohol or Fragile X syndrome. The study revealed that respondents' level of education, receipt of a degree, or years of experience teaching children were not associated with greater awareness or knowledge of Fragile X syndrome.

Disorders of Gestation

Various disorders of gestation of nonspecific etiology have been associated with mental retardation. One of the most common results of gestation disorders is prematurity, which may be associated with developmental and intellectual abnormalities. It has been suggested that cerebral hemorrhage, to which premature infants are susceptible, is the primary reason for mental retardation. Another factor that may be related to prematurity is a low socioeconomic level of the parents. It should be pointed out again, however, that it is not the socioeconomic level per se, but poor nutrition of the expectant mother, along with inadequate prenatal, obstetrical, and postnatal care, that are causes related to prematurity.

Psychogenic Factors

Most of the psychogenic factors contributing to mental retardation produce only mild levels of retardation. They may also produce educational retardation, for example, impaired motivation or negative achievement attitudes. Psychological deprivation could result in pseudoretardation, which may be modifiable by treatment.

In addition to psychological deprivation, environmental deprivation in infancy and early childhood has also been associated with mental retardation. This applies especially to disorders of nutrition. Our information about the relationship between nutrition and cognitive development is derived from animal research and the observation of humans subjected to adverse environmental conditions. Animal research reveals that nutritional deprivation is associated with reduced brain weight as well as histological and biochemical changes in brain tissue.

In humans, mental retardation is associated with nutritional disorders during the period of active brain growth that takes place during the last months of pregnancy and the early months of infancy. Kwashiorkor is a specific protein deficiency in humans associated with a high risk of mental retardation during this period.

Emotional Disabilities

When an individual's anxiety prevents the ability to function adequately under normal or average stress, he or she is usually referred to as emotionally maladjusted. There are various classification systems of emotional maladjustment. For our purposes, however, depending on the degree or severity of disturbance, it is convenient to divide emotional disturbance into mild, moderate, and severe. Degree of personality instability, pressure of anxiety, and degree of interference with behaviors of others should be the determining actors.

Mild Emotional Maladjustment

It is more difficult to describe mild emotional maladjustment than the more obvious moderate or severe. Furthermore, in children and adolescents, personality development is still in its formative stages, and some degree of fear and anxiety is to be expected. In children, most mild maladjustments are situational in nature and do not have such relatively permanent characteristics as in adults. Although we are dealing with developmental phenomena that, by definition, are distributed on a continuum and are a part of the process of socialization, for the sake of discussion, it is convenient to talk separately about mild emotional maladjustment in children and adults.

Children's mild emotional difficulties are related to problems that arise from the socialization process, whereas adolescent adjustment reactions are primarily related to the ego-identity crisis and psychosexual development.

Childhood adjustment problems have been described by Kirk (1972) as deviations from age-appropriate behavior that significantly interfere with a child's growth and development. Human development, speaking in broad psychological and social terms, is described as socialization. Socialization can be described as a process that helps children become functional members of society. Biologically and socially, the mother is the major agent of socialization in young children, so that it is only natural that maternal attitudes and personality are intrinsically related to the development of a child's personality. Any extreme rigidity or permissiveness, as well as inconsistency of parental discipline, are associated with behavior problems in children. One of the earlier studies (Behrens, 1954) reported a high correlation between a child's adjustment and such variables as maternal character structure, role, and conduct.

It is obvious that an infant and a young child have strong maternal dependency needs. Maternal rejection resulting in a child's partial or complete deprivation usually has serious repercussions for the child's emotional stability. Rejected children may manifest depressive phenomena described by such writers as Goldfarb (1943), Spitz (1948, 1951), and by Malmquist (1972). Many earlier studies dealt with children who were abandoned, orphaned by war, or born in institutions. Spitz indicates that partial deprivation refers to those children who, after establishing a satisfactory emotional relationship with the mother for the first six months of life, are thereafter frustrated by being separated from her. This leads to a condition that Spitz describes as anaclitic depression.

Some studies have been concerned with the influence of rejection on a child's intellectual development. Goldfarb (1943) indicated that children who grew up in institutions had IQs lower than children of comparable backgrounds who grew up in foster homes. The following is a partial description of children with depressive reactions:

> A physiognomy which records a sad, depressed or unhappy looking child . . .
> Withdrawal and inhibition with little interest in any activity. Low frustration
> tolerance coupled with self-punitive behavior. Reversal of affect . . . Under-
> lying depressive feelings [masked] by foolish or provocative behavior to
> detract from assets or achievements. (Malmquist, 1972, p. 513)

In addition to depressive phenomena, children sometimes manifest
strong anger outbursts as well as fears. Anger, frequently associated with so-
called temper tantrums in children, is a manifestation of primitive reaction to
frustration. Anger in children in our society is a very common occurrence.
Sears, Macoby, and Levin (1957) report that every one of 379 mothers whom
they interviewed indicated that they had to deal with anger outbursts in their
children, and 95 percent reported strong aggression.

An early comprehensive study of anger in children was conducted by
Goodenough (1931). In her study, anger outbursts were positively related to
such factors as time of day, conditions of health, and atypical social conditions. Anger usually becomes more intense either before mealtime, when a
child is hungry, or in the evening, when the child is tired. Conditions of health
influence a child's anger, for example, a low frustration tolerance induced by
a fever or fatigue. Finally, atypical social conditions, such as unfamiliar sur-
roundings or strange people, increase the potential for anger outbursts.

In addition to anger, the fears and anxieties that are normally found in
children, if exaggerated, can create emotional problems. A distinction between
fear and anxiety is frequently made by psychodynamically-oriented psychologists. Fear is usually thought to be associated with a known source, and one
is usually aware of the reason for the fear. On the other hand, anxiety is nonspecific. When anxiety is felt, one usually has difficulty in relating to the source
of the anxiety. As a child becomes older, fear responses become more specific, and fear of a more symbolic nature increase. In older children (CA 6 to 12),
fears and anxieties are usually related to school achievement or psychosexual
problems. Freud (1970) classifies fears into archaic, common, and those related to separation anxiety. Fears of darkness, noise, strangers, and solitude may
be described as archaic fears. General or common fears are those of punishment, rejection, desertion, thunderstorms, doctors, or dentists. Fears related to
separation anxiety bring about feelings of helplessness and loneliness.

Adolescent adjustment problems are intimately related to that period of
life, which is characterized by stress brought about by the major physiological, psychological, and social changes that occur in the process of maturation.
This stress is especially accentuated in our contemporary, technological, and
multicultural society. In relatively primitive and agrarian societies, which, in
most cases, are culturally homogeneous, the transition from childhood to adolescence is determined by specific role identification. Children mostly follow
in the footsteps of their parents' occupations, and since cultural roles are clear-

ly delineated, there is less likelihood for ego-identity crises to occur. On the other hand, in multicultural, technological societies, there are many conflicting and confusing roles with which adolescents may identify. Furthermore, confusing role images are often projected by the mass media.

Psychosexual maturation is one area in which anxiety in adolescents is most frequently manifested. From the psychoanalytical point of view, psychosexual adjustment reactions are related to the normal sequence of psychosexual behavior such as the discovery of sex differences, sexual curiosity, erotic genital exploration, and sexual play (Sours, 1972). Clinicians claim that anxiety in adolescents can be heightened by such behaviors as sex play, exhibitionism, masturbation, and attempted intercourse.

Kazdin (1992), in his review, stressed the importance of interaction between child, at-risk behavior, and parental neglect and abuse. He also emphasized that issues of mental health and mental illness in children and adolescents have been neglected when compared with similar work with adults. He also pointed out two well-known findings: (a) that many behaviors regarded by parents and teachers as problematic emerge over the course of normal development; and (b) that rates for dysfunction and specific diagnoses vary as a function of several factors, such as age, sex, parental education, and marital status.

Moderate Emotional Maladjustment

The distinction between a mild and moderate degree of emotional maladjustment is frequently difficult to determine. In general, one may assume that a moderate degree of emotional disturbance is manifested when an individual's behavior shows a consistent pattern of anxiety that interferes with everyday activity. Traditionally, individuals with such behavior patterns are described as neurotic. Words such as *anxiety, apprehension, worry,* and *uneasiness* frequently occur in discussions of neurotic behavior. At times, neurotics manifest physical or somatic symptoms, such as nausea, lack of appetite, indigestion, cold sweats, or palpitations. Frequently, a neurotic is dominated by feelings of doubt, loss of confidence, helplessness, or indecisiveness. Psychoanalyst Klein (1944) described neurosis as:

> A functional disturbance characterized by ambivalent emotional attitudes toward a conflict situation so that the patient feels himself trapped by those attitudes. Unlike the psychotic patient the neurotic is well oriented with respect to his physical and social environment and appreciates the abnormal nature of his disturbance. (p. 481)

Neurotic disorders are frequently difficult to treat since the symptoms serve the purpose of reinforcing what has been described as neurotic needs.

Psychological literature lists many syndromes of neurotic behaviors. For this overview, only those syndromes found frequently among school-age children and adolescents will be discussed. These disturbing conditions, although not necessarily in order of importance, are character disorders, hyperactivity syndrome, school phobia, and anorexia nervosa. Less frequently observed in this age group are hysterical reactions and disassociative reactions.

Character disorders occur when healthy personality needs, such as the need for achievement, acceptance, or affection, are frustrated. These basically healthy needs can turn into neurotic needs as a reaction to deep-seated feelings of insecurity and inferiority. A youngster who cannot find satisfaction in school achievement or competitive sports, who feels insecure or a failure, might find satisfaction in the rough power obtained by bullying and coercing other youngsters. A girl who might not have been appreciated at home, who has been neglected or rejected, might look for acceptance or affection from gang members. Frequently, youngsters who manifest character disorders also show other symptoms of neurotic behavior, such as nail biting, stuttering and stammering, or temper tantrums.

Character disorders are found most commonly in those delinquents whose antisocial conduct is determined by their neurotic needs. Some writers have described them as neurotic delinquents (Bennett, 1960). However, a majority of delinquents are not neurotic but simply products of an inadequate or inappropriate socialization process. In this respect, they manifest social rather than emotional maladjustment and will be discussed in the next chapter.

There are many school-age children characterized by excessive activity, compulsive and disruptive behavior, inability to learn quickly, short attention span, low frustration tolerance, speech impediments, and lack of inhibition. Such children have been described in the psychological literature as either hyperactive or hyperkinetic.

Although hyperactivity and hyperkinesis frequently have been used synonymously, Calhoun (1977) suggests that hyperactivity should refer primarily to psychological and/or neurological disorders. Similarly, Freedman et al. (1971) indicate that all hyperkinetic children are hyperactive, but not all hyperactive children are hyperkinetic. The behavior of hyperactive children has been reported to be fragmentary, disorganized, and continuously erratic (Sykes et al., 1971). Approximately 7 percent of all school-age children in the United States are estimated to be hyperactive, with boys significantly outnumbering girls (Renshaw, 1974).

Current data about ADHA (Attention Deficit Hyperactivity Disorder) has been reported by DuPaul, Guevremont, and Barkley (1991). Estimates of ADHD prevalence in school-age children range from 3 percent to 5 percent, with boys overrepresented 5:1 to 10:1 among those referred for treatment. It has been observed that with age, difficulties with activity level is becoming less pressing than concern with problems of sustained attention and impulse control. The writers also point out that in adolescents, attention and impulsivity deficits may be associated with other affective disorders, such as conduct disorders or emerging intrafamilial conflicts. They recommend that for the assessment of ADHD in adolescents, various procedures should be used, such as traditional clinical interviews with structural psychiatric interviews and standardized behavior rating scales.

Hakole (1992) pointed out that a student who has only ADD (Attention Deficit Disorder) and no other disability condition may not be entitled to special education services under the *IDEA (Individuals with Disabilities Education Act)* or state education laws. However, such a student may be entitled to special services under provisions of section 504 of Public Law 112.

A review of studies describing observations of parent-child interactions with hyperactive children has been reported by Denford, Barkley, and Stokes (1991). It is a well-known fact that children diagnosed with ADHD have difficulties with control of their activities and focusing of attention. Many of them also exhibit aggression. Results from observational studies suggest that hyperactive children may evoke certain behaviors in their parents. The writers suggested that medication for children and parent training should be the elements of comprehensive treatment programs.

In the past, hyperactivity was considered the result of either "organic" or "emotional" factors. However, it is now recognized that emotions themselves are related to complex factors of organism-environment interaction. It is conceivable that, as suggested by Block (1977), rapid cultural changes can contribute significantly to hyperactivity in children. Consider the changes that have taken place since the advent of television in the amount and kind of information to which children are exposed. Prior to the advent of television, the child of preschool age was exposed to visual or auditory input from only the immediate environment, which in most instances consisted of family and peers. Only older children and adolescents were able to absorb the kind of information that was available in printed form. Although the amount of information was limited, the child was not exposed to "emotionally" loaded information before being able to comprehend it. Complex, frequently irrelevant, and conflicting information to which children and adolescents are exposed contribute to insecurity and uncertainty.

In addition, one may consider such factors as changes in family patterns and changes in children's daily schedules that are related to recent cultural changes. Food additives and lighting have been known to affect children's behavior. Feingold (1976) reports that children's behavior is decidedly affected by artificial food additives, and Ott (1976) concludes from his investigation that the disruptive behavior of hyperactive children, who worked under full spectrum, shielded fluorescent lighting, diminished so sharply that special-class placement did not become necessary.

Clinicians interested in the emotional disturbances of childhood point toward phobic reactions aggravated by school setting and refer to such behavioral disorders as school phobia. A phobia is described as an irrational fear of an object or situation, for example, claustrophobia is a morbid fear of closed places. As pointed out by White (1964), "The word 'morbid' differentiates it from a normal fear and is inserted to indicate that we speak of phobia only when the thing that is feared offers no actual danger" (p. 254). In a phobic individual, the source of anxiety is different from the object of fear. Therefore, the mechanism in phobia is displacement, since anxiety is displaced in order to find a less terrifying object.

In the case of school phobia, it should be understood that it is not a fear of school that is of primary importance, but a fear of being separated from home, or, explicitly, the mother. Eisenberg (1958) considers school phobia to be a kind of separation anxiety that frequently is unconsciously reinforced by the mother. One frequently finds that the mother of a school phobic child is highly anxious or neurotic. The child fears that while at school, some unexpected tragedy will happen to the mother and leaves the child lost and abandoned. In such cases, the reluctance to go to school is transferred into anxiety reactions that, in turn, create a vicious circle by increasing maternal anxiety.

At the same time as the child is fearful of losing the safety of his or her mother, the child enjoys power over her. Kessler (1972) emphasizes this by stating that "any phobic child obtains extra attention and enjoys a perverted sense of power as the parents try helplessly to deal with the tyrannies of his symptoms" (p. 405). The same writer suggests that the dynamics of school phobia are generally more immature and dependent.

Not every fear of school or truancy should be interpreted as a school phobia. The pattern of absenteeism in truancy differs from that in school phobia. Although the absenteeism of a truant is haphazard, the child usually leaves home to go to school and then "skips" school. A school-phobic child presents the most severe symptoms when having to go to school after a prolonged absence, such as vacation. More important, however, is the obvious presence of strong anxiety, at times with psychosomatic symptoms.

Kerney and Silverman (1992) expressed a need for caution when diagnosing panic disorders in children and adolescents. They stress the need for more cautious inferences based on available data. In their opinion, further research should focus on correcting existing methodological errors.

A condition of severe weight loss associated with emotional difficulties is on the increase among adolescent girls. This condition is termed *anorexia nervosa*. Despite an emaciated appearance and considerable weight loss, the anoretic will continue to lose weight, claiming that hunger is not felt. Interest in this condition has increased (Duddle, 1974).

Anorexia nervosa was first recognized in the past century as a hysterical condition. A more current description of this syndrome (Dally, 1969) suggests that it is related to many other neurotic conditions. It would appear that anorexia nervosa does not exist as a single specific condition, but is rather a symbol of nervous malnutrition. Somatic complaints may result when an already weak organ or body part becomes the focal point for conversion symptoms. Some writers (Suinn, 1975) assume that anorexia nervosa is a visceral disturbance. Kessler (1972) suggests that anorexia nervosa is caused by a resistance to growing up, especially as it relates to sexual maturation.

Freehil (1973) maintains that there are two forms of anorexia nervosa. One is characterized by a severe neurotic or schizophrenic conflict, while the "true" anorexia nervosa is marked by disturbance of body image. If the youngster's inner tension is considerable and the environmental conditions difficult, the equilibrium may break down and hostility will take control to such an extent that self-hate becomes common and reaches formidable proportions with a considerable increase in frustration. The parents of anoretic children present no uniform type of psychopathology, although many of those who subsequently become anoretic probably have been overprotected.

Freedman and Kaplan (1972) describe anorexia nervosa as a nonclassic psychophysiological disorder in which it is difficult to determine the existence of a biological factor. Most of the symptoms can be explained on the basis of severe psychological difficulties resulting in a limitation of nutritional intake.

In anoretics, there seems to be a disturbance in the perception of stimuli arising from the body, especially those of hunger and body image. In most anoretics, the whole eating process is disturbed. Awareness of body sensations of hunger and fullness in normal controls and anorexia nervosa patients has been investigated by Garfinkel (1974). He reports that both groups experience similar gastric sensations, the only difference being the mood associated with hunger. Patients reported no gastric sensations at the end of the meal, while normals reported gastric fullness. Frequently in anoretics, awareness of hunger is associated with fear of eating. Those patients who gain and maintain weight do not rely on their sensations to determine food intake. They usually are served regularly by others, and they eat the exact amount served. Crisp, Harding, and McGuinness (1974) suggest that family conflict seems to be a major psychodynamic factor in anorexia nervosa. It is especially true when the child's illness may serve a protective function for both or one parent, especially in those situations where marital problems exist. Wold (1973) reports similar patterns of psychodynamic interaction in three cases of anorexia nervosa patients.

Sex differences in favor of females were found in anorexia nervosa, with females outnumbering males approximately four to one. There are two major reasons why anorexia nervosa assumes this sexual disproportion. In females, the bodily changes in adolescence are physically more profound, which makes sexual symbolism more important. It is also possible that females are more concerned about their body and physical appearance and do not like to look fat. On the other hand, a much simpler explanation is suggested by Toms and Crisp (1973), anoretic males might be less apt to seek help. In the case of anoretic males, it is also known that as children they are anoretic.

There is a dispute in the literature regarding the most appropriate treatment of anorexia nervosa. Some investigators (Garfinkel, Kline, & Stancer, 1973; Agras, 1974; Bhanji & Thompson, 1974) suggest the use of operant conditioning. On the other hand, Bruch (1974) is most outspoken against the use of behavior modification techniques. He feels that behavior modification will work only if it is interpreted as a part of a more comprehensive treatment plan involving correction of underlying individual and family problems. Schmurer, Rubin, and Roy (1973) proposed that alleviation of the fear of eating and gaining weight should be the most important focus of therapy. Likewise, Szyrynski (1973) proposes a psychotherapeutic approach, using behavior modification or tube feeding only to alleviate life-threatening situations or gross weight loss. Liebman, Minuchin, and Baker (1974) present an integrated model suggesting that family therapy should be a part of the treatment for anorexia nervosa.

Less frequently found than school phobia or anorexia nervosa are hysterical or disassociative reactions, such as voice loss, inability to swallow, tics, strange abdominal pains, somnambulism (sleepwalking), or hallucinations. These symptoms are usually associated with the onset of puberty. Inability to swallow is limited to certain types of foods; tics usually involve the musculature of the face, neck, and head, as in blinking, nose wrinkling, and twisting the mouth. It should be pointed out, however, that in each case of suspected hysterical symptomatology, detailed pediatric and neurological examination is essential to rule out organic reasons for the conditions.

Severe Emotional Maladjustment

In contrast to mild and moderate emotional disturbances in which the individual, although disturbed, is still able to maintain contact with reality, severe emotional disturbances (psychoses) are characterized by loss of contact with reality and personality disassociation. Although the literature identifies as separate conditions childhood schizophrenia (Bender, 1956), infantile autism (Kanner, 1949), and dementia infantilis (Dietze, 1963), for the purpose of our discussion, these conditions will be treated under the general heading of childhood psychosis. Although this book, for the sake of simplicity, discusses childhood autism as a severe emotional maladjustment of childhood, or childhood psychosis, the reader should be aware that there is an increased trend among psychologists to view childhood autism as a developmental disability rather than a clear-cut affective disorder.

A brief historical overview of the development of the concept of severe childhood emotional disturbances will help to place this discussion into proper perspective. For a long time, physicians and psychiatrists simply did not consider the possibility of the existence of childhood psychosis. As noted earlier, it was assumed, until the nineteenth century, that psychoses were the result of "stress of life," and children simply had not lived long enough to experience stress; therefore, psychoses were associated with chronological maturity. It was not until the nineteenth century that psychiatrists became interested in the discussion of "childhood insanity." As late as the turn of the twentieth century, there was still a common belief that childhood psychosis was related to heredity, fright, or masturbation.

A more contemporary view of childhood psychosis was introduced by Heller, who, in the 1920s, described a condition that he labeled "demential infantilis" (Dietze, 1963). His description corresponded in many respects to present-day infantile autism, with some major differences. In contrast to autistic children, those described by Heller exhibited normal overall development until two to four years of age, when deterioration began. Dietze described dementia infantilis as characterized by normal physical and mental development in the first years, with the illness beginning in the third and fourth years, including motor restlessness, anxious behavior, stereotypes, gradual loss of speech, complete lack of neurological localized signs, gradual but complete deterioration, and preservation of intelligent facial impressions. As a result of gradual deterioration, such children eventually become profoundly deficient in all respects while still retaining intelligent facial expressions.

More recently, Jordan, Libby, and Powell (1995) suggested that three cognitive theories should be considered for the explanation of autism. Those theoretical positions are a metarepresentational deficit, a social-affective dysfunction, and an executive functioning deficit. The writers believe that autistic thinking can be interpreted as a particular learning style. They also emphasize a need for better communication between professionals concerned with etiology and those who are educating autistic children.

Kanner's (1949) description of infantile autism differs in some respects from childhood schizophrenia as described by Bender (1956). In addition to inappropriate, bizarre behavior, autistic children manifest this disorder early in infancy with a corresponding lack of language development, while schizophrenic children may reveal the onset of their condition at any time in early childhood with gradual deterioration in language and cognitive skills. In addition, schizophrenic children are characterized by a variety of stereotyped and bizarre behaviors, whereas autistic children are characterized by the preservation of sameness. Elaborating on Kanner's and Bender's work, Mahler (1976) describes children whose psychotic behavior is related to problems in the weaning process. She describes this syndrome as symbiotic psychosis.

Psychological literature described the behavior of psychotic children as unpredictable, erratic, and bizarre. In general, disturbances of perception, developmental rate, language, and cognitive functioning have been noted. Ornitz (1976) reports that such children are frequently disturbed by wool blankets or clothing and seem to prefer smooth surfaces. The heightened awareness of sensation is often associated with a tendency to seek it out and to induce it. This might explain why psychotic children engage in various ritualistic stereotyped motor behaviors.

The most characteristic aspect of autistic children's behavior, and for that matter the behavior of all psychotic children, is peculiarity of verbal communication. The language of psychotic children is generally underdeveloped and in most instances echolalic. Frequently, psychotic children do not use pronouns appropriately and have a tendency to refer to themselves in the third person. Many investigators feel that the use of conversational language by psychotic children is the best indicator of prognosis. It is felt that the prognosis for recovery is poor if a psychotic child does not use language for meaningful conversation by the age of ten or twelve.

Frequently, the language of psychotic children reveals autistic thought disorder. An example of autistic thinking would be believing that "dreams come through windows at night," that other people can "feel my pain," or that the wind, moon, or sun are "alive." A note of caution has to be expressed, however, when interpreting autistic language. Some children may express seemingly autistic ideas in "make-believe" fashion, and such playful behavior is obviously normal. It is the difference between pretending in normal children and actually believing in distorted reality in autistic children that is the distinguishing feature. Being able to assess the difference requires skillful clinical experience.

Echolalia, or the mechanical repetition of the verbal expressions of others, has been noted in psychotic children. Earlier psychodynamic interpretations attributed echolalia to the child's refusal to communicate. More recently, however, it has been explained as the natural result of a failure to comprehend (Baker et al., 1976). The same investigators feel that the poor level of intellectual attainment frequently found in autistic children may be attributed to specific defects in language rather than a global defect in intellect.

Interest in the comparison of behavioral and cognitive variables of autistic and retarded children has been noted in the psychological literature

(Frankel & Graham, 1976; Holroyd & McArthur, 1976; DeMyer, 1976). DeMyer, in a survey of 155 autistic children, reports that most of them had an IQ of 67 or below, and 75 percent had an IQ below 51. However, some were able to advance from a subnormal level of intelligence to a verbal or performance IQ within an average range of intelligence.

PSYCHOLOGICAL EMPHASIS

From a psychological perspective, exceptionality implies disturbance in the equilibrium or balance between opposite emotions. In psychodynamic terms, it is expressed as a conflict between "id" and "ego" (neurotic anxiety), while in the neuropsychological terms, it can be expressed as an imbalance between excitation and inhibition.

As an intelligent, cognitive organism at the highest level of psychogenetic development, since ancient times Homo sapiens attempted to understand their own behavior. The current dualism of cognition and affect can be traced to the writings of Plato, who differentiated between intellect (nous) and soul (psyche). In more recent times, this dichotomy was expressed as "id"-"body," "intellect"-"emotions," "cognition"-"affect" issues. According to Vygotsky (1982), this psychological crisis manifested itself in the emergence of such theories as reflexology and behaviorism on the one hand, and psychoanalysis and humanistic psychology on the other.

Prior to the brief discussion of major current personality theories in psychology, an overview of basic theories of human emotions will be in order. The basic theories may be identified as evolutionary, physiological, cortico-thalamic, conditioning-learning, neuropsychological, and cognitive.

The evolutionary theory is associated with the seminal contribution of Darwin, especially in his book *The Origin of the Expressive Movements in Humans.* Viewing human emotions from a phylogenetic perspective, Darwin related human emotions to the corresponding affective and instinctive reactions of animals. A number of other nineteenth-century psychologists expressed similar views.

A physiological interpretation found its expression in a theory of emotions proposed independently by an American psychologist, James, and a Danish psychologist, Lange. Hence it is known as the James-Lange theory. Briefly stated, what we call an emotion is the cognitive perception of awareness of physiological changes, which take place in our organism following a strongly positive or negative event.

Cortico-thalamic theory emerged as a result of experiments conducted by Cannon and Bard. The theory suggests that basic profound emotions are associated with subcortical areas and can even be present in the absence of cortex. Cortex has been associated with inhibiting functions. The whole range of human emotions can be explained by inhibition-excitation-balance, or lack of it.

A notion that more complex human emotions or feelings are learned responses has been associated with conditioning theory. The theory itself has been identified as classical or orthodox (Pavlovian) and operant or Skinnerian. According to this theoretical position, emotions can be divided into unconditional or reflexive and conditional or learned.

More recent neuropsychological research, primarily with the limbic system, refined older cortico-thalamic findings about the inhibition-excitation properties of the central nervous system (CNS). Eysenck, a British psychologist, suggested that when the cortex is very easily aroused, it produces greater inhibition of impulses coming from the brain stem. As a result, the cortex is not flooded by emotional stimuli, and "less emotionality" is in evidence. Conversely, weak excitatory potential in the cortex allows for greater stimulation of the cortex by lower brain areas, resulting in "more manifest emotionality."

The cognitive psychology approach in the interpretation of human emotions is enjoying increasing popularity.

A more complex construct than emotionality is the concept of personality. Personality may be defined as a relatively stable set of behavioral characteristics acquired by an individual during the formative years. Complex interactions among biological-psychological and social variables influence formation of personality. Unconscious and conscious experiences, as well as learning and conditioning, should be kept in mind. Various degrees of importance attached to the above variable account for numerous theoretical interpretations about the nature of personality. Consequently, there are many theories of personality. In this chapter, discussion will be limited to five major theories: psychoanalytical, humanistic, existential, behavioristic, and dialectical. Within the limits of this chapter, only a broad overview will be presented.

Psychoanalytical theory, also known as Freudian theory, is probably the most widely known and popular. The basic assumption of this comprehensive theory is that human behavior is influenced by two opposing instinctual forces: the positive force, or Eros, which also includes libido, and the negative or destructive force known as Thanatos. The structure of personality consists of three constructs: id-representing biogenic drives and needs; ego-representing cultural models of behavior. Conflicts between id, ego, and superego result in anxiety, which could be, if excessive, detrimental to the integrity of personality. Freud suggested that a tension between ego and the external world results in fear, or objective anxiety; between ego and id, in neurotic anxiety; and between ego and superego, in moral anxiety. The extent of anxiety will determine the existence of mild, moderate, or severe emotional disturbance.

Strong anxiety may become debilitating to the individual's personality. Emotional disturbances traditionally referred to as neuroses are examples of moderate disturbances. Some of those conditions have been known as obsessive-compulsive, hysterical, hypochondrias, phobias, and anorexia nervosa. In order to defend itself from anxiety, ego employs defense mechanisms. The major defense mechanisms are known as repression, displacement, rationalization, and projection.

Repression is the basic defense mechanism. It occurs when unpleasant experience is "forgotten" or relegated to the unconscious. Displacement occurs when we relegate negative feelings toward someone else and not the object of our hostility. For example, youngsters may be angry at their fathers but afraid to express such feelings. They may instead turn their anger toward the young brother or sister.

Rationalization, simply, is "justification" for our otherwise unacceptable behavior.

Projection is defined as attributing our feelings to someone else in order to justify our behavior.

One of the more recent personality theories is humanistic theory. Major formulations of this theory are attributed to Maslow (1954). It is sometimes viewed as a "third force" between psychoanalysis and behaviorism. Unlike psychoanalysis, humanistic psychology does not emphasize unconscious influence or the primacy of instinctual libidinal force. Maslow suggested three major human assertions: human needs are arranged in hierarchy; self-actualized people are motivated by values of being. Maslow maintained that there are five levels of human needs, which in ascending order are: physiological; safety; love, affection, and belonging; esteem; and self-actualization. Maslow also assumed that in order to move to a higher level, one has to satisfy previous needs.

Roots of existential theory can be found in the writings of Danish philosopher Soren Kirkegaard in the nineteenth century. The movement gained in popularity in Europe in the context of disillusionment brought about by two major wars. The age-old notions of searching for the essence of human existence as suggested by the writings of Hegel, Freud, and most of the philosophers seemed irrelevant in light of the human tragedies brought about by the wars. Some writers, such as Heidegger and Sartre, turned their attention to the question of human existence. Their ideas were incorporated by Swiss psychiatrist Binswanger (1963) into the theoretical structure of existential psychology.

In general, existentialism can be described as an attempt to return emotional substance to the intellectual life of the individual. Existentialists view individual emotional problems as a result of alienation from society and a resulting loss of authenticity. As suggested by Heidegger, alienation arises in situations where there is a basic breakdown of morality, and humans stop caring about fellow humans. Individuals who feel alienated from the "establishment" attempt to seek authority outside of an established framework; hence, we notice the emergence, especially among alienated youth, of new identities. Some of those movements change extremely rapidly. Existentialists believe that alienated individuals can find new meaning and joy in life through commitment to causes of their choice.

Behaviorism is one of the popular contemporary schools of psychology dealing with human behavior. Physiologists and psychologists interested in the study of reflexes, such as Sechenov, Bechtiarev, and Pavlov, are considered its forerunners. Although other schools of psychology are interested in broad theoretical conceptualizations about the nature of human personality, behaviorism, in the tradition of reflexology, is interested in the study of behavior simply as behavior. Nineteenth-century reflexology, which subsequently became the foundation of radical or methodological behaviorism, denied the need for scientific psychology to deal with the question of "why?" of human behavior. It postulated the reduction of all experiences to physiological functions dependent on environmental determinism and an avoidance of a conscious process. As a result, it became reductionistic in nature. Recently, a shift is being seen in the behavioristic position toward explaining human behavior and emotions in broader terms.

Traditional behaviorism is associated in American psychology with Watson, who, in 1925, published his thesis on *Psychology as a Science of Behavior.* Contemporary behaviorism is associated with Skinner, who, in his 1931 dissertation, points out that a stimulus-response model can adequately explain behavior. Behaviorism is based on a set of empirical principles and generalizations. Its main principle is that for every organism, behavior will increase in frequency if followed by positive reinforcement and will decrease with negative reinforcement. Reinforcers can be divided into primary and secondary ones. Primary reinforcers are those that satisfy certain biological needs. Events or objects repeatedly paired with primary reinforcers may acquire reinforcing properties of their own, thus becoming secondary reinforcers.

A personality theory least known in the West but preeminent in the former Soviet Union could be described as dialectical. It was influenced by dialectical-materialist philosophy, Marxist ideology, and Vygotsky's cultural-historical position in psychology. The central notion of dialectical theory is the notion of collectivism or the primacy of society over an individual.

Collectivism as a social idea has been developed by Makarenko, a noted Soviet educator-ideologue (Holowinsky, 1990a). Makarenko maintained that the collective is the developer of personality and that personality can develop most effectively within collective. Collective can be defined as a group of individuals with the same goals and objectives who give up their individual identities for the sake of collective identity. As stated by Makarenko, membership in a collective is not based on friendship or love but on mutual interests.

Dialectical personality theory strongly criticized psychoanalytical views. More recently, however, in the context of the restructuring of the former Soviet psychology, more positive attitudes toward psychoanalysis can be noticed (Holowinsky, 1990a).

SOCIOLOGICAL EMPHASIS

In terms of consensus about the nature, etiology, and extent of exceptionality, socially exceptional, maladaptive, or different behaviors have the least degree of consensus. Lay people and social scientists reveal little agreement about the nature of socially maladaptive behaviors. This is understandable, since a socially maladaptive behavior can be defined only within the context of a given society or culture. Philosophical, ideological, or political orientation in any given society at any time can influence how socially maladaptive behaviors are viewed. In the opinion of this writer, such major orientation could be defined as autocratic, democratic, and Marxist-Leninist.

Within an autocratic system, it is generally assumed that rules of behavior emanate from a set of promulgated principles and are not dependent on the consent of those governed; for example, the Japanese concept of *tenns* or "heavenly sovereign"; Islamic rules promulgated in the Koran; reliance of fundamentalists on the Bible, and so forth. In such a context, socially maladaptive behavior will be a kind of behavior that deviates from the prescribed rules.

In the democratic system, the basic assumption is that the rules that govern behaviors should have the consent of those governed. In this context, socially maladaptive behaviors are less broadly defined. Only behaviors that directly infringe on the rights and freedoms of others can be classified as socially maladaptive, for example, crime and juvenile delinquency.

In Marxist-Leninist totalitarian societies, socially maladaptive behaviors are the kind of behaviors that interfere with the goals and objectives of a collective. The collective as a social organization is a concept introduced into Soviet educational literature in the late 1920s, and early 1930s and elaborated on by Makarenko. For a more detailed discussion of the concept of collective, see, for example, Holowinsky (1989).

The main difference between socially maladaptive or emotionally disturbed individuals, at least from the psychodynamic perspective, is the absence of anxiety. By definition, anxiety must be present to classify someone as emotionally disturbed. On the other hand, socially maladaptive behaviors may be, but not necessarily are, associated with anxiety.

In our culture, crime, juvenile delinquency, and behaviors related to these, such as substance abuse, cults, and runaway phenomena, can be broadly described as socially maladaptive behaviors.

A simple definition of criminal behavior, or crime, is illegal behavior. Crime, however, beyond the concise, simple definition, is a complex phenomenon that is influenced by cultural, social, philosophical, and political variables.

Major theoretical explanations for criminal behavior have been suggested by Sutherland and Cressey (1970) as classical, cartographic, sociological, socialist, and topological. The classical school explains criminal behavior in terms of hedonistic philosophy, which postulated that humans are attracted to pleasurable experiences and repelled by punishment. The cartographic view explains criminal behavior in terms of such variables as ecology, culture, and composition of population. The sociological school emphasizes the importance of group and social processes in the understanding of criminal behavior. The socialist interpretation, essentially based on Marxist ideology, views crime as a typical condition of "imperfect" societies, that is, those in which one class is exploited by the other. The topological school attempts to explain criminal behavior in terms of types of individuals who may be prone to criminal behavior, for example, feebleminded persons and psychopaths.

Difficulties in the determination of criminal statistics have been explained by Sutherland and Cressey (1970). They point out that the number of criminals known to police is not an adequate index of crime. They list five possible reasons for this discrepancy:

1. The number of known crimes is smaller than the number actually committed.
2. The accuracy of crime statistics depends on the efficiency of the police reporting them.
3. The ratio of crimes committed to crimes reported varies according to the offense.
4. Varieties in the criminal law may affect the volume of crimes known to the police.
5. The crime ratio is usually stated in proportion to the population surveyed, but the determination of this base is often difficult.

"Juvenile delinquency" as a label for antisocial behavior is primarily a legal definition that distinguishes between a juvenile and an adult offender. It should be pointed out that juvenile delinquency, as a separate group of offenses, is a rather recent development. No attempt was made in ancient and medieval times to distinguish between a juvenile and an adult offender; everyone who reached an "age of reason" was treated similarly.

Since there is no agreement on what constitutes delinquent behavior, it is difficult to obtain reliable data on the incidence and prevalence of delinquency. Peterson, Quay, and Tiffany (1963) point out that earlier formulations about juvenile delinquency were typically based on case history information, which is vulnerable to subjective bias. Authorities do agree, however, that the number of juvenile delinquents in the United States has been on the increase since the 1940s. Short (1966) reports that, prior to 1940, 1 percent of all youngsters were involved in acts of juvenile delinquency. Delinquency cases handled by the juvenile courts in the United States ranged from 200,000 in 1940 (the population between CA 10 to 17 was nineteen million) to 1,268,000 in 1966 (the population between CA 10 to 17, thirty million) (Sutherland & Cressey, 1970).

Bennett (1960) lists numerous characteristics of delinquent behavior: stealing, pilfering, forgery, embezzlement, lying, truancy, wandering, running away from home or school, aggression or destruction, quarrelsomeness, tormenting, provocation, extreme disobedience or defiance, open hostility to parents and teachers, cruelty to animals or young children, incorrigibility, and verbal aggression. Halleck (1972) provides a rather broad definition of delinquency in terms of those behaviors:

> [Behavior] that will bring a child to the attention of those clinicians and those social agencies which are involved in disciplining, rehabilitating or treating offenders. Such attention is called for when a child repeatedly engages in acts which are either illegal or offend the morality of the greater community, and which are defined as a problem by the child himself, by his parents or by the community. (p. 542)

Many investigations have provided behavioral descriptions of delinquent activities. For example, Harris (1974) reports on a group of delinquent boys in Honolulu. The boys ranged in age from 13 to 15 and were attending eighth and ninth grades. Approximately 20 percent attended school irregularly, had a police record, and occasionally ran away from home. Nearly 50 percent sniffed paint at least a few times a week. Harris observed that "the less often one engaged in socially unacceptable behavior, the less likely was that particular boy associated with known delinquents" (p. 31).

The literature reports various attempts to classify delinquent behaviors. Bennett (1960) lists nine specific "types" of delinquents:

1. Dull or handicapped delinquents
2. Delinquents who lack adequate social training
3. "Adolescent" delinquents who show no history of misconduct prior to puberty
4. Delinquents from vicious homes
5. Secondary antisocial conduct disorders (secondary to organic condition, epilepsy, encephalitis)
6. Deprived delinquents (suffering from chronic deprivation during the formative years)
7. Neurotic delinquents
8. Psychopathic delinquents
9. Psychotic delinquents

Halleck (1972) suggests that delinquents can be classified according to biological, psychological, or sociological theoretical positions. Major associative factors with juvenile delinquency are sex of the offender, age, and educational performance.

Earlier investigations (Merrill, 1948; Glueck & Glueck, 1934) pointed out that gender plays an important role in determining frequency and type of delinquent activity. Bowker, Gross, and Klein (1980) reminded us that the 1960s data showed that females were systematically excluded from the planning and action phases of delinquent activities. Despite the fact that delinquent girls are engaging increasingly in offenses that are similar to those of boys, wide sex differences still exist.

There exists a widely accepted generalization that boys are usually adjudged delinquent at a much younger age than girls. Sutherland and Cressey (1970) reported that the peak age for juvenile delinquency in the United States is from 15 to 16 years of age.

The educational achievement of delinquent boys and girls is below age and grade expectancy level. They present a general pattern of dislike for school and school authorities. Most exhibit poor motivation (Tutt, 1973) and lack of study habits. The reasons are usually rather complex. Some have experienced educational failures as early as second or third grade. Because they did not find enough help, support, and encouragement at home, their problems simply multiplied. Others, especially those who have not had a meaningful family relationship, simply did not acquire any positive study habits. An absence of positive support at home and the negative attitude toward school or their delinquent peers makes a rebellion against educational achievement very fashionable. After all, it is easier not to achieve than to achieve, especially when nonachievement is encouraged by other members of the group.

Murphy (1986) reported that "the prevalence of some handicapping conditions among juvenile delinquents particularly emotional disturbance, learning disabilities and mental retardation is disproportionate to the prevalence estimates reported among their non-delinquent counterparts or the general population."

Associated with delinquent behaviors are substance abuse and the "runaway" phenomenon. Multiple factors contribute to substance abuse. Some of those in various combinations could be lack of strong positive relationships with significant others, poor education, a dependent-submissive personality, boredom, association with antisocial individuals, physiological dependence, availability of drugs, and so forth.

Chapter 4

CLASSIFICATION

The classification of exceptional learners has its roots in an educational movement called pedology. Pedology emerged in Europe prior to the First World War. Its stated purpose was the scientific study of children. The movement attracted well-known pioneers of developmental psychology of that time, for example, A. Binet, V. Bekhtiarev, and G.S. Hall. Interest in pedology manifested itself considerably within the Russian psychology of the 1920s. Such world-renowned psychologists as L.S. Vygotsky and A.R. Luria were supporters of pedology (Holowinsky, 1988).

The focus of this chapter will be on classification and assessment in the United States, as well as in the former Soviet Union, primarily in Russia and Ukraine.

In the United States, the history of the assessment of exceptional children can be traced to the so-called Binet examiners of the early 1920s. Early examinations were primarily psychometric, administered by school psychologists. An important factor that contributed to the rapid growth of the assessment movement was state and federal legislation related to handicapped children. As grants became available, local school districts extended the scope and size of special education programs. The rapid growth of testing, assessment, and placement of children in self-contained special education programs resulted in a backlash and the emergence of a strong "anti-testing" movement in the 1970s. Among critics of standardized testing were teachers and elementary school principals (Rudman, 1977), university professors (Kamin, 1976), and publishers of scholarly publications (Piel, 1978). Arguments against the use of standardized intelligence tests, especially with ethnic minority group children, led to a moratorium on the use of standardized IQ tests for special education placement in a number of states.

The National School Psychology Inservice Training Network published a set of recommendations for the training and practice of school psychology (Ysseldyke et al., 1984). The main emphasis was to shift the focus from an individual child "with a problem" to the functioning of a child within school as a social system. In addition to school psychologists, other professionals are involved in the assessment of exceptional children, for example, a learning disabilities teacher-consultant, school social worker, speech pathologist, and others.

In the late 1970s and early 1980s, emphasis shifted from evaluation for special class placement toward assessment for instructional purposes and assessment of children with learning disabilities. A set of recommendations describing competencies needed to assess children with learning disabilities was proposed by Cegelka (1982). Among other recommendations, Cegelka suggested that a child should be observed in his or her regular classroom setting, and that no assessment of a child should be considered complete unless the parent has been actively involved in the evaluation process as a significant observer of the child and his or her performance.

McNutt and Mandelbaum (1980) suggested that at least a minimal level of proficiency is needed in a number of areas before educators can begin to assess students for educational purposes. They named the areas as educational philosophy and goals, child and adolescent development, subject matter content, and terminology. Morgan (1982) advocated that parents of handicapped children should be involved in the IEP process. Schools should begin to deal with parents programmatically. In the area of identification of learning-disabled children, Chalfont (1984) reported, based on a survey of state education agencies, that in most of the states, five criteria are used to identify LD children, namely: failure to achieve, psychological process disorder, exclusionary criteria, etiology of perceptual or neurological disorders, and severe potential-achievement discrepancy. As recent literature indicated (Raynolds, 1985), there is still considerable confusion in the field of special education related to the meaning of potential-achievement discrepancy.

Elliott (1991) described new trends in assessment, so-called curriculum based and authentic assessment. These trends resulted from the application of behavioral assessment techniques and observation techniques. With authentic assessment, the requirement is that the learner must produce something new, rather than reproduce prior knowledge. Portfolios are another common feature of an authentic approach to assessment. Currently, authentic assessment methods are being proposed as replacements for both standardized tests and typical pencil-and-paper classroom tests.

In a provocative article, "What Is So Special About Special Education?" Detterman and Thompson (1997) conclude that special education is not yet "special." They point out that the long history of education of individuals with mental retardation can be viewed "as a pendulum that swings back and forth between competing social philosophies that are unsubstantiated by fact." Detterman and Thompson argue for an individualized approach to education and express hope that with the new technologies, such as functional magnetic resonance imaging, average evoked potential, and the identification of genetic trait loci, cognitive abilities will be better related to brain functioning.

For an easy understanding of more prevalent classification systems, this discussion will be divided into clinical and educational emphases.

Clinical Emphasis

Classifications of exceptionalities in the United States have been formulated by the American Association on Mental Deficiency (presently, the American Association on Mental Retardation) and the American Psychiatric Association. These systems will be discussed more extensively. For an easy overview of exceptionalities, this writer suggests (Holowinsky, 1983a), the following grouping: physical disabilities (structural, neurological, sensory, perceptual, chronic); communication disorders (articulation, voice, aphasic conditions, psycholinguistic problems); cognitive disabilities (intellectual subnormality, mental retardation, mental deficiency, oligophrenia, learning disabilities); affective disorders (mild, moderate, severe); and socially maladaptive behaviors (crime, juvenile delinquency, substance abuse).

Historically, physical disabilities were first to be recognized as such. By their nature, they are easily recognizable and represent a high degree of agreement about their characteristics. It is reported that the ancient Greeks recognized seizures as a physical disability.

Neurological disorders as a rule do not always result in learning or emotional difficulties. However, some neurological conditions, for example, cerebral palsy and seizures, depending on their etiopathogenesis, might be associated with impaired intellectual functioning.

External sense organs (exteroceptors) play a crucial role in the adjustment of the organism to its environment. It is a well-known fact that impairment of visual, auditory, and tactile modalities can present learning difficulties. However, these impairments as such are not necessarily associated with mental retardation.

Communication disorders are frequently divided into speech and language disorders. Speech, as a concept, refers more specifically to voice production and the mechanics of talking. Language, as a concept, encompasses complex variables of a cultural, affective, and psycholinguistic nature.

This writer suggested the concept of cognitive disabilities as a generic terminology for a variety of disorders characterized by difficulties in symbolic and abstract learning. In this class of conditions are learning disabilities, intellectual subnormality, mental retardation, mental deficiency, and oligophrenia.

Emotional or affective disorders are characterized by the presence of anxiety, disassociative thought processes, and, in severe cases, concomitant physiological, biochemical, and neuropsychological complications. The degree of anxiety might be mild, moderate, or severe. Strong anxiety usually interferes with the individual's behavior and everyday adjustment. Emotional disorders may or may not be associated with cognitive disabilities. Differential diagnosis will depend on the etiology and strength of the affective disorders. For a simplistic overview, emotional disorders may be viewed as mild, moderate, or severe. Other generic terms found in the literature are *adjustment, reactions, neurosis, psychoneurosis,* and *psychosis.*

Behaviors that interfere with the rights and freedoms of others may be described as socially maladaptive. Crime, juvenile delinquency, drugs, and alcohol abuse are considered socially maladaptive behaviors.

Since 1984, AIDS has been of concern to educators and health professionals. In children, the disease is associated with failure to attain developmental milestones or with an actual neurological deterioration. Byers (1989) pointed out that in children, "the virus appears to have a more profound effect on brain development and subsequently on the attainment and maintenance of motor, intellectual, and language development milestones than is true for adults" (p. 7). With the implementation of Public Law 99-457 in the school year 1990–1991, which established a program of early intervention for handicapped or developmentally delayed infants, it is anticipated that children with AIDS will be able to profit from special education services.

Professional Classification

In the United States, classifications of the American Association on Mental Deficiency (AAMD, presently, the American Association on Mental Retardation [AAMR]) and the American Psychiatric Association are generally known and widely used.

The original AAMD classification was developed in 1919 by the American Association for the Study of the Feebleminded. The second edition of the *Manual on Terminology and Classification in Mental Retardation* (1933) and the third (1941) were prepared by the AAMD in cooperation with the National Committee for Mental Hygiene. Etiological classification was developed in 1957 by the AAMD Committee on Nomenclature. The fifth edition was published in 1959. A number of important features were included in the 1959 edition: "the dual medical-behavioral classification system, the definition of mental retardation in operational terms, the emphasis on current level of functioning, and the limitation of the use of the mental retardation label to those individuals whose mental disability has been manifested during the developmental period" (p. 4).

The 1961 edition of the *Manual on Terminology and Classification in Mental Retardation* defined that condition both in terms of a functioning level of intelligence and adaptive behavior as "sub-average general intellectual functioning, which originates during the developmental period and is associated with impairment in adaptive behavior" (p. 3).

The manual includes mental classification, classification of measured intelligence, and classification of adaptive behavior.

Medical classification is arranged into eight major etiological groups: (1) mental retardation associated with diseases and conditions due to infection; (2) associated with diseases and conditions due to intoxication; (3) associated with diseases and conditions due to trauma or physical agent; (4) associated with diseases and conditions due to disorder of metabolism, growth, or nutrition; (5) associated with diseases and conditions due to new growth; (6) associated with diseases and conditions due to (unknown) prenatal influence; (7) associated with diseases and conditions due to unknown or uncertain causes with the structural reactions manifest; and (8) due to uncertain (or presumed psychological) causes with the functional reaction alone manifest. Medical classification also includes two supplementary categories: convulsive disorders and motor dysfunction.

Measured intelligence has been classified into five levels which, in terms of the range of standard deviation units, correspond to the following ranges: borderline, −1 to −2 SD; mild, −2 to −3 SD; moderate −3 to −4 SD; severe −4 to −5 SD; profound, below −5 SD. In terms of IQ levels on the Revised Stanford-Binet Test of Intelligence, the following IQ ranges have been accepted: borderline, 68–83; mild, 52–67; moderate, 36–51; severe, 20–35; profound, less than 20.

The classification of adaptive behavior has been arranged in four levels, which, in terms of social and vocational adequacy in adulthood, can be described as follows: Level 1: "Capable of social and vocational adequacy with proper education and training. Frequently needs supervision and guidance under serious social or economic stress" (p. 63); Level 2: "Capable of self-maintenance in unskilled or semi-skilled occupation; needs supervision and guidance when under mild social and economic stress" (p. 63); Level 3: "Can contribute partially to self-support under complete supervision; can develop self-protection skills to a minimal useful level in a controlled environment" (p. 63); Level 4: "Some motor and speech development, totally incapable of self-maintenance; needs complete care and supervision" (p. 63).

The *Manual on Terminology and Classification in Mental Retardation,* 1973 revision, introduced two major changes: deletion of the borderline category and revision of the medical classification to bring it up-to-date with current medical knowledge. More elaborate examples of adaptive behavior functioning were provided. The definition of mental retardation was changed slightly to read: "Mental retardation refers to significantly subaverage general intelligence functioning existing concurrently with deficits in adaptive behavior and manifested during the developmental period" (p. 5).

Changes in the 1970s were incorporated into the new revision published in 1983 (Grossman, 1983). As stated in the manual, this revision was made "to reflect current thinking in the field and to make it consistent with the *International Classification of Diseases-9 (ICD-9)* of the World Health Organization and the American Psychiatric Association's *Diagnostic and Statistical Manual-3 (DSM-3),* particularly with reference to medical classification" (p. 7). Levels of retardation are described with the same terms as those used in the previous AAMD manuals. However, IQ cutoff points between levels are expressed as ranges rather than as fixed numbers. For example: mild retardation, IQ 50–55 to approximately 70; moderate retardation, IQ 35–40 to 50–55; severe retardation, 20–25 to 35–40; profound, below 20 or 25 IQ points.

In 1992, the most recent classification in the field of mental retardation was published. Schalock et al. (1994) reviewed the rationale for the new classification. They pointed out that over the past forty years, the concept of mental retardation and its definition have undergone numerous changes in terminology for example, cutoff levels and the diagnostic role of adaptive behavior. Since 1983, there has been a significant paradigm shift within the field of mental retardation. In the opinion of Schalock et al., the emphasis shifted from the concept of mental retardation as an absolute trait to the notion that mental retardation is the expression of functional impact of the interaction between a person, his or her adaptive skills, and environment. The writers pointed out that during the overview stage of the 1992 proposed classification, 30 percent of respondents saw problems with the definition, and 75 percent saw problems with the classification component. However, 95 percent of respondents felt that the proposed 1992 classification reflected emerging trends in mental retardation.

Greensham, MacMiller, and Siperstein (1995) call attention to the fact that the 1992 definition of mental retardation as formulated by the AAMR represented a radical departure from Heber's (1961) and Grossman's (1983) definitions. The 1992 definition eliminated the levels of retardation and replaced them with the intensity of needed support (pervasive, extensive, limited, intermittent). The authors recommend a dialogue between the Divisions of School Psychology and Mental Retardation of the American Psychological Association and the AAMR concerning the conceptualization and definition of mental retardation.

In a recent article, Baroff (1999) suggested that the label "mental retardation" should be replaced by the label "general learning disorder." He points out that within the general category of "cognitive disabilities," we can recognize such disabilities/disorders as specific learning disabilities, broad learning disabilities, and mental retardation. He anticipates that the new label will unite all three learning disorders and also help to remove the pejorative connotation of the term *mental retardation*.

Considerable discussion took place in professional journals throughout the 1970s about the use and relevance of the IQ concept. Criticism of norm-referenced testing has been widespread, expressed by parents of exceptional children, teachers, school principals, psychologists, and publishers of scholarly publications. For example, see Cardon, 1975; Kamin, 1976; Piel, 1978; Rudman, 1977; and Zigler and Trickett, 1978. This trend has been strongly underscored by Haywood (1977), who stated: "It is necessary for us to develop, construct, and use methods of clinical assessment that depart radically from the normative model" (p. 11). Literature also emphasized differences among individuals (Underwood, 1975; Ashby, 1976), as well as differences within individuals (Batting, 1975). This controversy has led to a moratorium on the use of standardized IQ tests for special education placement in public schools in New York City, Washington, D.C., and California.

Classification of affective (emotional) disorders is presented in the *Diagnostic and Statistical Manual* of the American Psychiatric Association *(DSM-3)*. The first edition of the manual appeared in 1952, the second in 1968, and the third in 1980. *DSM-3* was revised in 1987.

Clinical classification is organized along five axes (lines). Axes 1 and 2 include all of the known mental disorders. Personality disorders and specific developmental disorders are listed under Axis 2, while all other mental disorders are assigned to Axis 1. Axis 3 is used for physical disorders and conditions. Axes 4 and 5 are used in special clinical and research settings and are used to provide information that is additional to the official *DSM-3* diagnoses. *DSM-3* describes each disorder in terms of the following areas: "essential features, associated features, age at onset, course, impairment, complications, predisposing factors, prevalence, sex ratio, familial pattern, and differential diagnosis" (p. 9).

Educational Emphasis

Whereas clinical classification focuses on etiology and the nature of handicapping conditions, educational classification focuses on educational programming and services, while retaining a categorical approach. Historically, educational classifications were developed by the state departments of education and frequently differed in some respect. In general, however, pupils have been classified as auditorially handicapped, visually handicapped, physically handicapped, emotionally disturbed, and mentally retarded (trainable or educable). Since the 1960s, some states added such classifications as perceptually impaired or learning disabled.

The comprehensive federal law, Public Law 94-142, also known as the *Education for All Handicapped Children Act of 1975,* defines handicapped children as "mentally retarded, hard of hearing, deaf, speech impaired, visually handicapped, seriously emotionally disturbed, orthopedically impaired or other health impaired children or children with specific learning disabilities, who by reason thereof require special education and related services" (p. 2).

The main provision of this law is that free and appropriate public education is a basic right of every child. In accordance with the law, every handicapped child should be provided with special education and related services at public expense. Public Law 94-142 is implemented through the rules and regulations published in the *Federal Register* (1977). These rules and regulations became effective on October 1, 1977. Turnbull (1978) lists six major principles underlying Public Law 94-142: zero reject, nondiscriminatory assessment, individualized educational programs, least-restrictive alternative, due process, and parent participation.

Zero reject means that no child shall be rejected or deprived of services regardless of the type or severity of handicapping condition. Nondiscriminatory assessment process implies that the evaluation procedures should be broadly based, fairly administered, and given only with the informed consent of the parents. A far-reaching provision of the law requires that tests used to assess intellectual level and cognitive skills must be sensitive to cultural factors and administered in the child's native language. The term *individualized education program* is defined to mean an educational plan developed jointly by the local education agency and an appropriate teacher in consultation with the parents or guardian, and whenever appropriate, the child is to be placed in the least restrictive alternative (United States Senate, 1976, p. 151). Least-restrictive alternative implies that a child should be educated in such an educational setting where he or she will profit most. In some instances, the least-restrictive environment from the point of view of an individual child's self-fulfillment, emotional adjustment, and achievement might be a special class or a special program.

Under the provision of the due process of Public Law 94-142, parents have the right to examine all records that are related to the school evaluation of their child. They must also be consulted before the placement evaluation occurs. If the parents or guardian of the child are unknown, and if the child is a ward of the state, surrogate parents must be appointed. The law also mandates that parents or guardians must be provided with an opportunity to present complaints in matters related to the identification and evaluation of the individual placement of their child. It is becoming obvious that all professionals providing service to exceptional children should be familiar with federal and state legislation. Bateman (1982) called our attention to the fact that lack of legal knowledge is rapidly becoming a major concern for all special educators, from the director of the large school district to the teacher feeling pressure to describe children's needs only in terms of already available service.

In June 1997, President Clinton signed amendments to the *Individuals with Disabilities Education Act (IDEA),* which is a further extension of the basic *Education for All Handicapped Children Act* (Public Law 94-142), promulgated in 1975. Kubiszyn (1997) expressed an opinion that under existing amendments there is potential for psychology to enhance and expand services in the schools. The *IDEA* has several important provisions, such as: enables, at state or local discretion, the provision of services to children under 9 years of age without requiring a "special education" label; expands the focus of infant and toddler programs; requires continuation of related services regardless of placement; eliminates cessation of services as a discipline option; requires that consultation be provided to the regular education teacher regarding behavioral interventions; enables broad staff and professional development activities through State Program Improvement Grants for Children with Disabilities.

The most frequently used educational classification at the present time in the United States is learning disabilities. Children classified as learning disabled comprise more than 50 percent of all children classified as handicapped. Furthermore, the prevalence of this classification has nearly doubled since 1978. In the same period, according to data provided by the U.S. Office of Education, during the school year 1976–1977 there were 797,230 children classified as learning disabled. That number increased to 1,839,292 in 1984–1985, and to 2,559,019 in 1997. The total number of all classified children increased from 3,708,599 in 1976–1977 to 4,363,031 in 1984–1985 to 5,067,000 in 1997, or approximately 11 percent of the school-age population. During the same time, the category of mental retardation declined from 967,567 in 1976–1977 to 717,885 in 1984–1985 to 584,000 in 1997. The data show that at the time when the LD category more than doubled, the mentally retarded (MR) category declined by almost half. There have been a number of complex reasons for this trend, among them an aversion to the negative connotation of "mental retardation." For the past century, with the increase of services to exceptional learners, expenditures for such services also increased. As reported by the *New York Times* on December 28, 1997, the financial expenditure for special education reached $30 billion a year in federal, state, and local money. For the past century, attempts to provide services and educate exceptional learners have been influenced by complex issues of terminology, labeling, and cultural and sociopolitical factors. Figures 4.1 and 4.2 illustrate this trend.

This trend of classification of children with mental retardation and learning disabilities was discussed by MacMillan et al. (1996). The writers pointed out that from 1977 to 1994 a steady decline was noticed in children diagnosed by public schools as being mentally retarded. The number of mentally retarded children decreased approximately 335,000, or 38 percent. In the same period, more than 20 percent, or 1.5 million, more children have been diagnosed as being learning disabled. MacMillan et al. expressed the opinion that the learning disabled classification became a political issue rather than a question of educational classification.

It is obvious that the increase in the LD classification occurred at the expense of the decrease in the MR classification. Two major factors appear to be responsible for this trend: elimination of the borderline classification in mental retardation and more awareness of and attention to mild learning difficulties. An important development of the early 1970s was a change in the AAMR classification that profoundly influenced an estimated prevalence of the MR population. The so-called Grossman revision of 1973 eliminated the borderline range (70–82 IQ) from the classification system. This range contained the largest proportion of all those individuals previously classified as MR within the range of theoretical 0–82 IQs. As a result of this change, clinicians began to consider all of those individuals scoring higher than a 70 IQ as falling within the range of "normal" intelligence. Consequently, those who did not achieve academically within age expectation, and most of those between 70–80 IQs who did not, were, after 1973, labeled "learning disabled" instead of "educable mentally retarded." In reality, the strengths and weaknesses of this segment of the school population did not change much, with the exception in the way they were labeled. Gottlieb, Alter, Gottlieb, and Wiseman (1994) collected data on the educational achievement of children with learning disabilities over a period of time and concluded that LD children function in a very similar way to those children who were labeled as "educable mentally retarded" twenty-five years ago. As a matter of fact, a dissertation, completed in 1960 by Holowinsky, revealed that achievement in basic educational skills is more directly related to the level of intelligence than to any other variable affecting the educational process. The findings of this study indicated that the achievement of students scoring within the 80–100 IQ range was statistically different from those within the 100–110 IQ range. Holowinsky's (1960) dissertation research was based on a sample of 376 children, CA 12–17. The sample was divided into IQ groups 80–90, 90–100, and 100–110. Achievement in reading and arithmetic was investigated. The process of labeling children as falling into the category of specific learning dis-

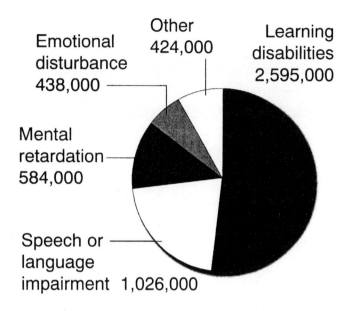

Figure 4.1. Who are they? About 11 percent of students are classified by their local school districts as disabled. Here are the most common disabilities. Source: U.S. Department of Education.

abilities created a situation where many children with nonspecific general learning disorders or learning disabilities were classified under the label "learning disabilities." This trend is supported by more recent studies that show that children labeled as "learning disabled" have many difficulties similar to those exhibited by poor learners in such areas as reading and arithmetic.

Mastropieri and Scruggs (1997) indicated that students with learning disabilities are characterized by language-based difficulties in such areas as reading, semantic memory, and verbal information processing. They exhibit a significant deficit in reading comprehension, which may include problems not only in remembering content, facts, and details, but also in interpreting and making inferences about the information presented.

After an extensive survey of the literature, Aaron (1997) concluded that the validity of the premise that there are qualitative differences between poor readers with learning disabilities and poor readers without learning disabilities cannot be substantiated. He pointed out that despite the belief held by educators that LD and non-LD poor readers require different instructional strategies, very little research is available to support such a premise.

For some time, psychologists and educators have recognized that there are children and adults who manifest learning difficulties despite the fact that

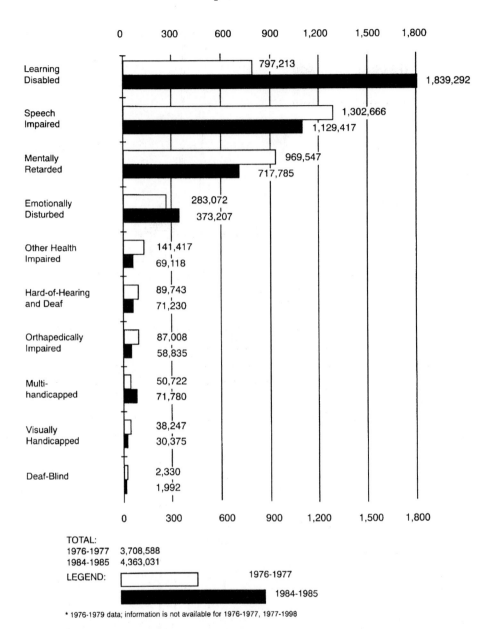

Figure 4.2. Distribution of children aged 3–21 years served under Chapter 1 of ECIA (SOP) and EHA-B by handicapping condition, school years 1976–1977 and 1984–1985.

they do not have serious sensory difficulties, are not mentally retarded, or seriously emotionally disturbed. Earlier notions about learning disabilities attributed this problem to the generalized perceptual-neurological weakness.

The idea that learning disorders have a neurological basis is attributed to the pioneering work of Goldstein, who observed in brain-injured patients difficulties in figure-ground relationship, perservation, distractibility, and rigidity. Following the tradition of Goldstein, Strauss and Werner (1942) concentrated their interest on children whose symptoms resembled those shown by brain-injured patients. Strauss and Lehtinen (1947) elaborated further on the difficulties of brain-injured children, observing that they manifested perceptual disorders, lack of visual closure, preservation, and conceptual and behavioral disorders.

Bonnet (1989) described learning disabilities from a neurological perspective. In the United States, some estimates suggest that about 15 percent or more of the general population have some form of learning difficulties.

The prevalence of dyslexia in males is almost ten times that of dyslexia in females.

Adults with posterior parietal lobe injury typically have visual impairment in tracking, localizing, and even in noticing stimuli. Injury to the inferior temporal cortex results in visual agnosia, a deficit in recognizing stimuli: "Developmental dyslexia can involve alterations in retinal, occipita-temporal, and occipita-parietal distribution of visual information processing" (p. 16).

In the 1960s, the term *psychoneurological learning disability* was introduced into the literature by Johnson and Myklebust (1967). Whereas Strauss and Werner emphasized perceptual components, Johnson and Myklebust emphasized language processing disorders. Following the influence of Kirk and Bateman (1962), education became the central terminological focus for an operational definition of learning disability: "A learning disability refers to a retardation disorder or delayed development in one or more of the processes of speech, language, reading, writing, arithmetic or other school subjects" (p. 73). Further elaboration of the concept of learning disabilities was suggested by Bateman (1965), who shifted attention from an emphasis on interindividual differences and pointed to discrepancies between estimated intellectual potential and actual level of performance. Since the 1960s, literature on learning disabilities has increased tremendously. Black (1974) reported that articles on learning disabilities in scholarly journals increased from very few in 1963 to a couple of hundred in 1972. Among noted contributors in the 1970s and 1980s, one may mention Wepman (1972), Denckla (1972), Algozzine and Sutherland (1977), Kosc (1987), and Kovale and Forness (1987).

The literature on learning disabilities in the past two decades has been very extensive. Summers (1986) reported that from 1968 to 1983, 2,270 articles on learning disabilities were published in 248 journals. Despite such a volume of publications, the question of the nature of the LD population can not yet be stated clearly. The problems are numerous and are related to conceptual, theoretical, and political issues. Frequently, learning disabilities are equated with any kind of learning problems, and this tends to obscure "the target" population. Furthermore, there is no single unique observable characteristic of LD children. Each child has his or her unique learning pattern. Some of the behavioral symptoms of LD children are also associated with other categories of exceptionalities. The lack of clarity of definition is also related to disagreements about the prevalence estimates within the school-age population. Some writers, for example, Tucker, Stevens, and Ysseldyke (1983), estimated the LD population to be as high as 10 percent of school-age children.

Based on available research evidence, Chalfant and Pych (1984) suggested five components of learning disabilities: (a) failure to achieve educationally with grade and age expectancy level, (b) deficiency in one or more psychological processes, (c) significant discrepancy between achievement and potential, (d) exclusionary definition, and (e) etiology of perceptual deficit.

There were various definitions of learning disabilities suggested in the literature throughout the 1960s. Eventually, a concise definition was formulated by the National Advisory Committee on Handicapped Children in their annual report to Congress in 1968:

> Children with special learning disabilities exhibit a disorder in one or more of the basic psychological processes involved in understanding or using spoken or written language. These may be manifested in disorders of listening, thinking, talking, reading, writing, spelling or arithmetic. They include conditions which have been referred to as perceptual handicaps, brain injury, minimal brain dysfunction, dyslexia, developmental aphasia, etc. They do not include learning problems which are due primarily to visual, hearing, or motor handicaps, to mental retardation, emotional disturbance, or to environmental disadvantage.

This definition with very minor changes has been included in Public Law 94-142, the *Education for All Handicapped Children Act of 1975*. It is still in use today by federal agencies.

In the opinion of this writer, the definition of learning disabilities is further complicated by the fact that there are actually two populations of individuals with learning disabilities: those whose disorder is associated with undifferentiated etiologies, and those whose learning difficulties are associated with specific neuropsychological impairments for example, agraphia, alexia-dyslexia, and acalculia-dyscaluculia.

With the emergence of the learning disabilities concept, an instrument was designed to "test" for this condition. A test developed by Kirk, McCarthy, and Kirk (1968), the Illinois Test of Psycholinguistic Abilities (ITPA), became very popular in the 1970s. However, subsequently the test was strongly criticized for its lack of technical adequacy and was virtually abandoned by practitioners in the mid-1980s. To study learning disabilities, the federal government established five research institutes in 1977. Each of the institutes eventually acquired a specific focus: the Institute for the Study of Learning Disabilities at Teachers College, Columbia University, focused on basic skills and information processing; at the University of Chicago: social competence of LD children; Kansas University: adolescent LD; the University of Minnesota: assessment of LD children; University of Virginia: attention deficit disorders. Despite so much effort in research and resources allocated to learning disabilities identification, problems with definition still persist.

Currently, the crucial criterion for LD definition is severe discrepancy between potential and achievement. There are, however, a number of problems with this rationale. To begin with, it is essential that intelligence tests that have strong predictive validity for academic achievement are employed in the LD determination process. Additionally, as suggested by Hessler (1986), the concept of multiple types of intelligence raises some critical questions and issues with respect to severe discrepancy analysis. Furthermore, as indicated by Danielson and Bauer (1978), students in the dull-normal range of intelligence, as well as those under 8 years of age, are more likely to be identified as learning disabled. We may agree with Lerner (1984) that in the final analysis, determination of LD status should be a value judgment and not based on measurements alone.

A modified definition of learning disabilities was proposed by Kosc (1987), who suggested that learning disabilities should be strictly distinguished from more educationally conceived "learning failures" as well as from more medically neurologically conceived "dysfunctions" of learning. In his opinion, the present LD label is too nebulous to be used in clinical practice as a diagnosis, or in research as an independent variable. Kosc proposed the following modified LD definition:

> Specific learning disabilities represent structural deficiencies in one or more psychological abilities basic for psychological process involved in the acquisition, understanding, and/or use of spoken or written language, in the development of perception, thinking, orientation in space, manipulation of space, etc., due to brain injury or minimal brain dysfunction, but not primarily to visual, auditory, or motor defects, to mental retardation, emotional disturbance, or to environmental disadvantage.

Swanson (1993) investigated LD children's mental processing during problem solving. The results of this study supported the notion that LD children's problem-solving performance reflects a weak interpretation of metacognitive skills. Swanson concluded that children with learning disabilities are of normal intelligence but have information-processing difficulties. They process high-order information in a manner qualitatively different from their peers.

Learning disabilities also became a political issue because of their complex sociocultural variables and potential social policy implications. Sleeter (1986) suggested that in the late 1950s school reform increased school failure, and the category of learning disabilities was created to explain the educational failure of white middle-class children. Kavale and Forness (1987) strongly criticized Sleeter's arguments. They argued that as the history of learning disabilities reveals, there is no empirical rationale to consider it the result of ideological conflict between social classes. Kavale and Forness (1987) stress that the question of LD definition should be resolved from "an empirical and not a rhetorical base."

Ogilvy (1994) suggested that the controversy surrounding the issue of specific learning difficulties may be in part attributed to the inappropriate application of the medical model of diagnosis to the educational context. Furthermore, the diagnostic picture is blurred by the politico-economic climate. Ogilvy argues for the broader approach to the diagnosis of learning disabilities. The writer states in the conclusion to his article that the identification of specific learning disabilities is an issue that assumed importance and became a law despite the fact that the empirical evidence for a separate diagnostic and educational category is incomplete.

Children with learning disabilities became an issue in a broader controversy of the regular education initiative (REI; Wang, 1988) versus special education (Kauffman & Pullen, 1989). Proponents of the REI suggest that many mildly handicapped LD children can be educated in the regular programs since their main difficulties are related to inadequate motivation, poor study habits, or inappropriate cognitive strategies. Opponents of the REI are concerned that such an approach at the time of shrinking financial resources will hurt special education efforts.

Fuchs, Fuchs, and Fernstrom (1993) reminded us that there is still a strong disagreement within the educational community about where to educate the majority of children with disabilities in special or regular education settings. The writers described the process of preparing students for transition from special education resource rooms to a regular classroom for mathematics instruction.

Desforges (1995) reported wide use of psychometric tests in the assessment of bilingual pupils. It is reported that there has been some misunderstanding about the role of linguistic factors in special needs assessment. Desforges suggests that children should not be considered as having learning difficulties if those difficulties are only directly related to the fact that they are learning English as a second language.

In a recent article, Holowinsky (in press) suggested that the learning disabilities concept is a logical and sociopolitical puzzle. It is generally accepted that an equation A = B is also accepted as B = A. However, this is only true in those situations where both A and B do not include subclasses or are unidimensional. In the case where one side of the equation is a subclass of a larger universe, or where we are dealing with unequal units, the equation does not hold. For example, it is perfect to say that "all criminals are humans" or C = H. However, we cannot reverse the equation and say that H = C, or that "all humans are criminals." Likewise, it is logical to say that all LD children manifest learning disorders. However, we cannot say that all children who manifest learning disorders should be classified as LD or manifesting specific learning disabilities. The reason is that many other exceptional learners manifest learning disorders, for example, children with mental retardation, aphasia, or emotional disturbances. In my judgment, LD as a clinical label and a category represents a specific subgroup of learning disorders and should not be used as a general label.

Lumping together into one category children who manifest general learning disorders with those classified as showing specific learning disabilities, as well as the use of discrepancy formula and the process of arriving at the LD classification, are responsible for what may be called a sociopolitical puzzle.

Former Soviet Union, Russia, and Ukraine

In the former Soviet Union, which was a country of many languages, the terminology in the field of exceptionalities was recognized as being of two types. For example, generic terminology as in the field of mental retardation was directly translatable and similar in many languages, for example, *umstvenno otstaly* (Russian) or *rozumovo nedorozvyneni* (Ukrainian).

In addition to generic terminology, there was also an official terminology used by the Institute of Defectology of the Academy of Pedagogical Sciences.

In the former Soviet Union, the field of special education has been traditionally divided into four areas: oligophreno-pedagogy (education of the mentally retarded), surdopedagogy (education of the deaf), typhlopedagogy (education of the blind), and logopedagogy (speech correction). Discussion of developmentally delayed children was a relatively recent phenomenon in the Soviet defectological literature. Research with this population began in 1965 at the Scientific Research Institute of the Academy of Pedagogical Sciences (Holowinsky, 1983).

The official view of mental retardation in the former Soviet Union suggested that it was related to a notion of diffuse maldevelopment or a defect of the cortical hemispheres that led to pathological inertia of the central nervous system. Intellectually impaired individuals were described in the Soviet Union either as *umstvenno otstaly* (Vlasova, 1971), which is a generic term and could be translated as "intellectually backward," or as oligophrenic (mentally deficient)–those in whom there is definite evidence of neurological insult (Luria, 1963; Pevzner, 1973). Because Soviet defectology did not acknowledge use of standardized IQ tests for the purpose of quantitative assessment of cognitive abilities, *umstvenno otstaly* as a group would compare to mildly retarded individuals of undifferentiated etiology. Oligophrenia more precisely would describe a condition within the range of profound to moderate retardation. Such individuals might be described in the United States as mentally deficient.

In Ukraine, the acceptable terminology for intellectual subnormality is *rozumove nedorozvynennia,* which translates directly as "intellectual backwardness" or "mental retardation." It should also be pointed out that official Soviet publications on defectology and oligophrenia until the 1980s were using outdated terminology in reference to the levels of mental retardation, for example, *idiocy, imbecility,* and *debility* (feeblemindedness).

In the late 1960s and early 1970s, a new term was introduced into the defectological literature. Studies began to appear that described children with *delayed mental development.* Pevzner and Rostiagalova (1981) reported that research with developmentally delayed children began in the former Soviet Union in 1965 at the Scientific Research Institute of the Soviet Academy of Pedagogical Sciences. In 1966, a book by Pevzner entitled *Children with Developmental Deviations* was published in Moscow.

Children described as developmentally delayed in the former Soviet Union were similar in many respects to those described in the United States as learning disabled. Many etiological factors are also similar to those found among mildly retarded children. Yavkin (1973) indicated that in both clinical groups, such etiological factors as mild intrauterine and perinatal trauma, prematurity, chromosomal aberrations, endocrine disorders, and infectious illnesses in early childhood are found. Yassman (1976) agreed with Yavkin that many developmentally delayed children were similar in their performance to oligophrenic children. Comparisons between characteristics of normal, developmentally delayed, and mentally retarded children were made by Tsymbaliuk (1973), Vlasova et al. (1975), Markovskaya (1977), Zharenkova (1981), and Strelkova (1981).

Classification of mental retardation usually involved medical or etiological factors, level of intellectual functioning, and adaptive behavior, as well as an estimate of educational potential. In the former Soviet Union, classification of the mentally retarded has been influenced by the writings of Pevzner and Luria. Pevzner (1973) suggested that oligophrenia is related to biological defects of the central nervous system, especially of the most complex and late-developing brain structures. She suggested (Pevzner, 1970) that there were five etiological groups among oligophrenics. The first group is characterized by diffuse maldevelopment of the cortical hemispheres without serious neurological implications. The second involves cortical defects with impaired perceptual abilities. The third involves various sensory, perceptual, and motor defects. The fourth is associated with psychopathological behavior. The fifth group is associated with maldevelopment of the frontal lobes, with behavior similar to that seen in people with serious psychopathologies.

Luria (1963) classified oligophrenics into five groups on the basis of behavioral manifestations of the central nervous system involvement. The basic group, composed primarily of the mildly retarded, has suffered localized damage to the cerebral cortex, with no serious behavioral characteristics. To the second group he assigns those oligophrenics who are uninhibited and poorly controlled. They are "excitable" oligophrenics in whom the balance of the nervous process is disrupted in favor of excitation. The third group consists of listless, weak, passive oligophrenics in whom inhibition predominates over excitation. The fourth group is composed of oligophrenics who suffer from specific impairment in auditory or visual areas in addition to diffuse central nervous system damage. To the fifth group, he assigns those oligophrenics who show gross underdevelopment of personality.

Individual intelligence tests were virtually unknown in the former Soviet Union and the assessment of cognitive skills was based on ideographic rather than nomothetic theory (Holowinsky, 1980). Levels of retardation were described primarily according to physiological characteristics (Luria, 1963). Luria suggested that idiots, the most severely deficient of the retarded, have suffered damage to the brain stem and subcortical areas as well as to the cerebral cortex; imbeciles have suffered lesser damage to subcortical and cortical areas. He maintained that feebleminded (mildly retarded) persons have only superficial damage to the cerebral hemispheres.

In the absence of standardized assessment of cognitive skills, achievement, and not a standardized test score, determines whether a child remains in a regular program or is placed in a special class in an auxiliary school. On admission to an auxiliary school, a youngster is subjected to two weeks of cognitive and educational evaluations. The evaluations take place within and outside the school environment. The general purpose of such evaluations is to determine developmental level, knowledge of arithmetic and reading, orientation to the environment, speed of performing practical tasks, level of understanding, and learning potential. Children entering an auxiliary school are divided into two classes based on higher or lower cognitive abilities.

A youngster is placed in the lower special class level if he or she cannot recognize letters, cannot read, has no concept of numbers, has no practical hobbies, and is disoriented within the environment. Children who are placed in the advanced special class can recognize letters of the alphabet, can write letters, have some concept of numbers, have practical hobbies, and are generally well oriented to the environment. Em (1974) described an evaluation and classification process as it has been developed by the staff of the Department of Clinical Study of Abnormal Children, Institute of Defectology, Academy of Pedagogical Sciences of the USSR. The evaluation data involved medical history, interviews with parents, interviews with siblings, and psychoeducational evaluation. Psychoeducational evaluation was based on comprehension of written stories and description of pictorial stories. On the basis of those findings, the children were classified into three groups: highly achieving, moderately achieving, and poorly achieving.

In the absence of standardized testing of intelligence, assessment and classification of exceptional children in the former Soviet Union has been based on a variety of informal techniques. Since the 1970s, there have been a number of attempts to reassess classification procedures. Yassman (1975) reported on a symposium devoted to the question of psychodiagnosis. In a paper presented at that symposium, Lubovsky argued for the appropriate use of quantitative data and statistical analysis to help determine qualitatively unique characteristics of developmental disabilities. The symposium participants decided to petition the Executive Council of the Soviet Psychological Association and the Academy of Pedagogical Sciences for permission to develop theoretical and practical approaches to psychodiagnosis. In a book written in 1974, Zamsky, although still critical of psychometrics, acknowledged that the long campaign against pedology prevented the development of legitimate attempts to determine the parameters of children's psychological, physical, and social development. In a symposium on psychodiagnosis in 1980 (Bogoyavlenskaya, 1980), more than one hundred scientists representing fifty scientific institutions resolved to develop a branch of psychodiagnosis within the Association of Soviet Psychologists. The symposium on psychodiagnosis took place in 1983.

Savchenko (1980) described a classification of oligophrenia that includes etiology, clinical psychopathology, and level of intellectual retardation. In reference to etiological factors, oligophrenia is divided into known and unknown. According to psychopathology, four types of oligophrenics have been identified: (a) those with general lack of mental development, (b) those with lethargic behavior and delayed personality development, (c) those with symptoms of dementia, and (d) those with concurrent low intellectual functioning and sensory motor defects.

Insufficient time has elapsed since the breakup of the Soviet Union in 1991 for any new trends to emerge in the classification and assessment of exceptional learners.

Chapter 5

GENERAL EDUCATION CONTEXT

The organization of education and schooling throughout the world is extremely complex, reflecting cultural, economic, and sociopolitical realities. It ranges from almost total decentralization as, for example, in the United States, where each school district controls many aspects of educational policy, to completely centralized, as in the former Soviet Union where in a huge country extending over nine time zones, the central ministry of education decided what textbooks should be used. In some countries, such as Switzerland or West Germany, education is the responsibility of cantons or states.

Almost all countries have mandatory education laws at least from 6 to 16 years of age. In Denmark, Great Britain, and the United States, formal education begins at 5 years of age. In the United States, formal education for handicapped students can extend until 21 years of age. In this chapter, general education content in various regions will be discussed. The regions under discussion are: the United States and Canada, South America, Central America and Mexico, the United Kingdom and western Europe, central and eastern Europe, Asia and the Pacific region, the Middle East, and Africa.

United States and Canada

Anyone familiar with the history of American education must have been impressed with the diversity and lack of centralization of the educational efforts throughout its history. Built on the tradition of individualism, Americans resisted the establishment of a centralized system of education, even at the state level, until the second half of the nineteenth century. The early state superintendents of education spent considerable effort in overcoming public apathy and opposition (Good, 1956). It is important to mention that American education never has been based on a single educational philosophy. This is not to say, however, that American educators in practice did not adhere to some broad philosophical notions relative to education. For the sake of brevity, let us consider three such notions. One broadly accepted notion is that "discipline" is inherently "bad." This attitude has its roots in the idealistic philosophy of Voltaire, Montesquieu, and Rousseau, which suggests that humans are essentially "good, but become corrupt by society." In reality, however, we are neither bad nor good, but become what we are in the process of growth, education, and socialization.

Since the colonial period, educational philosophy in the United States has stressed the ideology of democratic freedom and equality. This philosophy has been clearly expressed in the report of the President's Commission on Higher Education in 1947, as follows:

> The first goal in education for democracy is the full, rounded, and continuing development of the person. The discovery, training, and utilization of individual talents is of fundamental importance in a free society. To liberate and perfect the intrinsic powers of every citizen is the central purpose of democracy, and its furtherance of individual self-realization is its greatest glory. (p. 9)

After the launching of *Sputnik* by the Soviet Union in 1957, guided by the national policy statements concerning the importance of science and mathematics, general education in the judgment of some educators did not adequately emphasize humanities, fine arts, and social sciences. During the 1990s, leading colleges and universities began to reexamine existing curricula with the goal of achieving optimum balance. However, the philosophical foundations of democratic education have remained constant (Fanelli, 1997).

Common sense American educational philosophy has been so committed to the dichotomy of "democracy" and "authoritarianism" that, in the minds of many, authority became a negative concept. Unfortunately, the fact is overlooked that both democracy and authority are abstract verbal concepts that describe human relationships. Both concepts show a lack of transparency or easy understanding. Finally, many educators believe that teachers should avoid making value judgments. The paradox of this position is that, by not expressing a value judgment, the teacher is conveying a message that there are *no* values.

At the present time, however, many civic, political, and educational leaders agree that American education is in need of reorganization, both in terms of the achievement level of youngsters and the climate within the schools. Organization of public education is similar, as in many other countries. It is divided into preschool, elementary, and secondary levels. However, in terms of financial support, education is not directly supported by federal taxes; neither are teachers or school personnel considered state or federal employees. Responsibility for education still rests basically with the local educational authorities. The U.S. Office of Education has no authority or power comparable to that of the Ministry of Education in many European countries.

A relatively recent development is the formation of other than public schools, for example, private management schools, voucher schools, and charter schools. Although charter schools are accountable to the Local Education Agencies (LEAs) where they are located, voucher schools represent a fundamental challenge to public education. The debate continues among educators about the value of innovative approaches (Finn, Manno, Bierlein, & Vanourek, 1997; Moe & Gay, 1997).

It has been recognized for some time that with the mainstreaming of special education students, there is an apparent need to upgrade the skills of regular educators. Patton and Braithwaite (1990) reviewed trends in special education certification/recertification for regular educators. Their data indicated that in the 1980s, there was a significant change in state special education coursework requirements for certification of general education teachers. In 1990, 71 percent of the states required special education coursework for the initial certification of regular education teachers, whereas in 1978, 21 percent of the states mandated such requirements. However, states continue to be reluctant to require special education coursework for the recertification of regular education teachers. In 1990, only nine states required such recertification.

Based on an extensive survey of special education administrators (1,468 directors responded), Arick and Krug (1993) concluded that there is a need for extensive training of special education administrators at the preservice level. The survey revealed that special education directors who lacked college preparation in special education had higher in-service training needs. The need for preservice training of administrators is further emphasized by the fact that in the near future, more than 50 percent of the districts surveyed will need replacements.

In Canada, as in the United States, educational philosophy is based on ideas of democracy.

Canada is a nation that does not have a national education system. Instead, the authority with regard to education in terms of the initiation, administration, and evaluation of change and reform is entirely placed within the borders of the various provinces. The origins of this provincial jurisdiction go back to the *British North America Act of 1867,* which has been reinscribed most recently in the *Constitution Act of 1982.* This act makes it clear that education will remain the sole responsibility of the provinces (Goodson, 1995).

South America, Central America, and Mexico

Most of the South American countries established mandatory school attendance by the end of the nineteenth century. Among the countries of that continent, Argentina is reported to have the highest literacy rate (84%) (Wycke, 1987a). In Brazil, primary-level education extends for eight grades and secondary for three (Wechsler & Gomes, 1989). De la Meuse (1989) informs us that in Chile, schooling is divided into preschool, basic eight-grade elementary education, and four-year high school. Compulsory education extends through the eighth grade. According to Fish and Voorwald (1989), El Salvador provides free basic education for children 7 to 15 years of age. General education is divided into preschool, nine years of compulsory elementary schooling, and three years of secondary education. Holtzman (1989) reported that in Mexico, education is mandatory from the first to the sixth grade. Junior and senior high school is optional.

In 1990, an education interpretation law was enacted in Chile and since that time some progress was made with the inclusion of exceptional learners.

The differential classes within the regular schools were a step toward recognizing that children with disabilities are capable of learning and developing if given a chance. However, the parallel system is still a segregating system. It is a system that is still keeping children who may be able to manage in a regular class separate from their normal developing peers. Also, because of the labeling that is taking place, students are being shunned by their peers anyway. These students are being denied access to services and programs they need to facilitate their development. These concerns were valid enough to make further changes in the way services are being delivered.

In Chile, one of the biggest barriers facing integration is resistance from general education teachers. Teachers in Chile are against integration for many substantial reasons. For one, they themselves have to assume the most responsibility for the integration process. Teachers in Chile, like most teachers in developing countries, have to deal with many unfavorable work conditions. They have to deal with overpopulated classrooms, containing 40 or more students. Add to this number the varying levels of abilities one would find in any classroom, plus a handful of special needs students. Along with this factor are small classrooms. Teachers also face low wages, inadequate preparation to deal with children with special needs, few instructional materials, and very limited support, especially in the rural areas (Sius & Milicic, 1995). Coordination and a positive interaction between general education teachers and resource room (differential room) teachers are extremely important. According to Milicic, this is nonexistent in Chilean classrooms. The differential rooms are usually located at the back of the school buildings, which makes the physical structure very difficult. Teachers hardly see each other, and therefore communication is quite rare.

Teacher preparation in Chile does not include special education. It has an exclusive focus in general education, and therefore does not prepare teachers to deal with exceptional students. Teachers are not equipped to deal with disabled students, nor do they want to. Because they do have the desire to make inclusion successful, they may reject these students, which again will work against the whole process. Most teachers, as discussed earlier all feel they lack the training and expertise to deal with special needs students. These teachers have an extra hurdle to overcome when dealing with inclusion and that is economics. Chilean teachers do not have the financial support that industrialized nations have to make inclusion work. Yes, they may be integrating, but does that mean just the physical presence of handicapped children in the classroom, or does it mean everyone is learning and socializing together. Teacher attitude is one of the most important factors in the success of integration, but it costs money to provide the materials, to train the teachers, and provide the support. Most teachers indicated that if the conditions were right, they would be more positive toward inclusion. Chile is dealing with situational disadvantages such as poverty, malnutrition, and child labor.

United Kingdom and Western Europe

Public education in the United Kingdom reflects tension that exists in regions that claim their separate identities within large political systems. While educational policy is formulated in London, interpretation of the policy is made in Scotland and Wales according to local needs. For example, in Wales there is a separate institutional framework in education. There are schools with Welsh language of instruction.

In the United Kingdom, mandatory education applies to all children between the ages of 5 and 16 (Lindsay, 1989). For comparison, in the United States, free public education is provided until 21 years of age.

In Ireland, the educational system includes three levels: primary, secondary, and higher education. The state provides free primary education. There are approximately 3,550 primary schools that enroll children ranging in age from 4 to 13 (Chamberlain, 1989).

General education provisions in Europe differ in some respects from country to country. In Denmark, all public education is free for children 5 to 19 years of age. This also includes teaching materials as well as need-related services. In recent years, considerable emphasis has also been placed on adult education. Day nurseries, kindergartens, and preschool classes are considered an integral part of preschool education. Currently, everyone in Denmark has a basic education of nine years. Approximately 85 percent of those who complete basic education continue their education in a variety of vocational or academic settings (Ministry of Education, 1986). In France, education is divided into three levels: primary (pre-elementary and elementary); junior high school (12–15 CA); and senior high school (16–18 CA), which includes professional as well as technical curriculum (Guildemard, 1989).

Within the Federal Republic of Germany, each state (*Bundesland*) is responsible for its educational system. Compulsory education laws apply to nonhandicapped and handicapped youngsters. All children attend four- or six-year elementary schools. Secondary education is divided into three branches: *Hauptschule*–general high school; *Realschule*–technical school; *gymnasium*–a classical school where the emphasis is on university preparation.

In Italy, schooling is divided into preschool, primary (CA 6–10), lower secondary (CA 11–13) and higher secondary (CA 14–18). Preschool education is not mandatory. Free public education is provided only through the lower secondary grades (Nisi et al., 1989).

An interesting development in Europe is the close cooperation or consortium in the area of special education among countries (Denmark, Finland, Iceland, Norway, Sweden) (Juul, 1989). The Finnish education system was reorganized in the 1970s into a new comprehensive school system. The comprehensive school provides education for children 7 to 16 years of age. In 1986, there were 4,800 comprehensive schools with nearly sixty thousand children in attendance. For the first six grades, the homeroom teacher conducts instruction. The subject-teacher system is maintained in grades seven through nine. An optional tenth grade was introduced in the 1980s. The comprehensive school is free of charge. Local education agencies maintain schools, provide necessary study materials, free daily meals, and dental care. They also provide transportation (Lestinen, 1988).

In Spain, public education is free for children 6 to 14 years of age. Approximately 70 percent of schools are funded and administered by the state. The rest are parochial schools, mostly Catholic (Caro & Miralles, 1989).

Switzerland does not have a national ministry of education, as is the case with most European countries. Educational programs are the responsibility of regional authorities (cantons). School attendance is compulsory from 6 to 15 years of age (Burli, 1987).

Central and Eastern Europe

By contrast to the United States, the former Soviet educational system was diametrically opposed to the American system in many important aspects. To begin with, there were no private schools in the Soviet Union. All schools were state schools, run and operated by the state. The whole system of education was highly centralized. The Ministry of Education of the USSR developed guidelines for educational practices and determined the content of the curricula. The ministries of education of the Union republics were directly responsible to the Ministry of Education of the USSR. The major difference in education in the US and USSR was in educational philosophy and goals. In the Soviet Union, the main purpose of education was indoctrination in the communist philosophy and way of life. Soviet educators maintained that "schools should be, as Lenin emphasized, the tool of the dictatorship of the proletariat" (Kozhevnikov, 1973, p. 9). Communist education began with preschool experience, as has been emphasized by the leading Soviet authorities on preschool education (Zaporzhets, Markova, & Radina, 1968).

General education was compulsory. Children typically start school at the age of seven and attend classes for five or six hours a day, six days a week, for ten years. However, beginning in 1986, the duration of general education schools was changed to eleven years, with children starting school at six years of age. However, these changes and other educational reforms described in the Soviet *Guidelines for Reform and General and Vocational Schools* will be gradually implemented and become uniformly effective in 1990 (*Guidelines,* 1984). The school was divided into four quarters with vacations following each quarter.

Generally, the mandatory weekly classwork was twenty-four periods lasting forty-five minutes for children in the first four grades and thirty periods of forty-five minutes for pupils in grades five through ten. Students had some electives, ranging from two hours a week in the seventh grade to six hours in the tenth grade or senior year (Malkova, 1981).

The main tasks of general education were clearly spelled out in the Legal Foundations of Education of the USSR and the Union republics, as adopted by the Supreme Soviet of the USSR on July 19, 1973. In part, they called for:

> The implementation of general education of children and youth, conforming with contemporary requirements of social, scientific and technological progress, the inculcation of a solid knowledge of the bases of science, the encouragement of the striving for continuing improvement of knowledge and of the ability for self-improvement as well as of skills in practice. (Zimin, 1977, p. 42)

Education also called for the formation of a materialistic outlook, communist convictions, and a communist attitude toward work. Children were expected to acquire a spirit of collectivism, friendship, internationalism, and mutual aid based on social ideology and humanism (Kairov, 1963; Zimin, 1977).

In order to promote the total development of each youngster, Soviet education offered courses and experiences in mathematics, natural sciences, social sciences, humanities, workshop training, art, music, and physical education. Sciences and foreign languages, however, held a significant place in the curriculum as did polytechnical training and labor education. Moreover, education was closely linked to life and work.

Prior to 1939, Ukrainian SSR had about 14,500 elementary schools, 10,700 seventh grade schools, and 4,300 secondary schools. During the 1940–1941 school year, transition began to a universal seventh-grade education in villages and tenth-grade education in the cities (Chepelev, 1970).

In 1958, a new school reform was announced. The ten-year school was reorganized into an eleven-year school. Grades one to eight were designated as compulsory. Grades nine to eleven were designated as prevocational. In those grades, academic work was combined with vocational training. Students received four days a week of education and two days a week of work experience in a factory (Kreusler, 1976). In the 1966–1967 school year, there were 33,600 general education schools in Ukraine, 11,223 kindergarten and nursery schools, 138 higher education establishments, and 746 technical schools (Chepelev, 1970).

Since the declaration of independence of Ukraine in 1991, there has been a strong effort to restructure education. What complicates educational reforms within the context of Ukraine's sociopolitical reality is the fact that all educational cadres, including professors at universities, teacher-training institutes, school system administrators, and teachers, have been indoctrinated with Marxism-Leninism since the 1930s.

Prior to the declaration of independence, there were no private schools in Ukraine. All schools were state schools, and general education was compulsory. The emergence of private schools marks a radical departure from communist tradition and a significant development in Ukraine, in that it offers a choice that receives the support of government subsidies. One such private elementary school opened in 1992 in Lviv. The school began its gradual growth by accepting pupils into the first grade in the first year of its existence. Currently, there are three grades in the school.

Ukraine

Osvita Ukrainy (1997/Education in Ukraine) reported that in 1997, school-age population in Ukraine numbered 1.3 million preschoolers, approximately seven million elementary school students, and 1.6 million secondary school students. They are educated in 31,402 schools. The majority (15,898) are instructed in Ukrainian; 2,973 in Russian and 2,341 in both languages (Svorek, 1997).

In 1995, there were also 754 higher education establishments of the first and second level accreditation, including fourteen classical and forty-five technical universities, thirty academies, and seventy-two institutes. The faculties of these institutions included 6,250 doctors of science, professors and 36,650 assistant professors and candidates of science (Yablonsky, 1995).

Ukraine's Parliament passed in the Spring of 1999 a broad based education law that provides specific guidelines for general public education. The law provides a legal basis for new types of schools that have been introduced in Ukraine since the declaration of independence such as: classical high schools (gymnasia), lyceums and junior colleges. A major change in general education is the introduction of twelve grades beginning with the school year 2001. The school system will be divided into: elementary—four years; basic—five years; high school—three years. The children will enter the first grade at six years of age and graduate from high school at eighteen. This will approximate the structure of general education in most European countries. The law also will regulate the size of a class, which will be no more than thirty students, and the length of a lesson as forty-five minutes.

In Ukraine, there also exist numerous schools with non Ukrainian language of instruction. As reported by *Svoboda* (1997), schools with the Russian language of instruction are attended by approximately three million students. There are also 2,351 schools that offer bilingual instruction in Ukrainian and Russian (Svorak, 1997). Teachers of the Russian language are trained at eleven universities and twenty pedagogical institutes.

Unfortunately, due to decades of neglect by the former Soviet authorities, schools in Ukraine are in abysmal physical condition. As reported by Martyniv (1996), most of the schools cannot provide a basic sanitary environment for children without mentioning the need for capital improvement. Conditions are even worse in the rural schools. Forty percent of these schools operate in inadequate buildings. Classrooms are two or three times smaller than required, without central heating. The lighting is completely inadequate. Approximately 50 percent of the students are lacking one or two textbooks each. Up to thirty-five youngsters are crowded into one room. Normative tests have been introduced without preparing teachers how to use them. School psychological services, as we are familiar with them in the West, are virtually nonexistent.

At the same time, it should be stressed that the president of Ukraine and responsible educators recognize how crucial and indispensable quality education is in Ukraine at this time of nation building. This was highlighted by President Leonid Kuczma in his speech on the occasion of the fifth anniversary of independence of Ukraine. The president emphasized that education should be given priority in state planning. He also pointed out that education has a responsibility to lead the way toward a new social, economic, legislative, and political culture.

The new development of private classical secondary schools conforms to this market-oriented trend, an interesting spontaneous development that signifies a reaction to the past rigid, regimented system of education (Humeniuk, 1992). Today a number of such schools are mushrooming in Ukraine, especially in Stryj, Lviv, Berezhany, and Ternopil. Admissions to private secondary schools are based on new procedures, results of standardized test scores, and interviews, as commonly used in the West. This represents an important characteristic of the new educational plans of emerging eastern European nations, which react negatively to the collectivism of their past totalitarian socialist experience.

During the period of transition, where in some areas of education the views of old pedagogical "nomenclature" still prevail, it may be of interest to observe that some writers are beginning to question the ideological foundations of old Soviet pedagogy. Two examples will be provided from the writings of Krasovetsky (1995) and Skyba (1993, 1994).

Krasovetsky provides a critical overview of A. Makarenko's theory of education in a collective and through a collective. He points out that the concept of collective as a "tool" or "instrument" of education should be rejected, but the idea of a collective as a condition should be retained. Krasovetsky further emphasizes that a collective could have a positive role if education will be accomplished through humane children's activity guided by educators.

More specifically, Krasovetsky (1995) focuses on six principles of reconstructed pedagogy:

1. Ideological and political attempts to control school life, as well as attempts to create a single model of child personality, should be abandoned.
2. We should not accept as absolute every statement or recommendation suggested by Makarenko.
3. It is not true that the collective is the only instrument of upbringing and education. What was frequently underestimated was the strength of personality and intrinsic motivation.
4. We should absolutely reject the concept of collective responsibility for the actions of an individual. This clearly inhumane practice is open to serious abuses.
5. Humanistic pedagogy cannot accept a principle of unconditional surrender of the interests of the individual to the interests of a collective. This principle led to many tragedies because leaders frequently declared their own interests as interests of the collective.
6. We should reject the notion that the decision of a collective must always supersede the view of an individual.

Asia and the Pacific Region

General education provisions in Asia and the Pacific region vary significantly among regions. Some reflect British influence, for example, Australia, India, and New Zealand; others, U.S. influence, for example, Japan after 1945. In Australia, the state retains significant authority through the employment of all professional personnel and by providing most of the school funding. Since teachers are state employees and there is centralized educational planning, unlike in the United States, there is almost a total lack of litigation literature (Henderson, 1989).

Educational provisions differ throughout the three departments of education in Australia. For example, Queensland and New South Wales were contemplating using resource teachers to provide support in the classroom, while Victoria was using special education units and facilities and specialist staff. Educational settings also vary among states. For example, four settings are available in New South Wales. These settings include special schools, special classes, regular classes with support services, and regular school placement with no support services at all. Special classes here are held within the regular school. These same arrangements are also available in Queensland and Victoria; however, the majority of mentally handicapped children are segregated into special schools, whereas in New South Wales these students are in special classes within the regular school. Therefore, some contact does exist between special needs students and their normal developing peers (Jenkinson-Gow, 1989).

In China, a series of educational reforms beginning in 1985 were implemented when the CPC Central Committee enacted the Decision of the CPC Central Committee on the Reform of China's Educational Structure. The Compulsory Education Act, the first education law since 1949 was promulgated in 1986, marking a turning point in the universalization of education. The most important features of this fundamental reform were the legalization of a nine-year compulsory universal education, the decentralization of educational administration, and the diversification of educational financing (Zhu & Lan, 1996). [It should be noted that the State Education Commission was renamed the Ministry of Education in 1998 (Ota Wang, 1999).]

The current Japanese Constitution, promulgated on November 3, 1946, stressed the right to comprehensive, nondiscriminatory educational opportunities. As explained by Shinagawa, Kodama, and Manita (1989), general education in Japan consists of six years of elementary education, three years of junior high school, and three years of senior high school. Compulsory education is from six to fourteen years of age.

In India, as recently as 1987 (Nesbit, 1987), universal school attendance has not yet been achieved. The government survey in 1981 reported the literacy rate among the general population was only 41 percent. In 1986, the National Policy on Education was formulated.

In New Zealand, compulsory education extends from six to fifteen years of age. As in most countries, education is divided into elementary, secondary, and higher schooling (Brown, 1989).

Middle East

Educational provisions in the Middle East present an extremely complex picture. They are related to political, religious, and cultural diversities, as, for example, in Israel and Yeman, or Egypt and Iran.

In Jordan, as seems to be the trend in many countries, opportunity is provided for a twelve-year public education (Hamdi & Hamdi, 1989). In Turkey, however, only primary education of five years is compulsory. Six years of high school education is divided into three years of junior schooling and three years of senior schooling. However, only about 11 percent of high school graduates attend college (Dolek et al., 1989).

In Israel the educational system is divided along national and religious lines. However, there are almost no "private" K–12 schools. As explained by Horenczyk (1999), Arabs and Jews, for the most part, attend different schools; within the Jewish sector, there are separate "state-religious" and "state" (secular) schools. Within the Arab sector, most of the Muslim children are enrolled in "state" Arab schools while Christian children generally attend church-run educational institutions. In contrast to this national/religious segregation, the educational integration of Jewish immigrants has been traditionally described as reflecting a "melting pot" approach, although in practice, it has basically followed assimilationist policies and strategies.

Following the establishment of the state of Israel in 1948, the school population changed radically with the influx of survivors of Nazi camps and immigrants of Middle Eastern and North African origin (Raviv, 1989). In 1949, a compulsory education law was passed, which mandated schooling from five through fourteen years of age. In 1968, compulsory education was raised to sixteen, and in 1978, free secondary education for all was affirmed. A 1979 amendment to the compulsory education act provides that a child with special needs can be educated at the expense of the state from ages three through eighteen.

Africa

Although we in the United States advocate inclusion of severely handicapped students into regular classrooms, school attendance rates and literacy rates are abysmally low in developing nations. For example, the literacy rate in Afghanistan and Gambia is 12 percent. School attendance rates are 39 percent in Bangladesh, 12 percent in Afghanistan, and 15 percent in Bhutan (Cates, 1994).

The problems of education in some parts of Africa are staggering. This is the legacy of the colonial past, when most of the curricula originated from British or European sources and more recently from the United States (Baine, 1988). Schools for Africans based their curricula on European cultural contexts and values, which might have been of little interest or relevance to children in Africa. Furthermore, colonial powers had little interest in erasing illiteracy in Africa. For example, by some accounts (Wycke, 1987b), Nigeria still has an illiteracy rate of over 70 percent. The current educational system was introduced in 1983. It consists of six years of elementary education, followed by three years of junior high school and three years of senior high school education (Ezello, 1989).

In Swaziland, compulsory primary education of seven years (CA 6–13) is required of all children. Noncompulsory secondary education of five years is available, but enrollment in high school is monitored and restricted by society's needs (Csapo, 1988).

Prior to independence in 1980, the educational system of Zimbabwe was segregated along racial lines. School attendance for blacks was voluntary and depended on high scores on the entrance examination as well as ability to pay school fees (Kabzems, 1989). In 1980, the new government decreed free universal primary school education. By 1985, the number of primary schools had doubled, and the number of secondary schools rose nearly tenfold (Chikombah, 1988). The same writer also reported that as recently as 1982, 11 percent of primary school teachers and more than 40 percent of secondary school teachers were not trained professionally.

Because of long-standing racial discrimination in South Africa, separate schools existed for whites, Indians, blacks, and colored students. There were eighteen separate departments of education: one general, eleven for blacks, four for whites, one for colored, and one for Indians (Donald & Csapo, 1989). As of 1989, South Africa was the only country where education for blacks was not compulsory.

Currently, general education in South Africa represents a complex tapestry of compiling political, cultural, ethnic, and national forces. As stressed by Wedekind (1999), schooling and the politics of identity have long been linked in South Africa. Colonial and settler governments before the formal system of apartheid was introduced, attempted to separate not only the different new groups in South Africa, but also ethnic and linguistic groupings within the races. The new democratic government, after the fall of apartheid, inherited an educational system with separate education departments for each race and ethnic group. In addition to this major problem, there are many pressing pragmatic issues. As stated by Wedekind (1999), "Problems associated with racial desegregation and integration, or lack thereof, affect a very small percentage of relatively privileged schools while the remaining 90 percent of the schooling system buckles under the strains of too few classrooms, inadequately trained and qualified teachers, schools without water, toilets, telephones, and electricity, and a breakdown in what is described as a culture of teaching, learning and managing."

Since the new government assumed power, South Africa is moving in the direction of change and reconstruction. There are, however, difficult tasks that must be overcome in order to bring about significant changes in education. Among several problems, three are crucial: where to allocate limited economic resources, how to increase the literacy rate within the general population, and how to prepare teachers and professional personnel for the schools of South Africa.

Chapter 6

SPECIAL EDUCATION PROGRAMS

UNITED STATES AND CANADA

Geographic, linguistic, and cultural factors in the United States and Canada would suggest more similarities than differences in special education in both countries. In reality, however, there are significant differences. In Canada, education is the responsibility of the provincial governments rather than the federal government. Canada is a multicultural, multilingual society, with two official languages, English and French.

As recently as 1969, a number of provinces in Canada did not have special education services. In the 1960s, only about 3 percent of school-age children were receiving special education services (Kendall, 1969). In the 1970s and early 1980s, however, there was considerable growth of special education services in Canada.

In the United States, early efforts on behalf of exceptional individuals began during the nineteenth century. Some of those efforts are associated with Seguin, who, in 1850, arrived in the United States from France. In addition to the pioneering work of Itard, Seguin became well known for his work in the field of mental retardation in the nineteenth century. At the suggestion of Itard, Seguin began to teach mentally retarded children at a private school in Paris in 1837 and in 1842 became the director of the school. On his arrival in the United States, he established a small school for mentally retarded boys in Germantown, Pennsylvania (presently, a part of northwestern Philadelphia). His book, *Idiocy: Its Diagnosis and Treatment by the Physiological Method,* was published originally in French and subsequently translated into English (Sloan & Stevens, 1976). Seguin was also one of the founding members of the Association of Medical Officers of the American Institutions for Idiots and Feeble-minded Persons, the forerunner of the American Association on Mental

Deficiency, and known, since 1987, as the American Association on Mental Retardation.

Efforts to educate exceptional children in the United States have undergone several changes since the turn of the century. Initially, such efforts were largely located at private institutions such as the Elwyn Institute, the Fernald Training School, or the Training School at Vineland. Gradually self-contained special education schools and self-contained special education classes were organized under the auspices of public education. For example, the New Jersey state law of 1911 (Kendall, 1918) mandated that each board of education should establish special classes for children who are three years or more below the norm in their mental development. The number of children per class was limited to fifteen. For the past twenty years, efforts have been on the way to provide programs for children with learning disabilities. Today, we are witnessing progress toward the normalization and mainstreaming of special education pupils into regular programs, as well as in the area of the preschool education of the handicapped.

As mentioned by Paget (1985), the proliferation of programs for children aged five and below created a controversy over which kind of agency or agencies should have the major policymaking responsibility for early intervention services.

Mainstreaming issues continue to be debated in the professional literature. Ammer (1984) identified three factors that appear to influence teacher involvement and attitudes toward special education and mainstreaming: formal coursework in special education, grade level of the respondents taught, and communication and sharing responsibilities. Ammer recommends that regular educators should be given a more active role in the multidisciplinary team decision-making process and in designing any future in-service course to improve the implementation of mainstreaming.

Garver, Pinhas, and Schmelkin (1989) investigated administrators' and teachers' attitudes toward mainstreaming. They reported that classroom teachers manifested the least positive attitudes toward mainstreaming, followed by special education teachers. Principals and special education administrators had more positive attitudes toward mainstreaming. However, as Garver, Pinhas, and Schmelkin point out, despite the seemingly positive attitudes of principals, special educators do not believe that principals will support actively the mainstreaming efforts.

In general, the public reveals positive attitudes toward mainstreaming handicapped students with normal potential for learning (Berryman, 1989). Less positive attitudes were expressed toward mainstreaming of students with considerable academic difficulties.

Wang et al.'s study (1984) described implementation of a mainstreaming program known as ALEM (Adaptive Learning Environment Model). The data seemed to support mainstreaming efforts with moderately handicapped students enrolled in the ALEM program. The writers maintained that mainstreaming should be tried first, and, only if unsuccessful, should more restrictive self-contained programs be tried.

A strong debate emerged in the 1980s known as the regular education initiative (REI) (Davis, 1989; Reynolds, Wang, & Walberg, 1987). There were many reasons for this debate. To begin with, the prevalence of children with mild educational difficulties labeled as "learning disabled" has more than doubled in the past ten years.

In a nation that spends more on special education than any other in the world, and in a nation that has the best-trained teachers and the most sophisticated research, a twofold increase in prevalence should raise serious questions. Is it possible that most of those labeled as "learning disabled" in order to receive help have educational difficulties related to inadequate motivation, poor study habits, or inappropriate educational strategies? Why can they not receive help for their mild learning problems without being labeled or segregated into special education programs? Proponents of the REI argue that a more inclusive system of general education should serve well all groups of children, average as well as exceptional (Reynolds, Wang, & Walberg, 1987). As a major problem with the present system, they point to the complex special education organization with separate bearing for accountability, funding, and advocacy systems. Davis (1989) cautions that the problems are much more complex than the proponents of the REI admit.

Within the educational community, regular and special educators should be involved in the debate, and they should be convinced of the need and value of change. Furthermore, as pointed out by Davis (1989), this debate involves issues of a political, economic, and sociological nature.

A new development in special education in the United States is the use of microcomputers. Computers have been used in the assessment of special-needs students (Hasselbring, 1984), as well as for instructional purposes with elementary mildly handicapped children (Torgesen, 1984). More recently, Liber and Semmel (1985) reviewed studies that surveyed the use of microcomputers in the education of elementary-age, mildly handicapped children. The use of microcomputers is viewed as supplemental to traditional education. The writers suggest that new research is needed that focuses on the interaction between characteristics of the computer and the nature of the environment, both around the computer itself and within the school. A survey of special education administrators conducted by Goldman et al. (1984) revealed that 50 percent of special education programs surveyed owned at least one microcomputer. It was also reported that 75 percent of the school districts surveyed provided training to their special education personnel.

In this chapter, education of exceptional individuals will be discussed as a lifespan process covering preschool, elementary, secondary, and postsecondary programs.

Preschool Programs

The decades of the 1960s and 1970s can be described as the years of heightened interest in early intervention and preschool education. Since it has become evident that cognitive development depends on continuous interaction between the developing organism and the environment, educators and psychologists have become keenly aware of the need for positive intervention and early education. Education as a concept became redefined as not only relating to a child's experiences with formal schooling, but also as related to all sets of experiences involved in the development of preoperational and operational skills. Learning and development are currently viewed as interdependent growth processes, with the result that information processing psychology and developmental psychology are merging (Farnham-Diggory, 1972). Interest in early intervention and preschool education also generated the development of early assessment of cognitive and affective development.

However, trends toward early assessment created some controversy among educators and psychologists by raising a number of issues, which were summarized by Chase (1975): "First, many professionals are concerned about early "labeling" and premature diagnosis. Secondly, as all testing involves the sampling of behaviors, the fact that infants display a narrow repertoire of reaction delimits the amount of 'hard data' which can be drawn. A third problem arises in the assessment process per se, as many available scales and measures rely upon the reports of parents and other child-care agents rather than on direct administration" (p. 342).

Support from the U.S. Office of Education provided impetus and encouragement for the development of preschool programs. Financial support through the enactment of two laws became crucial. The laws in question are: the *Handicapped Children's Early Childhood Assistance Act* (Public Law 90-538) of 1968 and the *Education for All Handicapped Children Act* (Public Law 94-142) of 1975. Public Law 90-538 provides funding for programs in the education of preschool handicapped children. Public Law 94-142 mandated that all states should provide by 1980 education for all handicapped children three to five years of age.

Many states, however, are making provisions for infancy programs from birth through three years of age. More recently, another federal law (Public Law 98-199), promulgated in 1984, provided funds to the states for the development of delivery systems to provide special education to all handicapped and at-risk children. By the school year 1984–1985, there were in the United States close to two hundred preschool programs, also known as the "First Chance Network."

Public Law 90-457 established programs for handicapped or developmentally delayed infants (birth through CA 2). For program eligibility, the following developmental delays have to be in evidence: cognitive, physical, language and speech, psychosocial development, or self-help skills deficiency. The child may be eligible if she or he has a mental or physical condition with a high probability of developmental delay (Byers, 1989).

Heward and Orlansky (1988) suggested that preschool programs could be grouped into three models: home-based, center-based, and combined.

Home-based programs focus on training of parents, who, in turn, directly apply their new skills to the training of children at home. Some writers point to the advantages of home-based intervention because it takes place in the natural family environment. The Portage Project, operated by a consortium of school districts in Wisconsin, is considered one of the best-known, home-based programs.

A number of programs have been organized in special education settings located within hospitals, day-care centers, or preschools. An additional advantage of a center program or home-based program is the opportunity it provides for interaction with other children, thus enhancing socialization. As a good example of a center program, the Model Preschool Center for Handicapped Children at the University of Washington in Seattle should be mentioned.

Assael (1985) tells us that the most frequently used intervention in early childhood is the combined home-center model. A project at the University of Illinois, PEECH (Precise Early Education of Children with Handicaps) is frequently listed as an example of such a program. It serves children three years of age or older with moderate to mild handicapping conditions. According to Assael (1985), more than seventy cities have been using some components of the PEECH program.

Wood and Hurley (1977) told us that most developmentally based early intervention programs have five goals: remediation, teaching basic processes, teaching developmental tasks, psychological constructs, and preacademic skills.

Elementary Programs

Preschool education and early intervention programs are relatively new developments. They are generally based on a noncategorical approach. In contrast, elementary education of exceptional children has a long history and until recently has been generally categorical. The first educational programs were for individuals with serious physical and sensory disabilities, followed by the development of programs for the mentally retarded, emotionally disturbed, socially maladaptive, and, since the 1960s, the learning disabled. They will be discussed in order in this section.

Youngsters with physical disabilities and health problems are educated in various settings such as regular classrooms, special education programs, hospitals, and at home, if home instruction is required. In some specific instances, if no health care specialist is available, routine health care is the responsibility of the special education teacher. The *Federal Register* (1977, p. 42478) lists the following health conditions found among handicapped children: limited strength, vitality, or alertness due to chronic or acute health problems such as a heart condition, tuberculosis, rheumatic fever, nephritis, asthma, sickle cell anemia, hemophilia, epilepsy, lead poisoning, leukemia, or diabetes. It should be added here that acute problems for schools and educators are created by children with AIDS.

Special educators are of the opinion that even severely handicapped children should participate as much as possible in activities with their nonhandicapped peers. To that effect, Stainback and Stainback (1985) offered a number of suggestions about how to facilitate interaction among nonhandicapped youngsters. Sirvis (1962) suggested the following main goals in the education of the physically disabled: physical independence, including mastery of daily living skills; self-awareness and social maturation; academic achievement; and career education, including constructive leisure activities.

Blind and visually handicapped children require specialized educational programming since, as a group, they are extremely heterogeneous. However, they represent only a small percentage of school-age children who require special education services. Experts in the education of the blind (Napier, 1972) underscore the importance of attitudes by sighted people while interacting with the blind. A sighted person should be careful not to sound surprised when talking to a blind person. An attitude of pity should also be avoided. In turn, a blind child should be trained to behave in social situations as normally as possible. Teaching academic skills to blind children requires specialized techniques. It is emphasized that even a small amount of visual acuity should be utilized in visual efficiency training, which emphasized development of such skills as controlling eye movements, attention to visual stimuli, and processing of visual information. Depending on the degree of blindness, auditory modality is stressed in information processing. Tactile modality has been utilized extensively. One of the earliest systems of teaching and writing through touch was developed in 1830 by Louis Braille. His method is still extensively used. A more recent technological development with strong potential application is the Kurzweil Reading Machine.

Deaf and hard-of-hearing children present an equally strong challenge to special educators. Leaders of special education (Kirk, 1981) suggest that teaching deaf and hard-of-hearing youngsters is one of the most "special" areas in special education. As with blindness, deafness per se is not highly correlated with impaired intellectual capacity. As underscored by Moore (1987), deafness "imposes no limitation on the cognitive capabilities of individuals." The same writer suggested in another publication (Moore, 1985) that four conditions seem to be related to the academic success of hearing-impaired students: the severity of hearing impairment and the age of onset, the socioeconomic status of the family, and the hearing status of the parents.

There appears to be consensus in the literature that deaf and hard-of-hearing individuals manifest a variety of emotional problems, such as feelings of depression, withdrawal, and isolation. Such problems are more evident in individuals whose deafness developed later in life.

A variety of educational methods have been used in teaching deaf children. Those methods are described as cued speech, oral communication, and total communication. A total communication approach seems to be most favored. Visual and tactile methods of input are also frequently utilized.

More recently, new technology has been utilized, and telecommunication devices for deaf persons are being increasingly employed.

Children with communication difficulties represent heterogeneous groups of etiologies and conditions. Some writers differentiate communication disorders into two large groups: speech disorders and language disorders. Speech disorders in a narrow sense refer to various conditions associated with voice production, such as articulation, voice quality, and fluency. Complex speech disorders with a neurological basis are known as aphasias. Those of a receptive nature are known technically as Wernicke aphasia; those of an expressive nature are known as Broca's aphasia. Language more specifically is referred to as a complex pattern of communication associated with psychological and sociological variables.

Speech and language disorders are treated by a variety of techniques, depending on their etiology and pathology or absence of it. Perkins (1977) divided speech therapies into action, behavior, and insight therapies. Most action therapies are based on operant conditioning principles.

Some intervention techniques have been designed to help parents in the development of language skills in their preschool children. Blue and Beaty (1974) have informed us that the Peabody Language Development Kit (PLDK) is a helpful tool in planning for language subskills and remediation.

Difficult problems are presented by severely and multiply handicapped mentally retarded persons. A variety of approaches to speech therapy with the population have been described. Those approaches include: manual or sign language (Fristoe & Lloyd, 1977), oral language (Kahn, 1977); operant conditioning (Nelson et al., 1976), and nonspeech systems (Elder & Bergman, 1978; Vanderheiden & Harris-Vanderheiden, 1977).

Special educators recognize that unique problems in special therapy are presented by aphasic children. In this respect, Wepman (1972) identified three important areas of concern when initiating speech therapy with an aphasic child: what is done to and with the patient by an external agency (stimulation), what the impaired nervous system is capable of doing (facilitation), and what the state of the internalized drive of the patient might be (motivation) (Wepman, 1972, p. 203).

Three distinct trends can be recognized in the education of children. Throughout the nineteenth century, they were educated in private or public institutions or tutored individually by altruistic persons. Self-contained programs for the mentally retarded in public schools experienced their greatest expansion from the 1920s through the 1960s. The third trend—deemphasizing self-contained programs and emphasizing mainstreaming—began in the late 1960s.

Mainstreaming as a policy has been associated with changes in attitudes toward the mentally retarded brought about by normalization concerns. This philosophical view found its expression in Public Law 94-142, which mandates that exceptional children should be educated in the "least restrictive" environment.

Sandler (1999), in his discussion of the value of inclusion for children with severe disabilities, acknowledges improvement in social skills but points out that some studies raise concern regarding the acquisition of functional skills. Furthermore, he argues that the acquisition of functional skills in inclusive classrooms may be necessary to justify inclusion as an instructional model.

Cook and Semmel (1999) investigated peer acceptance of included students with disabilities. The sample included 285 students, 44 of whom had disabilities. The sample was drawn from 14 elementary classrooms in southern California. Peer acceptance was measured by nominations from classmates regarding with whom they would like to play and study. The data was treated statistically by the analysis of variance and multivariate analysis of variance. Cook and Semmel concluded that selecting or designing the student composition of inclusive classroom environments based on severity of disability, may improve the level of success for children with disabilities in the inclusive classrooms.

Mamlin (1999) investigated inclusion efforts at one elementary school that served as a site for the in-depth study. Inclusion effort was directed at children with moderate to mild disabilities, who had been previously educated in self-contained settings. This study pointed out three important factors that should be taken under consideration for inclusion practices to succeed. To begin with, not all schools are ready to make decisions on restructuring for inclusion. Furthermore, the "culture" of the school should be carefully assessed to determine if students, teachers, and administrators are ready to accept necessary changes in attitudes for the process of inclusion to succeed. Finally, leadership style of a school leader, principal or superintendent is crucial.

Mainstreaming and deinstitutionalization created changes in the characteristics of the mentally retarded population served by special education programs. As a result of mainstreaming, more capable youngsters were placed in regular programs. This resulted in the lowering of overall ability and cognitive levels in the self-contained EMR (educable mentally retarded) classes. Likewise, with fewer youngsters institutionalized, the more severely and multiply handicapped mentally retarded youngsters have been placed into classes for the trainable mentally retarded. Those demographic changes in the population have significant implications for professional personnel preparation and curriculum development. Research on associative clustering, verbal mediation, and applied behavioral analysis show promise for the curriculum development and education of mentally retarded children. Snell (1987) reports that applied behavioral analysis has been used effectively with mentally retarded youngsters. Change in adaptive behavior is considered the positive outcome of training.

Adaptive behavior scales have been designed to assess changes in behavior. The public school version of the AAMD scale was developed in 1981. This school version includes twenty-one domains, for example: independent functioning, physical development, language development, prevocational self-direction, interpersonal manners, and so forth (Lambert et al., 1981).

The research literature on educability and educational achievement of the mentally retarded is rather extensive. It has been summarized by Holowinsky (1983) as follows:

1. The educational achievement of EMR children in regular programs was found to be superior to that of children in self-contained special programs.
2. Within self-contained special classes, better relative educational achievement (in reference to their MA) was found among children with lower IQs than among those with higher IQs.
3. Reading achievement of the EMR children was found to be generally below their MA reading achievement expectancy level.
4. EMR children in regular programs tended to be isolated and rejected by their peers. This phenomenon, however, is manifested more in suburban than inner-city school districts.
5. EMR children in self-contained programs made better social adjustment than their matched peers in regular programs. (p. 105)

Emotionally disturbed and socially maladjusted children present a variety of educational challenges. The curriculum for those children is contingent on the degree of severity of emotional and personality changes. Behavioral intervention may include play therapy, behavior modification, individual psychotherapy, group psychotherapy, or psychoanalysis.

The term seriously emotionally disturbed is defined in Public Law 94-142 as follows: "a condition exhibiting one or more of the following characteristics over a long period of time and to a marked extent, which adversely affects educational performance." The *Federal Register* lists the following characteristics of seriously emotionally disturbed children: intellectual, sensory, or health factors; an inability to build or maintain satisfactory relationships with peers and teachers; inappropriate types of behavior or feelings under normal circumstances; general pervasive mood of unhappiness or depression; a tendency to develop physical symptoms or fears associated with personal or school problems (1977, p. 42478). The category of seriously emotionally disturbed included, until 1981, both schizophrenic and autistic children. However, the U.S. Department of Education decided in 1981 to include autistic children in the category of "other health impaired."

Kauffman (1985) listed six main theoretical approaches that influenced development of curriculum for the emotionally disturbed. Those approaches were identified as biogenic, psychodynamic, psychoeducational, humanistic, ecological, and behavioral. Generally, educational achievement has been reported below grade and age expectancy level with poor motivation.

Children with learning disabilities constitute the single largest category of exceptionality, estimated as 4.6 percent of public school enrollment. Currently, the generally accepted definition of learning disabilities is "potential-achievement" discrepancy. In addition to poor educational achievement, many other characteristics of LD children have been identified, such as: significant discrepancy, deficient learning process, hyperactivity, incoordination, memory disorders, overattention or attention fixation, perceptual disorders, and poor self-concept.

Hickson and Skvy (1990) call our attention to a growing realization among educators that disadvantaged children from low-income, ethnic, and racial minority groups represent a substantial source of talent.

From a study of gifted LD children, Vespi and Yewchuk (1991) concluded that these children have many positive social and emotional characteristics. However, their main area of need is in dealing with those academic tasks that they found difficult. It is in this area that gifted LD children develop negative work habits and attitudes.

Gottlieb, Alter, Gottlieb, and Wishner (1994) collected data on the achievement of children with learning disabilities over a ten-year period. They concluded that LD children today function very similarly to how EMR children performed twenty-five years ago. The writers discussed characteristics and needs of inner-city special education youngsters and difficult options facing school administrators. They concluded that educational inclusion is

not the solution. What is needed, in their judgment, is the delivery of intensive and effective instructional services to the children in need.

Gearheart, Weisbahn, and Gearheart (1988) list seven suggestions for program planning in the education of children with learning disabilities:

> There is no single "right" method to use with learning-disabled students; All
> other factors being equal, the method "newest" for the student should be
> used; Some types of positive reconditioning should be implemented; High
> motivation is a prerequisite to success; and deliberate consideration of the
> affective domain is essential; The existence of nonspecific or difficult-to-
> define disabilities, particularly with older students, must be recognized; It is
> important to be concerned and involved with both process- and task-orient-
> ed assistance and remediation; One should attempt to determine how the
> student approaches cognitive learning and then assist him or her to develop
> better learning strategies.

In the past twenty years, learning experiences known as cognitive training or cognitive behavior modification (CBM) have been utilized in the education of children with learning disabilities. Meichenbaum (1983), whose
name is prominently associated with the cognitive behavior modification
approach, suggested the following guidelines for the development of a curriculum for LD children:

> Try out target behaviors yourself to determine all the steps; Tune in to stu-
> dents as they perform tasks; Choose as a training task an actual task the stu-
> dent performs; Ask for the students' advice in devising the training; Train
> subtasks and metacognitive skills at the same time; Provide specific feedback
> indicating how the use of the strategy leads to improvement; Teach general-
> ization by using the strategy under new circumstances; Provide a coping
> model; Review the strategy on a planned basis.

Secondary Programs

The history of special education in the United States reveals a strong
emphasis on elementary programs, with less attention paid to special education at a secondary level. A number of reasons can be identified for such a
trend. First of all, at the time when compulsory attendance extended only
until sixteen years of age, those students who were less academically capable
left school as soon as possible. Secondly, almost none of the EMR youngsters
attended high school at that time. Furthermore, since EMR children require
more time for the acquisition of basic educational skills, most of their schooling has been devoted to the learning of reading, writing, and basic arithmetic.

However, since the 1970s, increased attention has been paid to the development of secondary curriculum for exceptional learners. The most fre-

quently utilized model has been the work-study program. The students spend half a school day in the classroom and a couple of hours in the afternoon in on-the-job training (Halahan & Kauffman, 1978). Interest in work-study programs stimulated the development of the Vocational Interest and Sophistication Assessment (VISA) technique. This instrument has been developed and standardized by Parnicky, Kahn, and Burdett (1971) to be used to assess the vocational potential of adolescent EMR students. As suggested by Mercer and Payne (1975); a typical work-study program has five major phases: vocational exploration, vocational evaluation, vocational training, vocational placement, and following.

In the area of curriculum development at the secondary level, a number of very helpful suggestions have been provided by Gearheart et al. (1988) that advise us to develop study guides, technical vocabularies and glossaries, summaries of concept, special texts, and modified lectures. The authors also list five important guidelines to make curriculum more meaningful for secondary learning disabled students:

> For students who cannot express themselves orally or in writing, a carefully taped response to an assignment might be acceptable; Peer tutors may be used in many ways and in a wide variety of subject areas; Study skills classes or sessions may be organized; Students might be taught different reading rates for different types of material; the study of critical new vocabulary words should be encouraged in order to enable students to study them before presentation in the class.

SPECIAL EDUCATION IN CANADA

As mentioned earlier in this chapter, provisions and services for exceptional children in Canada vary significantly among various provinces. For example, Ballance and Kendall (1969) informed us that by 1968 Ontario had legislative provisions for all categories of exceptionalities, while Prince Edward Island had a specific legislative mandate for only the education of the blind and deaf. Although in the United States, approximately 12 percent of school-age children are receiving some kind of special education service, the percentage in Canada ranges from as low as 0.16 percent in Newfoundland to 3.85 percent in Ontario.

Wilgosh (1991) discussed underachievement and related issues for culturally different gifted children in Canada. The paper demonstrated the inappropriateness of using the intelligence-achievement discrepancy formula for identifying underachievement among Eskimo children. The writer argues for new approaches in the identification of culturally different, underachieving gifted children.

By 1980, there were six Canadian provinces and territories, out of twelve, that proclaimed mandatory legislation for exceptional children. Three others expressed interest in similar legislation, and three expressed no concern for mandatory legislation (Goguen, 1980, p. 179). Some examples of legislation by categories are given below.

Health and physically handicapping conditions: British Columbia, Manitoba, Newfoundland, Nova Scotia, Ontario, Quebec, and Saskatchewan have enabling legislation.

Blind and deaf: Every Canadian province has enabling legislation related to the education and training of blind and deaf individuals.

Mentally retarded: Specific legislative provisions are found in all provinces except Prince Edward Island. However, the legislation is broadly interpreted and also includes services for the mentally retarded.

Emotionally disturbed: Manitoba, Saskatchewan, and Ontario have legislative provisions for the education of the emotionally disturbed.

In addition to special education branches and departments within the provincial departments of education, many large school districts (for example, Calgary, Edmonton, Regina, Saskatoon, Toronto, Vancouver, and Winnipeg) have their own departments. Owing to considerable diversity in legislation and services among provinces, the discussion here will be arranged geographically by province.

The Department of Education in Alberta employs a supervisor of special education who is responsible for implementing regulations. Prior to 1969 (Ballance & Kendall, 1969), mandatory attendance was required from 7 to 16 years of age. Special education services were provided to the deaf, blind, and mentally retarded. Significant growth occurred in the 1970s, while in 1960, only 728 youngsters within the province received special education services. By 1979, 23,701 children were in special education programs (Church, 1980).

In British Columbia, there was no special education branch prior to 1969 (Ballance & Kendall, 1969). However, individual school districts have been providing education to the blind and deaf as well as to the educable and trainable mentally retarded. Significant changes were introduced in the 1970s. De facto segregation was replaced by mainstreaming efforts (Gittins, 1980). Toward the end of the 1970s, there were educational programs for almost every category of exceptionality in the province.

The Department of Education in Manitoba has a special services branch consisting of a director, assistant director, and special education consultants. Since 1969, the education of all mentally retarded children, including trainable, become the responsibility of the state. Currently, provisions are made

for the mentally retarded, physically handicapped, blind, deaf, and emotionally disturbed.

All special education programs in the province of New Brunswick are
functioning under the authority of the minister of education. Services are provided for the mentally retarded, cerebral palsied, blind, deaf, and deaf-mute.

In Newfoundland, there was no special education branch in the Department of Education, and no director of special education prior to 1969 (Ballance & Kendall, 1969). Compulsory attendance is from 7 to 15 years of age.
However, deaf and blind youngsters may stay in school until 18 years of age.

The Northwest Territories present unique educational problems. As summarized by Watters (1980), some of these problems are: many native languages and dialects; transient teaching population; no consistent
understanding of special education by school personnel; and great variety in
delivery of services across the territories. The first government involvement
in education occurred in 1948. It was as late as 1972 when the territorial
school system adapted its own elementary school curriculum (Watters, 1980).

In Nova Scotia, each municipal school board may provide instruction for
physically or mentally handicapped children. An interesting provision in the
Nova Scotia school code made an exception in compulsory attendance for
rural youngsters. Although in urban settings, compulsory attendance is from
6 to 15 years of age, rural children are required to attend schools from 7 to 14
years of age (Ballance & Kendall, 1969).

Comparatively speaking, the most elaborate special education services in
Canada are in the province of Ontario, where mandatory legislation was
enacted in 1980. The *School Administration Act* provides for the establishment
of programs for the blind, visually handicapped, emotionally disturbed, gifted, neurologically impaired, deaf, hard-of-hearing, physically disabled, and
those with other health problems. Keeton (1980) informs us that in December
1978, the Ontario Ministry of Education sent two memoranda to all school
boards. One required the establishment of procedures for programs for children with learning disabilities, and another required the establishment of
early identification programs. In addition to the programs provided by the
Department of Education, hospital schools for mentally retarded children and
a hospital for emotionally disturbed children are administered by the Department of Health. However, the responsibility for educational programs within
those facilities has been assigned to the Department of Education. A considerable number of children with learning disabilities or other handicapping
conditions are enrolled in private schools and clinics supported by the Ministry of Community and Social Services (Keeton, 1980).

In Quebec, compulsory attendance is required by children 6 to 15 years
of age. The school principal and a special class teacher have authority to
admit children to a special class.

In Saskatchewan, prior to 1969, the *School Administration Act* provided for exclusion of any youngster who is "so mentally deficient as to be incapable of responding to class instruction by a skillful teacher" (Ballance & Kendall, 1969). In 1977, *Special Education: A Manual of Legislation Regulations, Policies and Guidelines* (Carlson, 1980) was published by the Saskatchewan Department of Education. Programs have been developed for eight categories of exceptionalities: visually impaired, hearing impaired, trainable mentally retarded, severely learning disabled, orthopedically handicapped, chronically health impaired, socially-emotionally (behaviorally) handicapped, and severely multiply handicapped.

Special education services in South America, Mexico, and Central America vary from very limited to comprehensive.

In Argentina, as reported by Wycke (1987a), the National Directorate of Special Education is responsible for providing special education services to mentally, physically, and socially handicapped students. Services are provided from preschool through adulthood. Early intervention programs for children CA 1-3 are not yet well organized.

In Brazil, as of 1981, the following categories were served: visually and auditorily impaired, physically disabled, mentally retarded educable and trainable, and multiply handicapped.

In Chile, special education service is at an early stage of development. In 1975, psychoeducational centers were established. According to 1986 information, 278 schools were providing services to handicapped children, of whom 74 percent were mentally deficient (de La Meuse, 1989). Currently, separate schools exist for youngsters with visual and hearing defects, mental retardation, speech disorders, and motor disorders.

In Ecuador, the National Department of Special Education, within the Ministry of Education, provides for these categories of exceptionalities: mentally retarded, visually and auditorily handicapped, children with cerebral palsy, and children with other handicapping conditions.

The beginning of special education in Mexico dates toward the end of the nineteenth century. In 1914, Jose Gonzalez organized a school for the mentally retarded. Today this population is estimated as 2.5 percent of the general population.

In 1973, a department of special education was created as part of the Secretariat of Public Education (Holtzman, 1989). Currently, special education is provided to children between 6 and 14 years of age. However, the need for education of the handicapped is overwhelming. In many rural villages, schooling is not yet available (Brand, 1987). Special education services generally focus on the more severely handicapped and are usually provided only in special schools. Mainstreaming is not practiced, and self-contained classes are the rule rather than exception (Holtzman, 1989).

In El Salvador, special education services are very limited. Panama provides the following special education services: early stimulation (birth through six years of age); for children with cerebral palsy; and for mentally retarded children, both middle and profoundly handicapped. There is also a Helen Keller school for the deaf and a vocational school for the handicapped.

WESTERN EUROPE

Programs for the handicapped in western Europe vary considerably from one country to another so that there is no unified "West European" approach. Furthermore, in some countries, as, for example, Switzerland and the German Federal Republic, special education provisions change from state to state.

In Europe, special education is generally defined broadly and overlaps with such fields as psychology, psychiatry, rehabilitation, physical therapy, social services, and even philosophy (Juul, 1980). Physical education, creative movements, gymnastics, sports, and the outdoors have long been an intrinsic part of European special education. Important and well-documented early work with exceptional children by such well-known pioneers are Itard, Binet, Braille, Pestalozzi, and Montessori took place in western Europe. Readers interested in overviews of European programs for the handicapped should consult Wolfensberger (1964), Schmidt and Baltes (1971), and Juul (1978).

In many European countries, there is close cooperation among health care workers, social agencies, and educators in planning and programming for handicapped children. For example, in Austria, a multidisciplinary team usually headed by a pediatrician is consulted as soon as a child manifests developmental or school problems (Braswell, 1987). In addition to educational programming, parents of handicapped children also receive disability support.

In Austria, in the school year 1984–1985, there were 283 general special schools and 288 classes for the severely handicapped (Verzcichnis der Lender-schulen, 1985). There are nine types of schools and programs for youngsters who are classified as: mildly handicapped with learning disabilities, physically handicapped, in need of speech correction, hard-of-hearing, deaf, visually handicapped, blind, behaviorally maladjusted, and severely multiply handicapped.

Special education in Belgium is governed by the law of 1980 and provides services for youngsters three to twenty-one years of age (Magerotte, 1987). Services are provided for severely, moderately, and mildly retarded, emotionally disturbed, physically handicapped, health impaired, visually and auditorily impaired; and those with special learning disabilities. Programs are available at the kindergarten, primary, and secondary levels.

In Denmark, special education is an integral part of regular education. The country also seems the most advanced in the utilization of the "camp school" concept in the education and treatment of emotionally disturbed and socially maladjusted youngsters. Denmark is a Scandinavian nation which offers superior services to students with disabilities. Career guidelines in Denmark begin as early as in the seventh grade, when guidance teachers or "Kurators" focus on the development of positive work behaviors in students. Kurators serve as mediators for students with disabilities in Denmark and are assigned to students aged thirteen and older. During the final years of a student's education, the Kurator identifies each student's strengths and areas of interest before developing employment opportunities in the local community.

Prior to 1980, the more severely handicapped children were viewed as the responsibility of the Ministry of Social Affairs. However, since 1980, principles of normalization, decentralization, and integration have been accepted in Denmark. Of the total number of youngsters attending Danish primary schools, less than 1 percent were in special schools, 1 percent in self-contained special classes within regular schools, while 12.5 percent were receiving supplemental or remedial help.

In the primary and lower secondary schools, special education is provided to children with the following handicapping conditions: visual and hearing disabilities, motor disabilities, speech and language impairments, behavioral disorders, general learning disabilities, and reading disorders.

The British *Education Act of 1944* pioneered educational legislation for the mentally retarded in that country. It also listed such health impairments as diabetes and epilepsy, which make ill children eligible for special education services. The revised classification, known as the *Mental Health Act of 1959*, included under the generic term *mental disorders* such conditions as psychotic disorders, mental illness, and intellectual subnormality. In 1970, responsibility for the educationally subnormal was transferred from health services to the Department of Education (Feniak, 1988). The publication in 1978 of the Warnock Report provided a landmark in the development of resources for children with special needs. It also provided an impetus for the 1981 legislation (Lindsay, 1988). Since 1981, the three major categories of disabilities recognized as the responsibility of education are educationally subnormal moderate, educationally subnormal severe, and behaviorally maladjusted. Children may be regarded as behaviorally (emotionally) maladjusted if their behavior has a negative effect on themselves or their environment and cannot be remediated without help by parents, teachers, or other significant adults. Current British special education law (Webster, 1989) places increased responsibilities on the LEAs (Local Education Agencies). Local health authorities are required to inform parents and the LEAs if it is suspected that a child has or is likely to have special education needs.

The new *National Curriculum Act* was formulated in 1988 and was introduced in the fall of 1989 (U.K. circular N 22/89). Accepted current terminology is *children with special education needs.* The act covers all children from birth to the upper limit of compulsory school age at sixteen, and any pupil over sixteen up to their nineteenth birthday who continues to attend school.

Laaksonen (1989) informs us that in Finland most of the children in need of special education were identified as manifesting learning difficulties, hyperactivity, and behavioral problems.

Parental involvement in education has an important place in schooling in Scandinavian countries (Finland, Norway, Sweden) (Galton & Blyth, 1989). Parents schedule at the very least, one meeting per year, per child in Finland. The educational authorities also have been encouraging home-school contact. The National Board of Education in Finland proposed a "verbal reporting system" on children's learning success along with a feedback form for parents to answer and send back to school. Since 1979, booklets on home-school cooperation were sent to parents to make sure there was communication between the parents and the school.

The Ministry of Education in Norway created a policy to encourage parental involvement. They created an advisory committee consisting of a parent and two educational consultants to provide guidance to parents and schools. In Sweden, early intervention and parental involvement has been a part of educational process for a long time.

Tyszka (1993) provides a brief history and current status of special education in France. The roots of special education in France can be found in the work and contribution of Alfred Binet at the beginning of the twentieth century. Initially, the special education system was segregated. The issue of whether French education was to be elitist or egalitarian was not resolved until 1925. The law of 1975 ordered mandatory education of impaired individuals in the least-restrictive setting, beginning with mainstreaming into a regular setting. Currently, four kinds of placement options are available: full-time integration (class size is reduced and support services are provided); part-time integration (students attend a combination of regular and special education classes); partial integration; and segregated facilities.

In France, as in the Scandinavian countries and Austria, there is a compulsory screening of all infants at birth and again at two years of age. Youngsters in need of special education services are grouped into fifteen categories. Approximately 4 percent of the total school-age children profit from special education services. The first special classes for mentally retarded children opened in Lyons in 1906, and the following year additional classes opened in Paris. As reported by Guillemard (1989), 73,000 children are educated in special classes at the elementary level and 126,000 at secondary levels. In addition to special classes within elementary schools, there are also separate schools administered by the Ministry of Health.

In the Federal Republic of Germany, an estimated 6.5 percent of school-age youngsters receive special education services. Special schools are available for students with the following handicapping conditions: blind, deaf, mentally retarded, physically handicapped, educationally subnormal, hearing impaired, visually impaired, with special defects, behaviorally disturbed, and those in need of prolonged hospitalization (Nagelschmitz, 1985). Children categorized as educationally subnormal are divided into two groups: educationally subnormal with marked intellectual deficit, and educationally subnormal with generalized learning disturbance.

Since the 1970s, European countries have made significant advances in policies aimed at bringing persons with disabilities into the social mainstream. However, as reported by Murray-Seegert (1992), integration of persons with disabilities is progressing very slowly in the Federal Republic of Germany. As a matter of fact, German schools continue to place a high priority on student homogeneity. There are ten separate types of special schools in the Federal Republic where children are segregated according to categories of disability.

In Ireland, provision is made for handicapped and disadvantaged children within the system of elementary education. Handicapped children attend special schools or special classes within regular schools. In 1983, there were more than eight thousand children identified as in need of special education. There are 118 schools for exceptional children. More than half of these are for youngsters described as intellectually subnormal (Chamberlain, 1989). Other categories usually listed are hearing impaired, blind, physically handicapped, and emotionally disturbed.

Prior to 1960, the most severely disabled youngsters in Italy were institutionalized and given only custodial care. Less severely handicapped children were kept in special classes within regular school (Nisi et al., 1989).

Italy has attempted to facilitate the total integration of its disabled population through education and training for future employment opportunities. The concept of integration became reality for students with disabilities in 1977 upon the enactment of Law 517. The main thrust of Law 517 was the requirement that all handicapped children be mainstreamed into regular classes, regardless of the nature of severity of their disabilities. Thus, the principle of normalization is said to underlie the Italian education system from the earliest elementary years, so that segregation and social isolation of the disabled does not typically occur. Students with disabilities and their general education peers interact daily so that when students finally reach the age when it is appropriate to begin employment training, securing a placement in an integrated work setting, rather than a sheltered workshop, is the primary goal.

The Genoa Project, a model for enabling students to transition from schooling into integrated employment, originated in Italy. The central philosophy underlying the Genoa Project is to locate the "right place for the right person." This philosophy is based on four premises:

- Work is conducive to motivating individuals to attain adult status.
- Integrated work settings encourage age-appropriate behaviors.
- Competitive employment secure one's adult status in society.
- Competitive employment allows individuals to establish independence.

After assessing each client's work and social skills, the Project's design differs from most other models in that it attempts to make use of coworkers and other natural supports in the workplace to provide training and ongoing support to the students, as opposed to providing a job coach for training.

Vitello (1991) informs us that in 1971 the new education law mandated total mainstreaming of disabled and handicapped children. This law, however, became unrealistic. The period from 1971 to 1977 was referred to as wild integration that did not work for a variety of reasons. To correct problems with mainstreaming, a new law was adopted in 1977. Among its provisions was the stipulation that integrated classes should contain a maximum of twenty students per class, and that only two severely handicapped children should be placed in one class.

In the Netherlands a number of schools for the deaf, blind, and mentally retarded were established in the nineteenth century. However, the *Compulsory Education Act* was promulgated in 1901. Currently, special education services are provided at three levels: for preschoolers three to six years of age; elementary-age children, six to twelve years of age; and continued special education services for those over twelve years of age.

Norway and Sweden are commonly referred to as Scandinavian countries. It is generally acknowledged by educators that their major contribution to the field of special education has been the idea of normalization. In the 1970s, normalization became accepted as a philosophy of treatment for all handicapped (Juul, 1989). Two other important innovative approaches are "fold" high school, of which there are about four hundred in operation and *lekotek* (toy libraries), which are an important part of preschool special education. Future trends in Scandinavian special education were discussed by Tuunainen (1988). Emphasis on life span and career education, increased parental advocacy, and concern for the special needs of the gifted and talented were mentioned.

Skaarbrevik and Gottlieb (1973) reported that in 1888 Norway was the first country that mandated education for all deaf, blind, and retarded children. This mandate was officially implemented in 1892. The *Education Act of 1951* provided further impetus for the establishment of more local schools for the retarded. In many cases, this eliminated the need for residential care and allowed many, even more severely retarded children an opportunity to live with their parents while receiving compensatory education or training. Special education of the physically disabled is viewed within the general context of rehabilitation.

The beginning of special education in Sweden can be traced to the early 1800s. As in other Scandinavian countries, children with high-risk potential are monitored from birth. All children of preschool age receive free health examinations, including hearing and vision screening. According to a 1978 report from the National Ministry of Education, 20 percent of all school-age children receive some sort of special education or remedial service. For example, there is even a special high school for deaf youngsters (Magne, 1988). Various opportunities are provided for emotionally disturbed children. There are "observation" teaching approaches (Lundstrom, 1969). In each such setting, a teacher is supported by mental health workers. Such therapeutic teaching takes place outside the regular classroom for varying lengths of time.

Administration of special education in Sweden is divided into five regions. Each region has a planning committee, which coordinates the activities of the region. Services are provided for the blind and visually handicapped, deaf and hard-of-hearing, orthopedically handicapped, and mentally retarded. Intellectually handicapped adolescents attend vocational schools for the mentally retarded, most of which are housed on the same premises as regular high schools. Starting with the 1988–1989 school year, an experimental three-year program of vocational education in close cooperation with industry was initiated. These experimental activities are coordinated with other programs already in existence.

An extensive survey of children with mild mental retardation in Swedish schools was published by Sommender, Emanuelsson, and Kelbon (1993). The data revealed that nearly 2 percent of students were identified with mental retardation, with a general tendency of more boys than girls being identified. As in other countries throughout the world, a significant overrepresentation of youngsters with a low socioeconomic background was identified among the mentally retarded. The students with mild mental retardation in public schools were low achieving, but they did not constitute a homogeneous group. The writers expressed an opinion that a psychometric criteria label should never be the only guide to service delivery.

In Switzerland, special education is decentralized and developed according to regional regulations. In the 1983–1984 school year, more than 4 percent of the school-age children attended special education classes (Burli, 1987). Currently, there is an effort to stress various itinerant school services and to deemphasize segregated school placement.

The Swiss Center for Coordination of Special Education is located in Lucerne and provides information about education, schooling, and vocational training of handicapped individuals. It also helps with the training of specialists and conducts research.

Children who are described as having emotional and behavioral difficulties represent complex problems for special education in the United Kingdom. Although the UK government abolished the use of specific labels, they recommended the use of the generic term "special educational needs." The specific lables are still widely used as reported recently by Farrell and Taskalidow (1999). As in the United States, children who are placed in the programs and classes for EBD (emotionally and behaviorally disturbed) tend to come from socially and economically disadvantaged families. According to Farrell and Taskalidow's findings among exceptional learners, EBD children are most difficult to mainstream into the regular programs. Their general conclusion is that once such children are placed into special programs, they are likely to return if they are under 13 years of age and if "plans to reintegrate are made within the first two or three years of their placement."

Related Services

Juul (1980) tells us that in western Europe there is much emphasis on vocational training. Most of the secondary schools provide academic and vocational training. From 12 years of age, children with limited academic potential receive training in technical skills. By the time they reach 15 or 16 years of age, many go into full employment. Some examples of related services are provided in this section.

In Denmark, apprenticeship training may start after nine years of basic education and terminates with a journeyman's certificate. Training in the commercial and clerical fields also consists of on-the-job practical training and theoretical training at a commercial school. Education of the handicapped is viewed as a lifelong process; and adults are provided with remedial instruction, which is provided for the speech handicapped, physically impaired, deaf, blind, and mentally retarded. An extensive leisure-time education is also provided.

In 1933, the *National Assistance Act* declared that the care and education of the retarded was the responsibility of the government. In 1959, the semi-independent Mental Retardation Service was created within the Ministry of Social Affairs. It is widely recognized (Juul, 1978) that Denmark has one of the most comprehensive, high-quality care systems for the mentally retarded.

As an innovative approach, one can mention a community where the mentally handicapped and nonhandicapped live and work together. Such a community has been organized in France by Jan Venier. A similar therapeutic home was established in London by a British psychiatrist, Laing (Braswell, 1987).

Holland has made significant progress in the employment of the handicapped. Industry and labor organizations are involved in developing the processes of placement, wages, and conditions of employment.

In Sweden, in 1969, a group of professionals initiated development of small therapeutic communities known as *Hassela* (collective) (Juul, 1989). Such therapeutic communities usually house fewer than twenty members. One of the basic requirements is that staff and students live together.

Burli (1987) reports that in Switzerland, various related services are provided to exceptional children, such as psychotherapy, speech, and language therapy. Vocational training is provided with emphasis on normalization through numerous sheltered workshops and rehabilitation centers.

Eastern Europe

The former Soviet Union (Union of the Soviet Socialist Republics) comprised fifteen constituent republics: Armenia, Azerbajdzan, Beylorussia, Estonia, Georgia, Kaskhstan, Kirgisia, Latvia, Lithuania, Moldava, Russia, Thaddzikistan, Turkmenia, Ukraine, and Uzbekistan.

The administration of special education in the former Soviet Union was centralized within the All-Union *(Vse-Souznaya)* Ministry of Education in Moscow. Each of the fifteen union republics had its own ministry of education and a department of special education. The ministries of education of the union republics were responsible to the Ministry of Education of the USSR. The scope and degree of comprehensiveness, however, of special education services was not identical in each of the Soviet republics.

In European Russia and in countries incorporated into the USSR after 1944, for example, Estonia, Latvia, and Lithuania, there were services for some types of handicapping conditions in the nineteenth century.

In Lithuania, the first school for deaf children opened in Vilnious in 1805. However, in the Asian part of the Soviet Union, Kazkhstan, Uszbekistan, and so forth, special education services are a rather recent development.

An interesting aspect of the history of special education in the USSR has been the movement called pedology, discussed in more detail elsewhere (Holowinsky, 1988). Among early supporters of pedology were such noted psychologists as Blonsky, Vygotsky, and Zamsky. In the early 1930s, strong opposition to pedology developed, led by Makarenko and Medinsky.

Medinsky, especially, strongly criticized pedology and the whole testing movement. In his words: "Intelligence and achievement tests were made with such calculations that the children of the indigent parents should appear as weakly endowed and nonachieving. Those tests claiming objective proof were in reality the means to enable the children of the bourgeois to continue their education and to except the children of toilers" (Medinsky, 1954, p. 179). Owing in part to much political and ideological arguments, the Central Committee of the Communist Party of the USSR declared in July 1936 that pedology was a pseudoscientific and anti-Marxist science (Shore, 1947).

In the former Soviet Union, the service delivery network for exceptional learners extends from nursery and kindergarten through vocational and adult continuing education. There existed an elaborate system of registration of infants and young children with developmental disabilities. Developmental abnormalities were noted at the time of birth in the delivery room (Aleksandrovskaya & Boitsova, 1974). Special schools grouped children according to chronological age and degree of severity of impairment.

In 1975, the council of ministers produced a document outlining education, training, and work placement of intellectually and physically handicapped. The main goal of Soviet special education was stated as preparation for school and life, academic learning and productive work, and the development of "appropriate social adjustment to socialist society" (Csapo, 1984).

Traditionally, the field of special education has been divided into four areas: oligophrenopedagogy (education of the mentally retarded), surdopedagogy (education of the deaf), typhlopedagogy (education of the blind), and logopedagogy (speech correction). Discussion of developmentally delayed children is a relatively recent phenomenon in the Soviet defectological literature. Research with this population began in 1965 at the Scientific Research Institute of the Academy of Pedagogical Sciences (Holowinsky, 1983b).

Mentally retarded children were trained and educated at various facilities such as hospitals, residential facilities, and auxiliary schools. Since 1976, a class limit of twelve has been set for children with auditory, visual, and speech defects, and sixteen for the mentally retarded. A curriculum for moderately retarded youngsters was described by Kuzmitskaya (1977). It emphasized nine objectives: personal communication; orientation to place; knowledge of occupation of residents of towns and villages; understanding of basic ideas of commerce; familiarity with everyday basic food preparation; knowledge of available health services in the neighborhood; use of a post office, telephone, and radio; knowledge of available recreation facilities in the neighborhood; and basic familiarity with work habits, work schedules, wages, and salaries.

In addition to special schools for the mentally retarded, blind, and deaf, there were also auxiliary schools for the intellectually backward and mildly handicapped. Programs in auxiliary schools were arranged in such a way that a youngster would be expected to reach an eighth-grade competency level after twelve years of schooling.

There were heavy emphasis on vocational training in auxiliary schools. Language stimulation and speech correction with exceptional children has been significantly increased since the 1976–1977 school year. The curriculum has been increased from four hours per week to eighteen hours per week.

In the past decade, considerable emphasis has been placed on program development for handicapped preschoolers. In 1970, there were 700 preschool facilities in the Soviet Union in which more than 11,000 handicapped children were educated (Filkina, 1977). In 1976, there were in existence 1,580 preschool facilities educating 19,648 children. As of 1982, preschool facilities in the former Soviet Union were providing training and education to approximately 140,000 handicapped children. Noskova and Kuznyetsova (1980) reported that there were four types of kindergarten facilities: kindergarten with full-day programming; residential homes for preschool children; preschool programs with special schools; and special groups for various categories of exceptional children within kindergartens for normal children.

In the 1980s, increased emphasis was placed on the teaching of arithmetic and vocational preparation (Ippolitova, 1985; Pinsky & Boganovskaya, 1985; Sukhova, 1985; Ek, 1985; Gazova, 1985). Ippolitova (1985) stressed the need to teach arithmetic to young mentally retarded children. Pinsky and Boganovskaya (1985) reported that most of the arithmetical errors made by children in the first through third grades are due to a lack of familiarity with concepts of equivalence and order. Inability to acquire mathematical concepts has been related by Sukhova (1985) to the limited verbal communication of exceptional children. An example of a highly structured arithmetic curriculum in the first grade was provided by Ek (1985). The activities are highly structured and organized by the teacher, with all children required to participate.

Developments in special education in the USSR were highlighted in an article by Lubovsky (1987). He informed us that deaf children of average ability were receiving high school-equivalent education in twelve years. Considerable progress has been made in clinical, genetic, neurophysiological, psychological, and educational studies of atypical children.

Lubovsky stresses that a considerable contribution in defectological research has been made by the Institute of Defectology of the Academy of Pedagogical Sciences of the USSR, the Institute of Pedagogy, and the Institute of Psychology of Ukrainian SSR. He acknowledges that more research is needed in the area of preschool education.

His comment that in the former USSR mentally retarded children constituted more than 80 percent of all atypical children is interesting. For comparison it should be pointed out that in the United States mentally retarded children account for approximately 15 percent of all school-age classified children. The two largest categories, accounting for approximately 55 percent of handicapped children, are learning disabled and communication handicapped.

A few examples of special education efforts in various former Soviet republics will be provided next. It should be kept in mind, however, that the extent of services and program development varies considerably among various republics. Minasian (1970) informed us that in Armenian SSR the first school for blind children opened in 1922. In the capital city of Yerevan, the first auxiliary school opened in 1928. Considerable growth of special education programs in Armenia took place in the 1960s and 1970s. Toward the end of the nineteenth century, a number of private schools were organized in Byelorussia (Bobla, 1987), primarily for the education of the deaf, blind, and deaf-mute. Since the 1970s, programs for developmentally delayed children have been established (Gaiduk, Slepovitch, & Asanova, 1984). The first class for children with this classification opened in Vitebsk in 1974, and by the school year 1982–1983 there were seventy-four such classes in existence. Currently (Bobla, 1987), there are approximately one hundred schools for exceptional children in Byelorussia.

In Estonia, the first school for the deaf was organized in 1867 and for the blind in 1883 (Korgessar, 1988). There were only three auxiliary schools in operation between 1923 and 1925. Currently, in auxiliary schools with a nine-year curriculum, the students are taught life skills, basic academic skills, and are exposed to some prevocational training. The number of students in auxiliary schools is limited to twelve to sixteen. In the 1985–1986 school year, there were five special schools of "remedial" type for children with delayed mental development, as well as twenty-three special classes. The development of special kindergarten began in the late 1960s. Between 1960 and 1984, the number of special schools in Estonia increased from eight to forty-one. Lutskina and Grushevskaya (1985) informed us that the development of special education services began in the Kazakh SSR in the early 1970s. As of the late 1970s, approximately 26,000 exceptional children of school and preschool age attended various programs organized within seventy-seven special classes. Considerable in-service training for teachers was provided through the Defectological Department of the Kazakh Pedagogical Institute.

At present, there are in Kazakhstan 112 special schools of eight types (Lutskina, 1987). This number included: 79 auxiliary schools, 12 for deaf, 6 for hard-of-hearing, 2 for blind, 4 for visually handicapped, 5 for children with speech disorders, 2 for children with sensory-motor difficulties, and 2 for children with 2 PR. For handicapped preschoolers existed 416 groups. This article concluded with the observation that many more defectologists are needed in Kazakhstan.

The first auxiliary schools for mentally retarded children in Lithuania opened in Vilnius in 1923 and in Kaunas in 1931. In the 1970s there were thirty-five auxiliary schools in existence, providing education to more than seven thousand exceptional children in the first through the eighth grade (Machikhina, 1975).

An integral part of the education of the mentally retarded has been labor training and prevocational preparation. This aspect was discussed by Karviali et al. (1986). They described a number of programs and pointed out that general aspects of labor education play an important role in the education of mentally retarded children.

Pavlova (1978) reports that the first program for the severely retarded was organized in Moldavia in 1946. The first auxiliary school for the mildly retarded opened in the early 1950s. In the twenty-year period (1950–1970), thirty-seven additional schools were organized for the mildly retarded, three evening schools for the deaf, and one school for the blind, as well as thirteen special correction clinics within public schools.

Special education in Ukraine, which is the largest non-Russian republic in the former USSR, should be viewed in the context of the size of Ukraine's general education (see Chapter 3).

The systematic instruction of blind children in Ukraine began in the nineteenth century when several schools were organized (Kyiv, 1840; Lviv, 1851; Kamenets-Podilsky, 1885; Odessa, 1887; Kharkiv, 1886; Chernyhiv, 1892; Poltava, 1894). Yeremenko (1984) reported that prior to the First World War, Sokolansky, Schcherbyna, and Korolenko were widely known as defectologists. Schcherbyna (1874–1934), a noted Ukrainian scholar-educator, was considered one of the founders of defectology. His most noted activity as an educator was associated with the Kyiv Pedagogical Institute, where, in 1929, a special education department was organized (Zolotnycka, 1977).

Sokolansky is also recognized as a noted special educator in the 1920s who developed in Kharkiv a program for the education of deaf, blind, and mute children. In the 1930s, Makarenko acquired prominence as an educator who contributed significantly to the development of the collective concept in the Soviet educational literature. The child's collective was viewed as an integral part of society. Makarenko viewed collective not just as an assembly or a group of individuals interacting, but as a goal-directed constellation of personalities responsive to their organizational structure.

Special education in Ukraine includes such traditional categories as blind, visually handicapped, deaf, hard-of-hearing, mentally retarded, and severely speech impaired. Acceptable terms for intellectual subnormality are *rozumova vidstalist* or *rosumove nedorozvynennia*, translatable as intellectual backwardness and mental retardation.

Children entering an auxiliary school are divided into two groups based on higher or lower cognitive abilities. During the 1978–1979 school year, individualized instruction was introduced into auxiliary schools serving mentally retarded children.

Yeremenko (1976) described individualized instruction as a new approach to the education of mentally retarded children, calling it one of the most pressing needs currently confronting defectologists.

Sixty-eight special schools are operating in Uzbekistan serving more than eighteen thousand children (Gordienko, 1985). Additionally, there are eighty-five special classes within public schools. It is reported that in five years (1971–1976), programs for preschool handicapped in Uzbekistan increased fourfold. Nearly 3,000 special educators are working in the special schools, of whom 520 have defectological preparation.

Other Eastern European countries prior to 1945 had a long history of special education efforts, mostly within the mainstream of European tradition, and almost no contact with special education in the former USSR. At the present time, there are still many differences, some of a historical nature, among special education systems in various eastern European countries. For the purposes of this discussion, countries formerly under the political influence of the Soviet Union, for example, Bulgaria, Czechoslovakia, East Germany, Hungary, Poland, Rumania, and Yugoslavia will be considered in this section.

The general administration of special education services was centralized within respective ministries of education. It has been estimated (Lipkowski, 1968) that exceptional children in Bulgaria constitute 1.1 percent of the general school population. Special schools exist for children CA 4–7 with children CA 7–15 attending eight grades of auxiliary schools. Facilities exist for deaf, hard-of-hearing, blind, visually handicapped, and speech-disordered children. Exceptional children of preschool age are included within the system of general preschool education.

Deaf and hard-of-hearing preschoolers are referred for consultation and pedagogical help to the centers of rehabilitation (Noskova & Kyznyetsova, 1980). Children who need speech therapy are trained in special kindergartens as well as in special therapy clinics. In addition to speech therapy, those children also receive clinical counseling. There are also special kindergartens for mentally retarded children. The main goal of the preschool education of the handicapped is the preparation of exceptional children for entrance into various types of special schools. Visually handicapped children beginning at age five are placed in special classes within public schools. Children with mild handicapping conditions are educated with nonhandicapped children.

Diagnosis of exceptionalities in school-age children in Bulgaria is made by medico-pedagogical committees consisting of physicians, psychologists, defectologists, and educators. If the committee is unable to agree on a diagnosis, the child in question is referred to a diagnostic camp for up to three weeks of evaluation. Special committees are set up for a comprehensive evaluation of preschoolers. To upgrade the qualifications of the members of medico-pedagogical committees, in-service training is systematically organized for them.

Lipkowski (1968) informed us that in the former Czechoslovakia (currently two countries: the Czech Republic and Slovakia), exceptional children were estimated to constitute about 2.35 of the school population. The Ministry of Education had centralized responsibility for ideological, political, and educational aspects of the program, as was the case in all socialist countries. The Ministry of Education approved syllabuses for all subjects, as well as textbooks and texts (Holmes, 1980).

The government makes attendance compulsory in kindergarten for children who are three years of age and who have perceptual mental and physical disorders. They remain there until they are able to be placed in the basic nine-year schools. Within a basic nine-year school, specialized classes are established for children who have developmental dyslexia as well as for children with perceptual and motor disorders. Special schools are also established for educable mentally retarded children. When it is not clear whether children are educable, they are placed in special auxiliary schools and classes where long-term observations can take place.

In the Czech Republic and Slovakia, health officials monitor infants with high-risk potential from birth through three years of age. The monitoring is the responsibility of district pediatricians. Children with various disorders are referred for additional examinations by physicians and psychologists. Programming for children aged three or older is conducted by a district psychoeducational committee. Comprehensive evaluation includes medical diagnosis, psychological evaluation of cognitive abilities, and educational evaluation of educability and learning potential. As a rule, a diagnostic study team includes physicians, psychologists, defectologists, and educators.

Prior to the unification in the former German Democratic Republic (East Germany), 57,000 handicapped children were educated in 478 special schools, special education classes, and other facilities. There were schools for the hard-of-hearing and deaf, visually handicapped and blind, those with special disorders, physically disabled, mentally retarded, behaviorally disturbed, and chronically ill. The average class size is nine students (*Documentation*, 1989). The length of schooling extends for eight years for the mentally retarded, ten years for the deaf, and ten years for other handicapping conditions. Approximately 32,000 special education students attend boarding schools or after-school centers.

Graduates of special schools are guaranteed vocational training and an opportunity for gainful employment.

In the nineteenth century in Hungary, efforts began on behalf of the mentally retarded. The first institute for the mentally retarded was organized in the 1880s, and the first preschool facility for blind children opened in 1908.

The current system of special education includes auxiliary schools, schools for severely retarded, deaf, hard-of-hearing, blind, visually handicapped, and physically disabled children. Educational programs for the exceptional are designed according to the chronological age of the child and the category of disability. Exceptional children, from three to six years of age attend preschool special education classes. Children between six and fourteen years of age attend special classes for the retarded in supplementary schools. Moderately retarded children between the ages of six and eight attend preparatory schools, and mildly retarded children between ages eight and sixteen attend the "practical" schools (Dziedzic, 1968). Children between three months and three years are eligible for training in preschool facilities. Special kindergartens exist for blind and deaf children, children with motor difficulties, and children who are mentally retarded (Noskova & Kuznyetsova, 1980). Children with severe speech disorders can be assigned into a program at three years of age and in cases with mild speech disorders at ages four or five.

Special education in Poland has a long history. In 1817, the Institute of Deaf-Mute and Blind was established in Warsaw. In 1922, Maria Grzegorzewska (1888–1967) established the Institute of Special Education, which conducted research and trained teachers. In 1924, a special education section of the Polish Teachers Association was established (Kirejczyk, 1975).

In the 1950s, programs for the mentally retarded were segregated into self-contained schools. In 1956, there were 120 special schools for the mentally retarded. In the 1960s, there were 331 special classes within elementary schools with an enrollment of more than 5000 youngsters. By the 1970s, the number of such classes increased to 698, with an enrollment of nearly eleven thousand.

In the 1986–1987 school year, special education in Poland served more than 64,000 mentally retarded children in 536 schools (Hulek, 1989). The same authority reported that there were 561 child guidance clinics employing 2,610 educators, 2,368 psychologists, 305 physicians, and 266 other specialists. Since 1985, classes and programs for the behaviorally disturbed have been introduced. More than 80 percent of special education graduates continue their training in prevocational or vocational facilities. However, in spite of significant efforts, only 20 percent of the eligible children in Poland receive special education services.

Handicapped pupils in Poland are educated in special preschool facilities, special elementary schools, special vocational schools, residential boarding schools, and rehabilitation and therapeutic facilities, and receive home instruction (Belcerek, 1977). Various levels of interaction of exceptional children within the mainstream of education are also provided (Hulek, 1989), for example, regular programs with some supplemental instruction; special classes within regular schools (there are presently in Poland more than 1,100 such classes for the mildly handicapped within public schools and 57 within vocational schools); selected activities in regular schools for children from special schools; and construction of special schools in the vicinity of regular schools and development between them of various forms of cooperation.

Special educators in Poland prefer the terms *therapeutic pedagogy* or *special pedagogy,* rather than *defectology,* a term widely used in the Soviet Union.

Hulek (1989) reported that in accordance with the classification proposed by the Ministry of Education (Circular N 40, 1984), twelve categories of exceptionalities are recognized in Poland: mentally and severely handicapped, mentally retarded moderately and severely handicapped, deaf and hard-of-hearing, deaf mildly retarded, deaf moderately and severely retarded, blind and visually handicapped, blind and visually handicapped mildly retarded, blind and visually handicapped moderately and severely retarded, chronically ill, chronically ill and mentally retarded, socially maladjusted, and socially maladjusted and mentally retarded. The mildly retarded attend eight years of basic special school, followed by three years of specialized vocational training. A new ten-year curriculum for the mentally retarded recommends the following areas of training and education: adaptation and social living, language stimulation, arithmetic, visual-motor tasks, music, physical exercise, technical-practical activities, and prevocational training. Training goals and objectives for the severely handicapped include: physical development and acquisition of manual skills, development of self-help and everyday activity skills, development of basic information, appropriate interpersonal relationships, and prevocational training.

The intellectually disabled population in Poland has been estimated to range from 1.3 percent to 1.87 percent of the general population. Polish psychologists are utilizing an IQ index in their classification of the mentally retarded. The ranges of the levels of classification are similar to the AAMD classification system. In addition to health examinations, psychological and social-developmental examinations are also conducted. An evaluation for the purpose of a special class placement consists of a detailed classroom observation, educational evaluation, and psychological and medical evaluation. Structural classroom observation usually lasts one school year. Additionally, a detailed anecdotal record of the child's activities is maintained. The record also includes a description of the role of parents and the extent of their cooperation with the school. Detailed records with samples of the child's performance are sent to the child study team as additional information. Slow learners and children who do not show good educational progress are directed to prevocational classes at fourteen or fifteen years of age.

Elska (1985) reported that the vocational curriculum for the mildly handicapped consists of two periods per week in first through third grade, four periods in the fourth grade, and six periods per week in the fifth through eighth grades.

Bogucka (1994) informs us that prior to 1989 there was a separate system of education at the preschool and primary school levels for handicapped and nonhandicapped children. The integration of the handicapped into the mainstream began in 1990. An attempt has been made to limit an integrated class size to fifteen to eighteen students, with a ratio of handicapped to nonhandicapped of one to four.

In Rumania (Rumanian People's Republic), the education and training of the mildly handicapped is the responsibility of the ministries of education and labor. Severely handicapped children and those in need of custodial care are the responsibility of the Ministry of Health. Children are selected for special school placement by evaluation committees consisting of a pediatrician, neurologist, psychologist, psychiatrist, special class teacher, and general education teachers. Since 1959, industrial establishments have been requested to reserve from 3 percent to 5 percent of their available positions for the handicapped and graduates of special schools (Lipkowski, 1968). Mentally retarded children ages four to seven attend preschool classes. Mentally retarded children ages seven to fourteen attend elementary special education schools. Older children attend residential special vocational schools (Dziedzic, 1968). Every school maintains students' records which are transferred to the employer on graduation. The educational system in Rumania was reorganized in 1979. The emphasis shifted toward a close integrated relationship between education and vocational preparation (Boyanjiu, 1985).

In Yugoslavia, the former Socialist Federal Republic of Yugoslavia, special schools were part of general public education from three to eighteen years of age. The number of children in special schools varies from fifty to four hundred. Depending on the category of handicapping condition, the number of children in a single class varies from eight (hard-of-hearing) to fifteen (mentally retarded, mild). The staff of each special school consists of a principal, assistant principal, speech therapist, psychologist, social worker, and pediatrician. Also depending on the category of handicapping condition, other professionals are assigned, such as a neuropsychologist for a school of mentally retarded children and an ophthalmologist for a school for the visually handicapped (Rozanova, 1974). In general, the mildly handicapped attend auxiliary or special schools for eight years. For youngsters who reach twelve years of age, education emphasizes vocational preparation.

There are special schools for the mentally retarded, visually and auditorily handicapped, orthopedically handicapped, and behaviorally disordered. Additionally, there are preschool facilities for handicapped children. An interesting innovation is the placement of children from undesirable homes into foster homes. This system of "alternate families" is viewed as an important part of the rehabilitation of exceptional children (Rozanova, 1974).

Middle East

Michael (1989) tells us that when the state of Israel was established in 1948, there existed only three larger special schools, a number of small residential centers, and three special classrooms within regular schools. Since 1950, the growth of special education in Israel can be described as phenomenal. The number of special education classes increased from 90 to 3,675, with an increase of special education students served from 1,534 to 57,000 (Michael, 1989). Raviv (1989) reported that a strong mainstreaming effort is presently in evidence. The number of special schools declined from 352 in 1960 to 208 in 1988. About 60 percent of handicapped children are integrated into regular schools. There are no private schools in Israel.

Gumpel (1996) compared the provisions of the Israel Special Education Law of 1988 to U.S. Public Law 94-142 and concluded that they differ in some important aspects. One major difference is the emphasis placed on parental involvement. Gumpel (1996) suggested that the special education bureaucratic system in Israel is empowered to act without parental input. A review of the law as well as relevant ministry regulations reveals a tightly controlled, central educational system that attempts to exclude the exceptional learner's family from the decision-making process regarding their child's educational experience. Gumpel explains that the Israeli legal system comprises a mixture of English common law, British mandate regulations, and some influence from the Jewish, Christian, and Muslim traditions.

Vance and Ashwal (1987) reported that in the past decade rapid development in special education in the Middle East has been noticed. In Egypt, special education focuses on services for the visually impaired, deaf, and mentally retarded. Youngsters classified as mentally retarded attend elementary education classes for eight years. Concentration for the first two years is on the acquisition of basic academic skills. The next six years are devoted to prevocational and vocational preparation. The more severely mentally retarded are institutionalized in hospitals. Egypt's influence in special education extends to Jordan, Kuwait, and Saudi Arabia.

Writing about the education of children with mental retardation in Arab countries, Yousef (1993) concluded that the education of exceptional children is largely neglected. In general, Arab countries lack recent data about children with mental retardation and the services provided for them. Existing schools for "mental education" or "intellectual development" are usually located in big cities and urban areas. Existing services are provided for school-age children with mild or moderate mental retardation. To appreciate the status of special education in Arab countries, we should note that not a single periodical on mental retardation or special education is published in the Arab language. Some isolated special education schools began to be established in the 1960s. However, there are countries, such as Yemen, that as recently as 1993 did not have any programs for the mentally retarded. Most programs have been established in Jordan (23). Yousef (1993) reported that as of 1989, a total of seventeen Arab countries have eighty-nine institutions offering services to approximately 14,124 mentally retarded individuals.

Hamdi and Hamdi (1989) informed us that in Jordan, special education and rehabilitation programs are provided to the mentally retarded, the physically handicapped, and the hearing and visually impaired through thirty special centers. About 12 percent of the estimated handicapped children receive services.

Asia and the Pacific Region

The overall impression of special education in Asia and the Pacific region is of vast differences in available services and tremendous potential for development. In comparison with Europe and the United States, special education services are reasonably well developed in Australia, Japan, Korea, Hong Kong, and Taiwan, and show only sporadic development in China, India, and Pakistan. On the other hand, considering the size of the population in these countries, the potential for the development of services is tremendous.

Australian special education traces its origins to the arrival of early settlers from Britain. The first private institutions toward the end of the nineteenth century were for the education of the blind and deaf (Safron, 1989). Rapid growth in services occurred after 1945. By 1976, 35,268 youngsters were enrolled in special school programs, with an additional 58,000 enrolled in regular programs (Safron, 1989). In Australia, there is no federal legislation for exceptional children comparable to U.S. Public Law 94-142. As a result, there are considerable differences in program implementation among regions. Educational personnel have considerable freedom in the choice of service-delivery models. Integration of the mildly retarded within the mainstream is accepted as a general practice, and services for the profoundly retarded are in the process of development (Valcante, 1987). In the area of mildly handicapped conditions, Australia has adopted a noncategorical learning difficulties model, free from formal identification procedures. Support-remedial services are offered within regular education (Safron, 1989).

Safron (1989) discussed the legal foundation of special education in Australia and the United States and pointed out the number of significant differences. For example, legal foundations in the United States are based on the Bill of Rights. There is no such bill in Australia. The United States has national legislation for the handicapped, but such legislation is absent in Australia. In Australia, school policy is under centralized state authority. In the United States, there is a substantial local school district input, and school authority in decentralized. Legislative, administrative, economic, and social means have been employed to develop educational programs for the disabled not only as an integral part of but as a precondition to the general human rights. The *Compulsory Education Act of the People's Republic of China* promulgated in 1986 has articles describing the rights and duties of handicapped children educationally, the Act on the Protection of the Handicapped has prescribed legal rights for the disabled including the development and implementation of special education programs in integrated schools and classrooms.

According to Chinese statistics from 1987 (Piao, 1989), China provides service to 2,677 blind persons, 40,622 deaf, and 9,937 mentally retarded, for a total population of 53,236. This number, however, is only a fraction of the estimated 6,000,000 handicapped school-age children.

Yang and Wang (1994) provided brief information on the status of the education of handicapped individuals in the People's Republic of China. According to their information, by 1989, there were nearly 52 million people with disabilities in China. Of that number, there were nearly 10 million children and adolescents with disabilities, including 5,390,000 mentally retarded, 866,000 hearing impaired, 181,000 visually impaired, 806,000 multiply handicapped, and 620,000 physically disabled. Following the establishment of the People's Republic of China in 1949, the new government took over all the special schools previously sponsored by foreign organizations and transferred all of those schools into public special schools. The growth of special education in China can be represented by the following statistics: in 1949, there were 42 special schools with 2,000 students; in 1992, there were 1,023 schools with 129,445 students. However, even this number represents a small percentage of the 10 million estimated children and adolescents with disabilities.

In Shanghai, a school for deaf-mute children was established in 1926 by an American missionary. Presently, the school consists of nine classes with a staff of forty-seven (Xu, 1989). In the period of its existence, the school has graduated more than one thousand students. In 1979, the school initiated education of the mentally retarded in China. At that time, only twenty-four youngsters attended school. We are told by Yin Chun-Ming (1989) that in 1985 there were 160 special classes in twelve provinces with two thousand students. In 1988, there were 158 special schools for the mentally retarded in twenty-five provinces. Additionally, there are 664 special classes within elementary schools. However, the total number of mentally retarded children in programs (13,800) is only a fraction of 1 percent of the mentally retarded in China if we assume 1 percent of the total population of more than one billion. Yin Chun-Ming also reported that the National Education Commission proposed instituting compulsory education for the retarded.

According to La Volve (1989), most of the special education schools in China serve the visually and auditorily handicapped. Schools for the deaf stress vocal training, while those for the blind emphasize music appreciation. On graduation, students become factory laborers, either in regular factories if they have mild handicapping difficulties or in special production facilities organized for the deaf and blind. As reported by Oinzhu (1989), the number of schools for the blind, deaf, and mute was 466 in 1988.

In contrast to mainland China, special education in Taiwan has implemented many Western ideas.

In Hong Kong, the special education section of the Education Department was established in 1960. By 1986, services were provided for more than eight thousand handicapped youngsters in seventy-one schools at the elementary and secondary levels (Hu, Oakland, & Salili, 1988). Youngsters, who were classified as blind, deaf, physically handicapped, mentally retarded, emotionally maladjusted, learning disabled, and socially deprived, were placed within appropriate programs. Residential services are also available.

India, the country second to China in terms of population, has equally tremendous needs in the area of the education of the handicapped. A home for mentally disabled children was established by the Children's Aid Society in 1941 in Bombay. Initially, the facilities in the country were organized by the parents. In 1944, a school for children in need of special care was started by a parent in Bombay. There were about thirteen schools in the 1950s. In the 1960s, there was a remarkable increase in the number of schools for the retarded in the country. There were fifty-one schools in the 1960s, which increased to ninety-one in the 1970s. Today there are more than three hundred special schools and institutions in the country.

The facilities have increased not only in number but also in the variety of services offered. The schools and agencies initially catered to the care and education of retarded children. At present, most schools have extended their facilities to provide preschool and postschool programs. This includes early stimulation and prevocational programs, respectively.

As reported by Roy (1989), until recently, even mildly retarded children were considered uneducable. It was not until 1986 that the Ministry of Human Resources Development formulated a National Policy on Education, which envisions comprehensive services by the year 2000. Nesbit (1987) estimated that there are about 1.4 million disabled children in the CA 0–4 range who still require identification, assessment, and program placement. Only 0.5 percent of the mentally retarded attend special schools. In rural areas, nearly 80 percent of the mentally retarded do not attend any educational programs. It is also estimated that more than ten thousand schools will be needed to accommodate approximately two million severely handicapped children.

In 1940, Harutaro Suzuki, who introduced the Binet test to Japan, provided the initiative for the development of a school for the mentally retarded in Osaka (Egani, 1981).

As of 1987, more than 95,000 children were receiving education in 924 special schools and an additional 90,000 children in special classes in elementary and secondary schools. Prefectural governments are obliged to organize special education institutions for the physically and mentally handicapped (Shinagawa, Kodama, & Manita, 1989). Eligibility for special education placement is described in "Educational Placement of Pupils and Students Who Need Special Education Treatment" (*Notification*, 1978).

In Japan, schools for exceptional children are grouped into three categories: those for the blind, deaf, and handicapped other than blind or deaf. Schools for the handicapped are further subdivided into schools for the mentally retarded, physically handicapped, and health impaired. For mildly handicapped youngsters, special classes are established in elementary and secondary schools. There are seven types of special classes: for the mentally retarded, physically handicapped, health impaired, partially sighted, hard-of-hearing, speech handicapped, and emotionally disturbed. Placement in small classes is emphasized. Special classes in regular public schools have a maximum of ten students, seven in special schools, and only three in classes for the multiply handicapped. Emotionally disturbed children are subdivided into two groups: those with "mutism" and problem behavior, and those with "weak" emotional attachment and autism. In 1987, there were approximately three thousand special classes for emotionally disturbed children in Japan. For visually and auditorily handicapped students of average intelligence, the national junior college, known as Tsukuba College of Technology, was established in 1987.

There are eighty-nine institutions for the handicapped in Korea, with a total of more than five thousand students (Korea, 1988). Of those facilities, forty-six are for the mentally retarded, twenty for the deaf and mute, twelve for the blind, and eleven for the physically handicapped. No information was provided in the above publication on the special education programs in regular public schools.

Miles (1988) informs us that in Pakistan, the first schools for the mentally retarded were organized in Lahore and Krachi in 1961. By the early 1970s, only 75 visually-impaired and 193 hearing-impaired youngsters profited from special education services in Pakistan. A government survey from 1981 indicated there were twenty-four schools for deaf children, fifteen for the mentally retarded, and ten for the blind.

In the Philippines, special education services for exceptional children are provided in fifty-eight special schools, thirty-five special education centers, and a number of self-contained special education classes in public and private schools.

In New Zealand, a survey was conducted in 1982 to obtain information on issues of policy and organization of special education (Panckhurst, Panckhurst, & Elkins, 1987). The survey investigated such leading questions as: support necessary, professional training, early assessment and intervention, and involvement of parents. The survey revealed as strengths existing guidance and support services. However, the need to improve communication among agencies was also noted. The survey recommended expanding services for the more severely handicapped, those with specific learning difficulties, the behaviorally disturbed, and for the delinquent culturally different (Polynesian) youngsters. As of July 1983, a total of 31,557 children were receiving special education services. Presently, the major trend has been toward integration and mainstreaming, and as a result, many special education classes are becoming resource classes. Off-campus centers for disruptive adolescents are separated from mainstream facilities. There are seven such centers (Valcante, 1987). Current epidemiological prevalence studies in New Zealand suggest estimates very similar to those in the United States, Europe, or Australia (Valcante, 1987).

In New Zealand, the Crippled Children Society was founded in 1935, which soon initiated programs for children with physical and mental handicaps. In 1940, programs for the mentally retarded were expanded.

In 1987, a reappraisal of special education services since the 1940s was published under the title "The Draft Review of Special Education" (Brown, 1989). Recently, an itinerant model became popular. The child is retained in the regular classroom, and the support teachers assist the regular classroom teacher.

Boorer and Kirubia (1987) informed us that in Papua New Guinea, traditionally the family and village cared for the handicapped. Limited special education services are primarily supported by charitable efforts. As of 1987, thirteen special education centers provided service to mostly physically handicapped, blind, and deaf individuals, of whom 111 were residential and 276 nonresidential.

Africa

In Africa, special education programs have to overcome challenges created by past colonial practices, poverty, lack of educational opportunities, discrimination, and racism. For example, in South Africa, a dual educational system exists even at the present time. On the other hand, because of the scarcity of available services, opportunities for program development are immense. It also should be emphasized that special education in Africa is a very recent development. Most of the existing programs are for children with physical and sensory disabilities.

Nkabinda (1993) reminds us that special education for blacks can be seen as a very recent development in South Africa's educational system. Historically, such programs have been neglected.

Baine (1988) clearly presented a number of serious problems facing education in the developing countries. Initially, education in general was based on west European cultural content, which had little relevance for children in Africa. Not only was such curriculum culturally irrelevant, but it was also foreign to the village life that surrounded the child. As a result, until recently school and community life have been separated.

Although the life of children in developing countries is activity oriented, and problem solving is done by doing, the school curriculum emphasized overwhelmingly the rote memory approach. In many developing countries, special education curricula are simply "watered-down" versions of regular education curricula. In the area of selection of children for special education programs, a real problem exists in the indiscriminatory application of Western tests, most of which have not been restandardized according to local norms. Baine (1988) suggests that when a test is translated from one language to another, the validity and reliability of the revised test must be reestablished. However, it should also be kept in mind that the cultural environment in developing countries is changing, with such developments as the introduction of mass communication, increased industrialization, migration from rural to urban centers, and increased technology.

Donald and Csapo (1989) reported that in South Africa special education provisions for black students are extremely limited. Only a few schools accommodate severely mentally handicapped, blind, and deaf students.

In Swaziland, existing special education provisions are limited to the needs of the mentally retarded and the physically and sensory handicapped. Four schools were established by charitable organizations (Csapo, 1988). A similar situation exists in Nigeria. As we are told by Wycke (1987b), available special education services focus primarily on physically handicapped or mentally retarded elementary-age school children. Early detection and intervention programs are nonexistent.

In Zimbabwe, prior to 1980, there existed schools for the blind, deaf, and mentally retarded, but they were sponsored by nongovernmental agencies (Kabzems, 1989). However, in 1988 there were 2,579 primary and 473 secondary students enrolled in special education programs. Nevertheless, as pointed out by Kabzems (1989), despite increased access to schooling, many disabled students are still denied access to appropriate educational services. At present, as in most African countries, programs are provided for the more severely handicapped. Mildly handicapped children, as well as those with learning disabilities, are just beginning to receive special services.

Chapter 7

COMMUNITY ADJUSTMENT

Society's attitudes toward community adjustment of exceptional individuals have deep historical roots. Since the emergence of the most elementary form of social organization, members of society who were different and unable to adjust have been considered deviant. It is clear that attitudes toward exceptional individuals have been influenced by cultural, economics, and sociopolitical realities. From the perspective of an individual with a handicapping condition, four major factors influence community adjustment: level of overall intellectual development; adaptive skills acquired; severity of the actual handicapping condition; and personality variables, including perception or misperception of one's own potential. Developing societies did not tolerate any deviations. They were concerned primarily with physical survival and did not attempt to create conditions favorable for the survival of the physically or mentally disabled. Furthermore, because of harsh conditions and nonexistent medical services, the infant mortality rate was very high, and children with developmental disabilities simply did not survive past infancy. Although agrarian societies were more accepting of individuals with handicapping conditions than nomadic societies, it was not until the seventeenth and eighteenth centuries that some systematic attempts were made by various societies to care for less fortunate members. However, those attempts were motivated primarily by a need to protect society from "deviant" individuals. Consequently, they were segregated and isolated in large institutions located away from population centers. Such a trend existed well into the first half of the twentieth century. Since the middle of the twentieth century, society's attitudes changed from segregation and institutionalization to normalization and deinstitutionalization. The normalization movement originated in Sweden after World War II, in part as a reaction against the inhumanities of the war. It should be pointed out, however, that from a global perspective, attitudes and services for exceptional individuals depend very much on the level of socioeconomic development of a given society.

There were no residential facilities for the handicapped in the United States prior to the nineteenth century. The first institutions were those for the blind and deaf. Institutions for the education of the deaf were established in Hartford, Connecticut, in 1817, and a school for the blind was established in Watertown, Massachusetts in 1819. Toward the end of the nineteenth century, a number of states established residential schools for the deaf, blind, and the mentally retarded (National Advisory Committee for the Handicapped, 1976). By 1900, more than 7,000 handicapped individuals were residing in institutions, and the number increased to 190,000 by 1969 (Cegelka & Prehm, 1982).

In the 1970s, Scheerenberger (1976) surveyed 191 residential facilities for the mentally retarded and reported 130,973 residents. Very few of the residents were below 2 years of age, and about 5 percent were older than 62 years of age. The majority were between 3 and 61 years of age. Most of the residents were severely or profoundly retarded; 17.9 percent were of moderate retardation, and 8.1 percent were mildly retarded.

A later survey by Scheerenberger (1981) revealed that since 1976, the number of residents in facilities for the mentally retarded has been steadily declining. The resident population in facilities for the mentally retarded decreased 7.74 percent between 1976–1977 and 1978–1979 (Scheerenberger, 1981, p. 59). By the early 1980s, one-eighth of the state-operated institutions that existed in the United States in 1965 had been closed. The combination of a variety of political, social, and economic factors created in many states an appropriate climate for the closure of institutions. By the end of the 1980s, some larger, very well-known institutions had been closed.

Simultaneously with the closure of large institutions, many new types of facilities were constructed. Hill and Lakin (1986) identified nearly 108 separate categories of facilities for the care of the mentally retarded. Based on a survey of 22,150 facilities, they grouped them into the following clusters: foster homes, group residences, semi-independent living programs, board and supervision facilities, general care homes, and nursing homes. Institutions built more recently were smaller and housed fewer residents (Westling, 1986).

With the deinstitutionalization process, we are witnessing how the emphasis for individuals with disabilities is shifting from large care facilities, such as institutions or nursing homes, to smaller residential living facilities. These facilities can be identified as group homes, semi-independent apartments or homes, foster families, or a surrogate family setting. A group home employs professionals to provide ongoing training and support, emphasizing daily living experiences. A semi-independent apartment or home provides living arrangements for individuals with disabilities who need less supervision. A goal of foster care or a surrogate family setting is to integrate individuals with disabilities into a family setting, which will enable them to learn necessary adaptive skills for community living. One of the major problems with small community-based homes is the retention of qualified staff. Larson and Lakin investigated turnover in 110 Minnesota group homes between December 1993 and 1996. Some of the major problems identified were: support needs, low pay, few tenured supervisors, and few direct support professionals. Larson and Lakin concluded that future plans of facilities for the developmentally disabled should consider "increased amounts and attractive options in compensation; more comprehensive and more effective recruitment initiatives; improved quality, recognition, and transferability of training; expanded career opportunities; more effective supervision; better matching of employees to work roles; and more effective team building. Successes in these efforts are among the most important components to assuring that community living is a viable option for all Americans with developmental disabilities" (p. 279).

A shift from large state institutions to community services necessitated a new pattern of fiscal spending. Braddock et al. (1999) conducted a comprehensive analysis of spending patterns based on published state executive budgets for the fiscal years 1977 through 1986. In comparing 1977 to 1986, a trend has been noticed, with states dramatically increasing expenditures for community services. In 1977, the United States spent 2.5 times as much for institutional care as for various community facilities. However, in 1986, the United States was spending approximately equal sums in both sectors. The current population in public residential facilities comprises primarily severely and profoundly retarded multiply handicapped individuals. More recently, Braddock (1989) provided a detailed analysis of services to the aging population in the United States with developmental disabilities. As of 1996 there were 394,284 individuals in residential placements. Of that number, only 15 percent or 59,726 were housed in state institutions. Approximately 200,000 lived in one- to six-person settings, such as "small group homes, supervised apartments, foster care, and supported living placements" (p. 155). This data supports clearly the deinstitutionalization trend that began in the 1970s. Two strong demographic trends are evident in the United States: longevity of the person with developmental disabilities and aging of caregivers. This reality will require development of new policy and programs of services for individuals with developmental disabilities.

A recent article by Stancliffe and Lakin (1998) presents data on the long-term adjustment of individuals with mental retardation who have moved from large residential facilities into community programs. The study compared two groups of adults with mental retardation. In one group were 116 adults with profound to severe retardation, who moved from a state institution in Minnesota to a community living setting. In the second group were 71 adults of a similar level of retardation, who remained institutionalized. The writers argue that a major challenge for policymakers and service providers will be to provide as much as possible individually tailored services to a large number of clients, while continuing the deinstitutionalization policy.

Although some of the ideas of deinstitutionalization were expressed in the early 1920s, real efforts at mass deinstitutionalization began in the 1970s, and a goal was announced of reducing institutions by 50 percent (Braddock, 1977). However, some writers (Lakin, 1981) expressed concern that the social philosophy and policy that gave impetus to the deinstitutionalization move-ment was not based on the research data of mental retardation professionals. As a matter of fact, there are very few longitudinal studies that follow the mentally retarded population through the developmental stages into adult-hood (Richardson, 1977).

It should be mentioned here that deinstitutionalization is but a part of a rather complex process that should lead to total habilitation and normaliza-tion. There are obviously a number of steps in such a process. A problem not clearly elucidated is the transitional stage between institution and community, which also should involve preparation for community return. There are many psychological and social variables associated with the transitional period.

Based on information obtained from a hundred families who have chil-dren with severe mental retardation, Hanneman and Blacher (1998) reached a couple of general conclusions. Perhaps not surprising, independent of other factors, prior behavior significantly predicted actual placement outside the homes. Two important variables that influenced the decision making were: the number of children within the family, and the socioeconomic standing of the mothers. Families with higher socioeconomic standing of mothers and families with a larger number of siblings promoted more serious considera-tion of the out-of-home placement for the child with mental retardation. It was interesting, however, that if the mother reported that she was coping well with the burdens of care, serious consideration of out-of-home placement was less likely, regardless of other factors.

A major philosophical thrust toward deinstitutionalization and communi-ty living was provided by the concept of "normalization," which had its ori-gin in the Scandinavian countries (Westling, 1986). Deinstitutionalization, which began in the United States in the 1970s, is the third stage in the efforts of society to deal with community adjustment of individuals with mental retardation. Toward the late nineteenth century, institutions were established with the idea of providing short-term education and training for the mentally retarded in order to facilitate their return to the community. Unfortunately, they soon became custodial in nature, viewed as protection for the society. Currently, the preference is for smaller regional facilities and community-based homes. This writer tends to agree with Westling (1986) that "the smaller size and home style of the building is no more likely to influence this development than is a large facility likely to depress it. In the final analysis, it will be the quality of the programs offered and the people who offer them that make the difference" (p. 218).

Persons with mental retardation, especially the elderly or senile, find security in consistent, somewhat rigid schedules. Relocation may evoke stressful reactions manifested in emotional and behavioral changes. In this context, Braddock and Heller (1985) recommend that every closure of a residential facility be accompanied by a longitudinal study of that closure. Additionally, efforts at deinstitutionalization are complicated by attitudes of the community (Vitello, 1991), which ultimately has to determine the future development of programs for the mentally retarded. Unfortunately, however, also in many instances, families of the institutionalized mentally retarded persons are not eager to accept them at home. Willen, Intaglieta, and Atkinson (1981) told us that complex reasons are related to parental attitudes. Parents who are both working or are of higher socioeconomic status are the least likely to accept deinstitutionalized individuals. When release was mentioned, most families were extremely anxious and many opposed the move. Similar tendencies were reported by Bercovici (1981). It is obvious that the success of persons with retardation in a community depends on the degree of community support.

Smith (1997) surveyed needs and knowledge of services among aging families of adults with mental retardation. Two hundred and thirty-five older mothers (CA 70.3) of adult subjects with mental retardation were surveyed to assess their familiarity and use of support services. Although the offspring were generally reported to have a moderate degree of retardation, their mothers tended to report high ability and low strain in their caregiver's role. One interesting finding of the survey was that the older offspring with mental retardation were found to use fewer services than did their younger counterparts. Smith concluded that the use of community support services is a familiar activity that is determined by the needs and behaviors of the adult offspring with mental retardation, his or her primary caregiver, and other key family members.

Various community services may include residential options, vocational opportunities, and recreational-leisure activities. Different models of service delivery are related to philosophical, political, and economic reasons. Baldwin (1985) identified the following models of service delivery: (child) developmental, medical, and socioecological, behavioral, and psychoeducational.

Schalock (1985) informs us that comprehensive community-based services for the handicapped include community living alternatives, habilitation programs, and support programs.

The question of how to integrate individuals with mental retardation into the community has been reviewed by Menolascino (1977), who made several suggestions. The more important suggestions are: programs and facilities for the mentally retarded should be socially and physically integrated into the community; no more mentally retarded people should be congregated in one service facility than can be supported in the community; and daily routines should be comparable to those of nonretarded persons of the same age.

One of the options for deinstitutionalized persons is a foster home placement. That option has been discussed in the literature by Intagliata, Crosby, and Neider (1981), as well as by Intagliata and Willer (1981). Intagliata et al. pointed out that foster family care presently provides an important component in the continuum of residential alternatives. Foster home care can provide a normalizing, reasonably cost-effective living environment. However, it is important to develop an efficient monitoring system to assure high-quality care by foster home parents. This arrangement raises a number of important issues. Intagliata and Willer (1981) discussed a number of training programs for the providers of foster family care. Their review mentioned a variety of available materials and strategies. However, they also listed additional needs that should be addressed, among those: wider implementation of existing programs, development of new programs and materials, and more systematic and regular evaluations of care providers.

Vocational preparation and employability are very important aspects of the total process of normalization. In addition to work skills, personality characteristics are very important. It has been acknowledged for a long time that most employers regard good working habits and positive attitudes as crucial for success on the job. "Appropriate" social skills were found to be more important than the level of intellectual functioning for community adjustment and individuals with mental retardation as reported by Black and Lampone (1997). They suggested that preparing students with intellectual disabilities for the transition from school to work requires creation of instruction in social competence. Black and Lampone (1997) stress that educators must facilitate social and vocational transitions for students. Parmenter (1993) pointed out that, much as in the area of community living, development in the area of employment for individuals with mental retardation has been influenced not only by research findings but also by our value system. Unemployment presents a challenge, especially for young handicapped individuals. One challenge for policy development in the labor market is the creation of community-based employment for individuals with mental retardation. To some extent, training in those skills has been provided by sheltered workshops. Their efforts, however, have not been uniformly strong. Whitehead (1986) suggested that approximately one-third of the sheltered workshops are significantly involved in transitional services leading to integrated employment options; one-third are currently modifying their programs; and another one-third are simply content with their current program focus.

Employment inequalities between men and women are investigated by Doren and Benz (1978). They concluded that, in general, having work experience while in high school facilitates post-school employment opportunity. However, young women with disabilities are more likely to experience poorer employment outcome than young men with disabilities. The writers conclude that the needs of young women with disabilities have received in the past too little attention in special education and transition research. Disabled females as a group have been also neglected as a specific priority in funding.

Since most developmentally disabled adolescents and young adults also have reading difficulties, reading-free vocational interest inventories have been developed. Becker and Becker (1983) reported that the latest revision of the Reading-Free Vocational Interest Inventory has been edited in order to include the learning disabled, adult mentally retarded, and young EMR individuals. Becker (1987) completed a cluster analytic study of the Reading-Free Vocational Interest Inventory. The analysis identified five clusters: (A) outdoor, natural interests, such as animal care and horticultural activities; (B) mechanical attributes with interests in the automotive and building trades; (C) combination of mechanical and natural attributes; (D) personal service, food service, materials handling; (E) social service and general assistance category.

More recently, a total habilitation movement in mental retardation has been proposed as a goal. Drash, Raver, and Murrin (1987) pointed out that by establishing total habilitation as a goal, society will stress the need for comprehensive intervention that includes prevention, total habilitation, and amelioration.

Cimera (1998) conducted a study to determine whether serving supported employees with severe mental retardation or multiple disabilities is cost-efficient. This question was examined from the perspectives of the worker, the taxpayer, and society. The data revealed that all individuals, regardless of severity or number of disabilities, are cost-efficient when served through supported employment; that is, the level was reported to be an important factor. The writer concludes that African-American and male supported employees were more cost-efficient to serve than were European-American and female employees. However, when examining the projected, lifelong benefit-costs of supported employees, no personal characteristics significantly predicted efficiency.

Morningstar (1997) pointed out that "transition services" for individuals with disabilities could be found as early as the 1930s for deaf students and the 1940s for students with mental retardation. However, since the 1960s, educational and vocational models have been developed to address employment and career issues for students with disabilities. In her article, Morningstar proposed five recommendations to foster career development and employment preparation for students with disabilities: consider the developmental nature of career preparation across the life span; provide opportunities for students with disabilities to develop the skills necessary for career maturity; provide meaningful work experiences; encourage the participation of families in career development, and encourage student involvement in career development.

The enactment of the *Individuals with Disabilities Education Act of 1990* focuses on ensuring that students with disabilities receive a coordinated education designed to enhance the transition to employment, further education and training, and independent living. Recently, Phelps and Henley-Maxwell (1997) identified what they described as promising practices that merit attention in improving programs and advancing the knowledge base. The writers emphasized the need for school-supervised work experiences and functionally-oriented curricula in which occupationally specified skills, employability skills, and academic skills are systematically connected for students. Among the group of exceptional learners, students with mild and moderate retardation had significantly poorer outcome when compared with other groups. Among the students with mental retardation, only 2 percent enrolled in postsecondary academic programs and only 6 percent in postsecondary vocational programs.

A transition from school to adult life was mandated into law through the *Individuals with Disabilities Education Act of 1990 (IDEA)* (Public Law 101-476). As interpreted by Hardman, Derew, and Egan (1996), transition services can be defined as: "a coordinated set of activities for a student designed within an outcome oriented process, which promoted movement from school to post school activities, including postsecondary education, vocational training, integrated employment (including supported employment), continuing and adult education, adult services, independent living, or community participation" (p. 146).

There are a number of important components of a transition system. McDonnell et al. (1995) suggested three important components of a good transition program: school programs that integrate instruction with community activities and expectations; a cooperative transition planning to ensure access to needed postschool services; and a variety of adult services to meet the individualized educational, employment, residential, and leisure needs of youngsters with disabilities.

Some of the insight into the problems of social work in developing countries has been provided recently by Badri (1998). The writer described school social work and school effectiveness in the Gulf states. According to Badri (1998), all schools in the United Arab Emirates employ full-time social workers, whose functions are similar in many aspects to those of school psychologists in the West. Although in theory, the description of their responsibilities is impressive, in reality their main task is to work with disturbed youngsters and to deal with disruptive behaviors. In conclusion, the writer pointed out that most of the developing countries face two key problems that reduce the effectiveness of their educational institutions: the shortage of resources and insufficient scientific know-how.

Chapter 8

TEACHER TRAINING AND PROFESSIONAL PERSONNEL PREPARATION

Teacher training and professional personnel preparation is extremely diversified throughout the world.

In some countries, for example, the United States, western Europe, and Scandinavia, there is a full range of professional personnel preparation such as classroom teachers, resource room teachers, and related service personnel.

Oakland and Cunningham (1997) discussed new guidelines for school psychological services adopted by the International School Psychology Association (ISPA). The guidelines were approved by the General Assembly of the ISPA in 1996. They discuss academic preparation, professional membership, and the nature of services. The areas included are assessment, intervention, consultation, organizational and program development, and supervision and research. It is emphasized that a person delivering school psychological services should be trained both as a psychologist and as an educator. In the opinion of Oakland and Cunningham, from an international perspective about the quality of programs, they can be divided into three groups: those with a long history of service, those with a brief history, and those that are just emerging. It is obvious that for some of the countries the guidelines are aspirational in nature.

In a number of countries, special educators are trained at all university levels, undergraduate and graduate. However, in other countries, there is hardly any special education teacher-training effort, and in some, special educators are prepared at the high school level. This chapter will provide a capsule view of the teacher training efforts by focusing as much as possible on several countries and continents.

United States

Systematic teacher training in the United States for persons interested in educating exceptional children began early in the twentieth century. In 1897, the University of Pennsylvania offered a three-course sequence in the education of the mentally retarded (Lilly, 1979). Prior to 1910, the Training School at Vineland, New Jersey, conducted summer workshops for teachers of the mentally retarded. One of the earliest state certification requirements for teachers of the mentally retarded was issued in New Jersey in 1911. It required that the applicant for the certificate should hold a permanent elementary or secondary certificate, and should pass examinations in psychology, elementary manual training, and physical training (Kendall, 1918).

The rapid growth of teacher-training programs began during the 1950s and 1960s, in part as response to federal support manifested by the enactment of Public Laws 85-926 and 88-164. In the 1970s, many special educators stressed the need to reexamine teacher-training programs.

In the late 1970s (Hartman, 1979; Lilly, 1979), many models of teacher training had been identified in the literature, such as: competency-based, generic, directive teaching, diagnostic-prescriptive, clinical, consulting teacher, learning disabilities teacher consultant, and special education complementary teaching.

Discussion continues about the nature of teaching as a profession, the relative value of a categorical versus a noncategorical approach, and the need for specialized training.

The federal commitment to the training of personnel in special education was initiated in 1970 with Public Law 91-230. By 1980, financial support for the Division of Personnel Preparation had increased from less than a million dollars in 1960 to 55 million dollars (Ysseldyke & Algozzine, 1982). The same writers reported that, as of 1980, there were in the United States nearly 1400 "institutions of higher learning" providing training for special education teachers.

Iano (1986), in a theoretical article, discussed the development of teaching as a process with implications for special education. He pointed out that since the beginning of the twentieth century, education has been developed according to a "natural science-technical model." In his opinion, teaching, student learning, and the preparation of teachers cannot all be brought under technical control. Iano sees a problem in what he calls the separation of theory and practice, with research and theoretical work located at universities, while practice is located in schools.

Assumptions of the value of categorical models in teacher preparation have been questioned by O'Sullivan, Matson, and Magnusson (1987). They evaluated the behavior of special educators holding categorical certificates and the behavior of children labeled "EMR" and "LD." The results of their study did not indicate any differences in teachers' behaviors that could be associated with their specialized preparation.

It has been generally recognized that a significant shortage of teachers exists in penal institutions and juvenile detention homes. Leone (1986) tells us that isolation of teachers in institutions, lack of administrative support, and inadequate financial resources contribute to low morale among teachers and may interfere with effective delivery of educational services. Leone also pointed out that there is a difference in how special educators and correctional educators perceive the importance of the knowledge, information, and skills required of successful teachers. For example, while special educators ranked individualized instruction fourth among fifteen skills, it was ranked fifteenth by correctional educators. Special educators ranked knowledge of assessment and test interpretation in first place, but it was ranked sixth by correctional educators.

The new realities and challenges of Public Law 94-142 require a common body of knowledge and practices for teachers in the 1980s. A number of recommendations toward this goal have been supplied by Reynolds (1980). Some of the competencies listed are: firsthand knowledge and experience with curricular principles, guides, and structure; competency in teaching and class management; knowledge of effective consultation and professional communication; and competencies in the assessment of the individual student's educational needs.

One of the central issues in education has to do with the question of how beginning teachers learn to teach. A critical analysis of research related to this problem has been conducted by Wideen, Mayer-Smith, and Moon (1998). The researchers reviewed ninety-three empirical studies on learning to teach. The review revealed tensions between the hopes and expectations of teacher educators and the expectations and experiences of beginning teachers. In summary, the writers point out a number of interesting conclusions:

> It is generally recognized that beginning teachers represent homogeneous populations of mostly females and middle class, while students in schools are heterogenous in terms of social standing and abilities. Some programs of teacher preparation are more successful than others, depending on their duration and consistency of approach. Some researchers raise serious questions about programs of teacher education that do not take into account the preparation of beginning teachers to teach in a diverse and multicultural society.

It is to be expected that an ever-increasing accumulation of knowledge, as well as complex social, political, and technological realities, will create new challenges for exceptional education.

Wilson, Gutkin, Hapen, and Oats (1998) investigated general education teachers' knowledge and self-reported use of classroom instruction for working with difficult-to-teach children. Their findings were based on interviews with twenty general education teachers, who were working with mildly handicapped students in their classrooms. Unfortunately, most participants demonstrated incomplete knowledge of classroom intervention techniques. The writers considered it surprising that the teachers consulted primarily with other general educators and seldom with special educators or school psychologists. Wilson et al.'s study suggests that school psychologists should work to familiarize teachers with classroom interventions, as well as with the processes, goals, and expectations involved in consultations and prereferral interventions. The writers emphasized that school psychologists should learn how to influence the attitudes, perceptions, expectations, and behaviors of general education teachers. In this way, they will be able to assist teachers, who serve exceptional learners in inclusive environments.

Kauffman, Strang, and Loper (1985) summarized a number of studies and listed six areas of competency that all teachers, including special educators, should master. These are:

> Ensuring a high level of success by presenting tasks at an appropriate level of difficulty; Giving students immediate and appropriate (accurate and specific) feedback on performance; Maintaining a high level of student's time on task in academic lessons (i.e., a high level of academic engaged time); Proceeding at an appropriate pace through lessons; Establishing and maintaining behavioral rules; Monitoring one's expectations to eliminate bias, that is, awareness of self and theirs, of cultural and ethnic differences, and of the influence of perceptions of information from cumulative records or other sources. (p. 135)

A new approach in teacher training is the utilization of microcomputers for simulation purposes (Kauffman, Strang, & Loper, 1985). The writers acknowledge that simulation cannot replace actual experience in a real classroom but also list several potential benefits if simulation training is used properly. There is a realization of the continuous need for in-service training for all personnel involved in the education of exceptional children. Harding (1982) maintained that exemplary professionalism can be maintained only if professionals keep abreast of the changes. With increasing frequency over the past fifteen years, educators have been concerned with the issue of occupational stress, burnout, and health among teachers. This problem was investigated recently by Guglielmi and Tatrow (1998), who suggested five stress-and-strain models. They identified those models as: person-environment fit model, demand-control model, effort-reward model, demands-supports-constraints model, and effort-distress model. The writers point out that it is unfortunate that the clinical literature on stress management for the teaching profession is larger than the literature that has focused on establishing relationships between teacher stress and health. However, the literature review supports the notion that occupational stress and burnout in teachers are associated with their poor health. It is obvious that special educators must become actively involved in continuing education if they are to provide optional opportunities for exceptional children.

Efforts to develop uniform standards for special educators have been carried out under the auspices of the Council of Exceptional Children (CEC) and through the accreditation process of the National Council for Accreditation of Teacher Education. CEC guidelines published in 1976 are entitled *Guidelines for Personnel in the Education of Exceptional Children.* This document was formally adopted in 1979. Heller (1982) believes that licensing of special educators should replace certification. A new effort in the area of certification is an attempt to develop the guidelines for certification of special education paraprofessionals. Frith and Lindsay (1982) surveyed fifty state agencies in an attempt to find out how paraprofessionals are utilized. The states that responded revealed that paraprofessionals were employed in all of the related service areas specifically mentioned in Public Law 94-142. Paraprofessionals are most frequently used in the following related service areas: transportation, physical therapy, speech stimulation, occupational therapy, recreation, and early identification.

A unique model of special educators, as developed in New Jersey, is a learning disabilities teacher-consultant (LDTC). The role of such a professional, as practiced since early 1979, includes educational assessment of exceptional children, individualized instruction, and remediation of learning difficulties. LDTC functions as a member of the child study team and a consultant to special education teachers. Certification requires three years of successful teaching experience, certification as a teacher of the handicapped, and additional concentration in such areas as learning theory, educational measurement, identification of learning disabilities, remediation of learning disabilities, the neuropsychological basis of human learning, and one semester of appropriate internship.

There is increased realization of the need for innovative programs in teacher preparation. Chalfont and Van Dusen Psyh (1989) discussed the various functions of teacher assistance teams. They define such teams as "school-based problem solving units," whose function is to assist classroom teachers in the development of various intervention strategies. The need is apparent, owing to the existence of a number of school districts that have many youngsters exhibiting learning difficulties. A new training model, somewhat similar to the LDTC, is a "resource-consulting teacher model" described by Idol (1989). A resource-consulting teacher is expected to function as a liaison between resource room teacher and a consulting teacher, providing services for youngsters with mild academic and behavioral problems.

Farrell, Smith, and Brownell (1998) discussed the effectiveness of level-system programs on the behavior of students with emotional and behavioral disorders (EBD). It is a generally recognized fact that students with EBD present significant challenges for educators. As a result of their behavior, EBD students tend to be placed in more restrictive and segregated educational settings. Farrell, Smith, and Brownell (1998) discussed a level system that teaches EBD students appropriate behaviors through a series of steps. Each step has clearly defined behavioral expectations, schedules of reinforcements, specific rewards, privileges, and criteria for advancement to the next steps. The writers claim that level systems can influence student behavior so that students can be academically and socially successful and return to regular classes.

Idol (1989) expects the resource-consulting teacher to be skilled in several areas, such as: (a) use of curriculum-based assessment, (b) direct instruction of specific skill deficits, (c) monitoring of students' programs, (d) familiarity with criterion-referenced mastery learning, (e) stages of learning, and (f) application of the principles of applied behavior analysis.

Two topics with which educators are currently preoccupied are students with learning disabilities and the program of inclusion. Vaughn and Klingner (1998) pointed out that prior to Public Law 94-142, most students with learning disabilities received all of their education within general classroom settings. As a result of this practice, many students with learning disabilities were provided special services from special education teachers in "pull-out" resource room settings. In their study, Vaughn and Klingner (1998) investigated students' perceptions of inclusion and resource room settings. Their conclusions were based on a review of eight studies on students' perception of instructional settings, resource rooms, and inclusion. It is interesting that both at the elementary and secondary level, many students with learning disabilities prefer to receive specialized instruction outside of the general education classroom for part of the school day.

A recent study by Soodak, Podell, and Lehman (1998) surveyed attitudes among 188 general educators toward inclusion. Two types of responses were identified: those falling on the continuum of hostility-receptivity and anxiety-calmness. Not surprisingly, results revealed that teacher attributes and beliefs, student characteristics, and school climate related to both dimensions. It is clear from this study that teachers' responses reveal the complex nature of their thinking about this new movement. The writers point out that, as is the case with many reforms in education, the movement to include students with disabilities was not necessarily initiated by those most affected by its implementation. However, general educators' cooperation is absolutely necessary for the success of exceptional learners within the mainstream environment.

In addition to the LDTCs, other professionals are utilized in special education. Recently, Ysseldyke and Algozzine (1990) listed among related services personnel: school counselors, school psychologists, educational diagnosticians, occupational therapists, physical therapists, speech-language pathologists, audiologists, and school social workers.

The roots of school psychology in the United States can be traced to the pioneering work of Henry Goddard at the Training School at Vineland, New Jersey, and the introduction of the Binet-Simon test by Goddard to the United States in 1911.

In the early 1920s, Goddard was training "Binet examiners" at the Glassboro Normal School (now Glassboro State College in New Jersey).

With the influx into the schools of psychologists trained by the Veterans Administration clinical training programs, a strong debate emerged among psychologists about the role of a school psychologist. Some of the models debated were: the school psychologist as "educational" psychologist, "clinical" psychologist; the psychologist as "scientist-practitioner" defined by the Boulder Conference in 1949 (Raimy, 1950). This debate was reflected in another report published in 1955, entitled *School Psychologist at Mid-Century* (Cutts, 1955).

It is generally acknowledged that school psychology in the United States presents a rather heterogeneous picture in terms of professional practice, state certification requirements, and professional accreditation requirements. School psychologists are currently employed with various academic degrees (MEd, MA, PsyD, EdD, and PhD). Furthermore, school psychology certification requirements vary considerably from state to state. Finally, a minority of doctoral-level school psychology training programs meets the full accreditation requirement of the American Psychological Association (American Psychological Association, 1984).

More recently, the National School Psychology Inservice Training Network began deliberations that resulted in the set of recommendations described as a "blueprint" for the training and practice of school psychology (Ysseldyke et al., 1984). The main emphasis of the recommendations is to shift focus from an individual child "with a problem" to the functioning of a child within school as a social system. It is anticipated that school psychologists will continue to work with exceptional children, but only as a part of a broad educational environment.

Gerner (1990) provided interesting information about school psychologists in American international schools. As of 1990, more than 25,000 teachers and administrators have been employed in more than one thousand American, British, and other international schools around the world. Of this number, American schools overseas exceed six hundred institutions. Those schools range from small community schools of twenty children to large, fully equipped campuses that educate thousands of students. In the early 1990s, there were an estimated three hundred thousand American children temporarily living overseas with their parents.

Since 1990, renewed emphasis has been placed by national leaders and the National Academy of Science on science education in the United States. In keeping with this spirit, the National Science Foundation has targeted individuals with disabilities as a priority for science education. Mastropieri and Scruggs (1992) reviewed sixty-six reports involving science education for students with disabilities. Those reports support previous recommendations for science education for students with disabilities. The writers emphasized the importance of focusing on concepts of science rather than language usage. It is also important that science teachers should cooperate with special education teachers to develop appropriate methodology for a variety of special learning needs.

Taking into consideration the way that economic, medical, social, ethical, and demographic conditions influence educational policies and procedures, Simpson, Whelan, and Zabel (1993) suggested some ideas of how special education personnel preparation should be modified in the next century. They stress the importance of professional development schools, as was also suggested in 1990 by the Holmes Group. The main focus of the PDS program is to: share resources between universities and public schools to reform education, prepare new educators, and promote the professional renewal of existing personnel.

Canada

Prior to 1969, standards for teachers in Canada who aspired to teach exceptional children varied considerably from province to province (Ballance & Kendall, 1969). Only four provinces–Newfoundland, Nova Scotia, Ontario, and Quebec–had teacher-training and certification provisions on special education (Ballance & Kendall, 1969). Alberta and British Columbia had no special requirements for certification. However, in Alberta, school psychologists, special therapists, and guidance counselors held general teachers certificates, including a basic teaching certificate, two years of teaching experience, and at least one year of special training in teaching mentally retarded or physically handicapped children. A separate certification is required for a person interested in teaching the deaf. All teachers who wish to teach exceptional children in Ontario must have a basic teaching certificate and successful teaching experience of two years in regular classes. To upgrade teacher education, summer courses are available for eligible candidates.

In 1972, *Standards for Educators of Exceptional Children in Canada* was published, which suggested a three-stage model in teacher preparation (Little,

1980). At the first stage of training, preparation includes the study of normal psychology and development identification of exceptional children and orientation to borderline exceptionalities in the regular classroom. Stage-one teachers are encouraged to work with educational consultants. At the second stage of preparation, teachers are trained as master diagnosticians and are usually employed as itinerant or resource room teachers. Stage three involves continuous specialization.

A number of Canadian universities offer special education programs. Few will be mentioned here. The University of Alberta and the University of British Columbia have special education programs. In 1971, the University of Alberta began to offer a four-year BEd degree with specialization in special education. The University of Saskatchewan, Saskatoon, developed a competency-based special education program based on the three-stage model mentioned above (Little, 1980). York University in Toronto has a training program in the education of exceptional children which includes field-based training and a practicum.

Social, political, and educational influences on inclusion practices in Canada were discussed by Winze (1998). The writer points out that educators in general accept the philosophical goals of inclusion, but differ in their assessment of how those goals should be implemented. At this time, inclusion is not universally accepted. In many areas, there is little or no advance training for receiving teachers and no formal support system. There is also a failure of official agencies to respond with the needed economic and human resources.

South America, Mexico, and Central America

Preparation of special education teachers in South America shows considerable diversity from country to country. In Brazil, only graduation from a normal school is required in order to teach at the primary level (Wechsler & Gomes, 1989). In Chile, special education teachers are trained at six universities and three professional institutes. However, only 1 percent of teachers who teach in grades one through eight have a degree in special education (de la Meuse, 1989).

Brend (1987) reported that in Mexico, teacher training in special education was still at the beginning stage. Presently, the focus is in the areas of speech and hearing disorders, mental retardation, and learning disabilities. Holtzman (1989) informs us that in Mexico the Teachers School of Special Education opened in 1942. However, to this day, Mexico has only a limited number of trained special education teachers.

Unfortunately, in El Salvador there are no certification requirements for teachers, and teacher training is not regulated (Fish & Vorwald, 1989).

United Kingdom and Western Europe

In Great Britain, there is no uniform pattern for the training of special educators. However, there exists an extensive and comprehensive program of in-service training. In Scotland, special education training is at a graduate level, and the candidates must have prior experience teaching one year in a regular classroom.

In western Europe and the Scandinavian countries, preparation for special educators is provided through the pedagogical institutes (teacher colleges), universities (which have departments of education), or the graduate schools of special education. In most instances, candidates for special education are experienced elementary classroom teachers.

In Denmark, where all teachers receive common basic training, teaching in special education has been an optional specialization chosen by almost half of the teachers. The revised Teacher Training Law of 1983 requires instruction in the teaching of handicapped students, a compulsory subject for all trainee teachers (Commission of the European Communities, 1986).

To become a special educator in France, one has to have prior experience as a regular classroom teacher. Basic requirements include one year of theoretical studies and one year of practicum. After completion of required coursework, the candidate for the teaching certificate takes an examination to become a special educator. Six distinct preparations are offered: teachers of the deaf and hard-of-hearing; teachers of the blind; teachers of the physically or mentally handicapped; teachers of the psychologically disturbed; special educators for "unadjusted" children of elementary school age; and special educators for "unadjusted" adolescents (Braswell, 1987a). Special educators trained to work with behaviorally and socially maladjusted children are known as *educateurs*. They are trained in sports, performing arts, and arts and crafts. Educateurs are known as orthopedagogues in the Netherlands and as milieu therapists in Scandinavia.

In the Federal Republic of West Germany, special educators are trained at thirteen universities and four teachers colleges. The universities with the most special education programs are in Dorfmund, Hamburg, Koln, and the Teachers College *(Hochschule)* in Heidelberg (Nagelschwitz, 1985).

In Italy, after the passage of Law 517, the Ministry of Public Instruction initiated a two-year specialization program for teacher aids (Nisi et al., 1989). Teachers aids or support teachers (Vitello, 1989) would be assigned by the state to assist regular teachers in the education of handicapped students. For every four handicapped students in the school, there would be one support teacher.

Vitello (1991) informs us that proposals had been made that elementary regular and special educators obtain a university degree. (Currently, they

attend an *institute magistrate* after high school for four years.) It has been recommended that the curriculum for regular education teachers include special
education content. The expectation is that the adoption of these proposals will
strengthen the link between regular teachers to deal more effectively with difficult-to-teach students, particularly those who are not classified and cause
regular teachers the greatest difficulties.

As reported by Chamberlain (1989), in Ireland, teachers of the handicapped have a dual certification. There were 852 special education teachers
in Ireland, of whom 501 were teachers of the mentally retarded.

In Oslo, Norway, exists the State Graduate School of Special Education.
A prerequisite for acceptance is a degree in elementary education or the
equivalent. Tuunainen (1988) sees a need among special educators in Nordic
countries to establish their own identity. There is also a need to increase special education knowledge among regular educators, either through preservice
or in-service programs. Emphasis should also be placed on the teamwork
skills of both regular and special educators.

In Switzerland, the best-recognized facility for the training of special education is the Institute of Science of Education in Geneva.

As reported by Burli (1987), most candidates for teachers of special education in Switzerland are regular classroom teachers, who specialize through
an additional two- or three-year program leading to a special education diploma.

In Sweden, special education teacher training comes after basic teacher
education. Prospective special education teachers must have acquired at least
three years of professional experience.

Inclusion implementation and practices in Scandinavian countries were
discussed recently by Vormeland (1998); who suggested that the three Scandinavian countries, Norway, Denmark, and Sweden share many similar ideas
about the integration of disabled students within ordinary schools. However,
there are a number of important issues, such as heterogeneity of students and
professionals and the development of caring social relations, that need to be
addressed before inclusion will succeed.

Central and Eastern Europe

Since the dissolution of the Soviet Union in 1991, too few years have
passed for any meaningful changes to be noticed in teacher training. Seventy
years of totalitarian control by the Communist Party left a strong ideological
legacy and the same structure in control.

In Russia, regardless of the areas of specialization, all students studied
several required courses, such as Marxist-Leninist philosophy, history of the

Communist Party, scientific communism, political economy, scientific atheism, Marxist-Leninist ethics and esthetics, and a foreign language.

Usually, kindergarten and elementary school teachers were trained in pedagogical schools, whereas secondary school teachers were trained in pedagogical institutes and universities. In 1980, there were 426 pedagogical schools, 200 pedagogical institutes, and 68 universities (Panachin, 1982). The pedagogical school curriculum consisted of general education and specialized subjects (e.g., teaching methodology in elementary school, school hygiene, psychology). After completing all the requirements, including student teaching and other practical work, the graduating students are examined and, if successful, receive their diplomas.

Professional personnel preparation to work with exceptional children was carried out at two types of facilities. Special education teachers were usually trained at the two-year teacher training institutes. Those trained at the universities were referred to as defectologists. After graduation, in-service training was frequently organized. Prior to the October revolution, preparation of special educators was sporadic, based on short-term in-service training. In 1918, a department of pathological pedagogy was organized in Leningrad. The State Institute of a Defective Child was organized in Moscow in 1920, and in 1921, the Pedagogical Institute of Child's Abnormalities. These two institutes were combined in 1924 and reorganized into the defectological section of the Pedagogical Department of the Moscow Second State University. The Moscow State Pedagogical-Defectological Institute was organized in 1938. From 1959 to 1981, ten additional defectological departments were organized: Shauley (1960), Minsk (1961), Sverdlovsky (1962), Irkutsk (1963), Slavyansk (1966), Tashkent (1967), Tartu (1968), Lyepay (1969), Kishinev (1970), and Alma-Ata (1979) (Lapshin & Zhivina, 1981). The curriculum to train defectologists was reorganized in 1963 and currently includes a four-year sequence of full-time study. Courses of study include: introduction to defectology, physics, chemistry, biology, anatomy, psychopathology, neuropathology of children, geography, pedagogical psychopathology, developmental psychopathology, sexual psychopathology, and a clinical practicum (Zhivina, 1974).

An interesting current approach to the training of defectologists are conferences organized for graduate students, where papers are presented that integrate learning material with research findings (Shakhovskaya, Rechitskaya, & Zabramnaya, 1989).

In keeping with the Soviet Union's political indoctrination as an integral part of professional preparation, defectologists were required to study historical materialism, political economy, and political education.

Even in the year of perestroika, Morgulis (1989) emphasized that the education and upbringing of children should be influenced by teachers' ideological efforts.

In 1976, a Council of Defectology was formed within the Ministry of Education of the USSR. Medicopedagogical committees were formed to facilitate cooperation between educators and physicians.

Guidelines for future preparation of teachers-defectologists were published in the directive $N = 1320$ of the Central Committee of the Communist Party of the Soviet Union (N.N. Defectologia, 1983). The document states that the Soviet specialists should know, among other information: the foundations of theoretical disciplines to the extent necessary to enable them to make pedagogical and administrative decisions; the disciplines of psychopedagogical areas, including pedagogy, psychology, developmental physiology, foundations of neuropathology, anatomy, physiology, pathology of hearing, speech, vision, foundation of genetics, and clinical oligophrenia; the basic ideas of teaching children with physical and cognitive deviation, as well as the methodology of teaching basic subjects.

Defectology departments are devoting considerable time to recruitment and professional orientation of interested applicants (Nazarova, 1985).

Miminova (1989) reported that a May 1989 conference in Tashkent discussed the training of educators-defectologists in view of current educational restructuring. One hundred fifty scholars took part in the conference, which formulated a number of recommendations, such as: improving the preparation of specialists-defectologists to work with learning-disabled children, strengthening interdisciplinary efforts, emphasizing students' initiative, and developing independent study habits. The participants also expressed a need to improve cooperation between departments of defectology and the Institute of Defectology of the Academy of Pedagogical Science. Some conference participants also suggested that the journal *Defectology* should print more materials representing various viewpoints.

In Ukraine, the defectological department was established in 1920 as a medicopedagogical section within the department of special education at the Kyiv State Pedagogical Institute.

In 1939, the section achieved the status of a separate department and functions as such until the present time (Bondar & Sasenko, 1983).

Presently, the Kyiv State Pedagogical Institute contains eight departments with nineteen subspecialties. In 1963, a new four-year study plan was introduced. In 1965, the Department of Defectology was divided into two departments: the Department of the Education of the Deaf and Speech Impaired and the Department of Oligophrenopedagogy. Starting in 1981, the extension division of the Kyiv State Pedagogical Institute began to offer in-service training to teachers with advanced pedagogical training who wanted to become speech therapists.

Litvak, Ushakova, and Pivovarova (1987) emphasized that the need exists to improve training of defectologists. A number of problems were identified:

insufficient material support, existence of small defectological departments that do not have highly qualified professional staff; and deepening differences between theory and practice in the education of atypical children. The authors stressed the need to upgrade the level of professional preparation and the "ideological-political maturity" of defectologists.

Lutskina (1987) described the education of defectologists in the Abay's Kazakh Pedagogical Institute, which began to accept students in the fall of 1928. The first year, 124 students were enrolled. Currently, the institute offers eleven specialties organized into seven departments.

Broad restructuring, or perestroika, in the Soviet Union affected all spheres of life, including education. However, in spite of initial discussion and attempts to change, Russian educators claimed significant difficulty in changing teachers' attitudes. Orlov (1988) viewed these difficulties as related to the philosophy of education, which for a long time has seen the child as only "material" and teachers as "operators" who control technology as teaching-learning process.

This authoritarian attitude on the part of teachers was very much in evidence in the Soviet Union (Bodaliov & Demidova, 1987). The training of school psychologists in the Soviet Union received considerable attention—for example, see Holowinsky (1986b) and Pambookian and Holowinsky (1987).

However, there are still numerous issues of concern, as identified by Bozhovich (1983). Some of the most important issues are: the need to develop better communication between psychologists and educators, the need for more research to clarify the impact of basic research on educational practice, and an improvement of coordinated efforts between psychological science and educational practice. In the 1980s, two roundtable discussions of Soviet psychologists were organized (Voprosy Psikhologii, 1982, *2* and *4*) to explore issues related to the establishment of school psychological services. A broad spectrum of responsibilities for school psychologists were suggested, for example, the psychological process of learning and communication (Matiushkyn, 1982); consultation, diagnosis, and therapy (Markova, 1982); individual work with students who have educational difficulties (Dubrovyna & Prykhozhan, 1982); in-service training for teachers; and consultation with parents and teachers (Tsybenova, 1982). It is also evident from a new book written by Kahanov, Lyshko, and Smirnov (*Methods of Psychological Diagnosis and Clinical Remediation*) (Lebedinsky, 1985) that such widely known tests as TAT, Rorschach, the Rosenzweig Picture Story Test, and the Wechsler Intelligence Scales were being gradually introduced on a limited scale in the former Soviet Union.

In the former Czechoslovakia, teacher education takes place in one of twelve colleges of education. Although Czechoslovakia was similar in form to the Soviet Union, prior to employment teachers had to pass examinations in ideological-political knowledge, psychology of education, art, language, and mathematics (Holes, 1980).

The Hungarian Institute of Therapeutic Pedagogy in Budapest was organized in 1900 and continues to train teacher-defectologists. All students are trained in the pedagogy of the mentally retarded. They can also add areas of specialization such as pedagogy of the deaf, blind, emotionally disturbed, physically handicapped, and speech disabled. The course work for teacher-defectologists lasts four years. In 1972, the institute added a specialized defectological research and consultation service (Noskova & Kuznyetsova, 1980). The institute provides comprehensive evaluations of infants and preschool children who manifest high-risk potential for disability, preparation of instructor-defectologists familiar with early identification and intervention, and research work with young children. The institute works closely with children's hospitals and educational facilities. Currently, 59 percent of special education teachers in Hungary have defectological preparation.

Training of special educators in Poland has a long history and has been associated with the movement of pedology (Holowinsky, 1988) and the pioneering work of Maria Grzegorzcwska. As a young student, she traveled extensively throughout Europe, studying in Paris and Brussels with pioneers in the field of child study. She returned to Poland in 1919 and was active in the field of special education until her death in 1967. Lipkowski (1977) considers altruism and concern for the handicapped to be her primary motivating factors.

Initial efforts in professional personnel preparation were sporadic, and the numbers of teachers graduating were inadequate for the needs. As was the case in the United States, the first efforts in special education teacher training were in the area of mental retardation. From 1918 to 1920, short-term courses were organized for teachers of mentally retarded children, which were reorganized in 1921 into a half-year seminar in special education. In 1922, the Institute of Special Education was organized, and Grzegorzcwska became its first director (Dziedzic, S., 1977). The institute's goal was to train teachers for various conditions of exceptionalities and to conduct methodological research. Initially, the institute accepted as students only experienced elementary and secondary teachers. The duration of the Institute's program was one year. Very few teachers of special education were trained at the university level prior to 1970. Since 1922, the Institute of Special Education in Warsaw has been the only higher-level school training special education teachers in Poland. Since 1970, the institute has been allowed to offer master's degrees (Tomasik & Zabczynaka, 1975). The first university-level chair of special education was established in 1958 at the University of Warsaw.

Significant expansion of teacher-training programs in special education in Poland occurred in the 1970s. A plan suggested by the Committee of Experts began to be implemented in the early 1970s (Pawula, 1981). In 1976, the State

Institute of Special Education in Warsaw was reorganized into the Graduate School of Special Education, which, in 1977 by permission of the Polish Ministry of Education, began to offer postgraduate studies in special education. The areas of specialization include diagnosis and assessment of exceptionalities as well as the study of deaf, hard-of-hearing, chronically ill, and socially maladaptive children.

Since 1983, 600 candidates, on average, have received master's degrees in special education each year. In the 1986–1987 school year, 5,410 teacher candidates studied special education, of whom 400 attended postgraduate studies (Hulek, 1987).

Guidelines for the training of special educators have been developed by the special education team of the Pedagogical Science Committee of the Polish Academy of Sciences (Hulek, 1978).

The guidelines recommend that a student in special education should first acquire experience in teaching nonhandicapped children before teaching the handicapped. The proposal stresses the need to know how to cooperate with various agencies and institutions.

Present programs of study include preservice and in-service preparation. Areas of study include: blind, visually handicapped, deaf, hard-of-hearing, mentally retarded, seriously handicapped, orthopedically handicapped, and socially maladjusted. Polish educational psychologists (Strupczewska & Doroszewicz, 1980; Klar-Stefanska, 1980) stressed the importance of including psychological foundations in special education teacher training. They argue that teachers should be able to appreciate knowledge about the learning process, individual differences of human development, and value systems. In addition to preservice education and training, considerable emphasis has been placed on in-service education. Most of the in-service training is conducted and coordinated by the Institute of Teacher Training and Educational Research (*Instytut Ksztalcenia Nauczcieli i Badan Oswiatwych*).

In the former Yugoslavia, special educators were prepared in two-year schools (after graduation from high school) or four-year schools. Two-year schools for special education exist in Belgrade and Lublany. Four-year schools exist in Zagreb, now Croatia. The curriculum for special educators includes general and child psychology, anatomy, physiology, "special" psychology, introduction to psychodiagnosis, psychopathology, and special education (Rosanova, 1974).

Asia and Africa

In most countries of Asia, special education teacher training programs are either in their infancy or are nonexistent. In China, the government recommends that each province establish special education teacher training at the secondary level. Piao (1989) informed us that only ten years ago there were no special programs in China for the training of special educators. Currently, there are three programs that train teachers of the mentally retarded, blind, and deaf. The universities of Beijing and Shanghai are preparing teacher trainers (Oinzhu, 1989). Each facility plans to admit twenty-five applicants per year.

It is estimated that in India, four thousand special education teachers will be required immediately if the proposed special education schools become functional (Nesbit, 1987). Furthermore, Roy (1989) estimated that more than six thousand teachers would have to be trained in India each year for the next ten years in order to meet anticipated needs by the year 2000. An interesting cooperative project in teacher training was described by Zirpoli, Hallahan, and Kneedler (1988). The University of Virginia and the Norwegian Institute of Special Education obtained a grant from the Republic of Indonesia to offer a two-year training program leading to a master's degree in special education. Nineteen students from Indonesia were selected by the government to participate in the project.

Prior to 1970, few training opportunities were available in Australia for special education teachers (Valcante, 1987). In the 1970s and 1980s, Australia made considerable advances in the training of special educators.

In Japan, teachers of exceptional children are required to study for four years. Two certificates can be issued: the regular certificate for teachers of the blind, deaf, and handicapped, for which one must first have regular teaching certification, and a separate certification for teaching specialized courses in schools for the handicapped.

In New Zealand, Auckland and Christchurch Teachers Colleges, as well as Palmerston North Teachers College, offer courses in special education. In 1984, a training course for teachers of the visually impaired was established at Auckland College (Panckhurst, Panckhurst, & Elkins, 1987). The same source reported that in 1986, Christchurch Teachers College and Cantonbury University began a four-year-degree training program in speech and language therapy.

Because of the low priority accorded to special education in Papua, New Guinea, there is minimal input from the government in terms of staff training (Boorer & Kirchia, 1987).

There is a tremendous need to train special education teachers in Africa. In general, teachers are not trained to recognize or to attend to the specific needs of handicapped or learning-disabled children. As stated by Shown (1987), the burden of education for handicapped students is frequently carried by less-well trained aides rather than by highly skilled teachers. In 1974, the government of Nigeria established a special education unit within the Federal Ministry of Education (Wycke, 1987b). There is a teacher-training college for special educators in Ibadan, which offers a three-year training curriculum. Swaziland has three teacher-training colleges (Csapo, 1988).

An interesting educational initiative in Africa, described by founder Renee C. Neblitt as a "unique twenty-first century educational model" is the Kokrobitey School outside of Accre in Ghana. The school is described as an American-based resource center offering short-term programs to American and Ghanian high school and college students and educators (Carlson & Simcoe, 1999, personal communication).

Kabzems (1989) reported that Zimbabwe had been expanding its special education teacher-training program. Prior to 1985, teacher training in special education was available only for the teachers of the blind, and fewer than thirty specialists were trained. By 1988, teacher-training facilities had graduated 101 teachers of the visually handicapped, hearing impaired, and the mentally retarded.

Change (1992) suggested a conceptual model for the training of special educators for underdeveloped countries. The model includes four phases: (a) identification of prerequisite skills and need assessment; (b) selection of course content and field experiences; (c) evaluation of learning outcome; and (d) designing of follow-up studies after students return to their home countries.

Chapter 9

RESEARCH WITH EXCEPTIONAL LEARNERS

It is beyond the scope of this chapter to review in depth worldwide research with exceptional learners. Instead this chapter will review more important findings and trends. There is an initial impression that research activities, as is the case with programs and services, are directly related to complex variables of a historical, cultural, and socioeconomic nature. For an easy overview, our discussion will focus on five geographical areas: the United States, western Europe, central and eastern Europe, Asia, and Africa. It should be noted that areas that have been emphasized by various researchers include: developmental psychology, etiology, motor and sensory disorders, mental retardation, learning disabilities, special education policy, and others. The chapter will point out how research findings are disseminated. The reader will notice that the most extensive research with exceptional learners has been conducted in the United States at major universities and at research and development centers.

United States

Prior to the 1950s, most of the money spent in educational research was related to test development and construction. Organized educational research originated in 1957 with the passage of the *Cooperative Research Act*.

A major federal breakthrough occurred in 1963 with Public Law 88-164. This law authorized funds for research and demonstration projects related to the education of the handicapped. In November 1966, with the enactment of Public Law 89-750, the Bureau of Education for the Handicapped was established.

In 1976, the National Institute of Education (NIE) funded the American Registry of Research and research-related organizations in education. Most of the funds were allocated to academic institutions where most of the staff was located. In 1981, $163 million was targeted for research and development activities (Ysseldyke & Algozzine, 1982).

The Council for Exceptional Children 1980 Fact Sheets and the ERIC Clearinghouse publications on handicapped and gifted children list 420 doctoral programs located at eighty-four universities throughout the United States. The programs are organized into the following areas of study: administration, hearing impaired, emotionally disturbed, behaviorally disordered, gifted, visually impaired, learning disabilities, speech and language disorders, mental retardation, multiply handicapped, severely handicapped, physically handicapped, early childhood, special education, generic, resource room specialists, and adaptive physical education.

The most frequently occurring programs nationwide are in mental retardation, emotional disturbance, learning disabilities, special education administration, and general special education. They account for more than 50 percent of all programs. The least frequently occurring are programs in adaptive physical education and resource room specialists. The highest concentration of programs is in region V (Indiana, Kentucky, Ohio, Tennessee).

Under President Kennedy, university-based research and development centers were initiated. They were expanded while President Johnson was in office, and new programs were initiated, such as regional educational laboratories (RELs) (Chase & Walter, 1982).

Sindelar and Schloss (1986) evaluated the reputation of doctoral training programs in special education. Questionnaires were sent to eighty-one programs that offer doctorates in special education. Respondents were asked to list five programs with the most distinguished faculties and five programs that graduate the best-prepared students. It should be pointed out as an interesting finding that the reputations of these programs are largely independent of the reputation of the colleges with which they are affiliated.

A new emerging area of research is the complex interaction between HIV infection in children and developmental stages. Recently, it has been reported that children with AIDS often exhibit signs and symptoms of neurological dysfunction (Diamond, 1989). Children of mothers who are intravenous drug users frequently have central nervous system (CNS) involvement. Incidence of CNS dysfunction in infants and children with HIV infection ranges from 78 to 90 percent. Developmental delays and a variety of neurological impairments in children with HIV infection usually appear during the first five years of life. Diamond suggested that planning for special education services should take into consideration the large numbers of children with infections who are surviving longer because of the effective use of chemotherapies.

A new area of emphasis in research is children with Attention Deficit Hyperactivity Disorder (ADHD). In a recent article, Reid and Katsiyannis

(1995) point out that the number of children diagnosed with ADHD appears to be increasing. Experts estimate that up to two million school-age children manifest symptoms of ADHD. Currently, ADHD is conceptualized as a medical-psychiatric condition. However, the initial medical focus began to shift to a discipline of education. Reid and Katsiyannis are of the opinion that, in contrast to other categories of disabilities, ADHD is as much a general education problem as a special education problem, since most of the students with ADHD will spend the majority of their time in general education classrooms.

At the beginning of their review, Reid, Maag, Vasa, and Wright (1994) remind us that ADHD has become one of the most commonly diagnosed and researched childhood disorders. Numerous studies in such fields as medicine, psychology, and education have appeared on this topic. The results of the study by Reid et al. suggest several areas that should be addressed by future research. The authors also suggest that in the case of learning disabilities, when *IDEA (Individuals with Disabilities Education Act)* eligibility criteria are strictly applied, students with ADHD may be overidentified. They warn us that focusing attention primarily on special education eligibility diverts attention from the fact that ADHD is also a problem in general education.

In the United States, attention has also been directed to the dual-diagnosis issue in mental retardation. Myers (1989) reported that in preschool children, infantile autism is more likely to be diagnosed than mental retardation. However, many children diagnosed as autistic are mentally retarded. Myers has also pointed out that unlike language development, gross motor development is a poor predictor of future intelligence. Normal motor development in autistic children has no implications for future mental development.

In comparison with deaf and cerebral-palsied children, not much has been reported on blind children. One possible explanation may be their low prevalence in comparison with other exceptionalities. In the 1980s, a good overview and update on issues of the education of the visually handicapped was presented by Hatlen, Hall, and Tuttle (1980).

Goetzinger and Proud (1975) made an extensive survey of studies dealing with the psychological development and educational achievement of deaf children. Among the important findings of their survey were the following: (a) children with a 25–40 decibel range of hearing loss in the better ear are likely to show significant retardation on verbal tests of intelligence; (b) children with a 40 decibel loss in the better ear may be significantly retarded in educational achievement and may manifest emotional and social maladjustment; (c) children with profound early deafness are seriously educationally retarded; and (d) deaf children compare favorably with hearing children on abstract verbal reasoning tasks, when the tasks are within their understanding.

In the field of exceptionalities, intellectual subnormality, mental retardation, and learning disorders received considerable attention. In the United

States, research in the field is published in the *American Journal on Mental Retardation, Mental Retardation,* and in *Applied Research in Mental Retardation.* In addition, a number of other journals not directly involved in mental retardation publish research articles in this field, for example, *Remedial and Special Education, The Journal of Special Education,* and *Exceptional Child.*

A few examples of research in mental retardation will be mentioned here. The language behavior of mentally retarded youngsters was found to be related to the complex interaction of such factors as sex, socioeconomic status, and chronological and mental age (Ogland, 1972). In general, the lower the cognitive development, the more severe the communication problems. In reality, many severely and profoundly retarded individuals are functionally nonverbal. These individuals have been described by Elder and Bergman (1978), Fristoe and Lloyd (1978), and Vanderheiden and Harris-Vanderheiden (1977).

The misuse of psychotropic drugs to control the behavior of exceptional populations has received some attention. An extensive review of the use of psychotropic drugs with handicapped children was presented by Sprague and Werry (1974). The psychotropic drug prescription pattern for 474 mentally retarded persons over a ten-year period was analyzed by Poindexter (1989). Results indicate a progressive, marked decrease in total psychotropic drug usage and changes in the type of drugs prescribed. The majority of subjects in this study were severely and profoundly retarded. The evidence of decline in drug prescriptions was clearly evident. For example, in 1979, 33 percent of 474 subjects were receiving drugs. By 1987, this percentage dropped to 9.5 percent.

An issue that received attention in mental retardation literature is the advisability of plastic surgery for children with Down's syndrome. This topic was discussed by May (1988) and Katz and Kravetz (1989).

May pointed out that since the 1970s, corrective facial surgery has been performed on children with Down's syndrome. The main purpose of the operation is to eliminate some of the physical stigma. The usual procedure involves reduction of the size of the tongue and elimination of the epicanthal fold. Unfortunately, such operations do not improve learning skills and will not eliminate many problems. This fact was underscored by Katz and Kravetz (1989), who recommend that the operation not be evaluated as an isolated intervention but as a part of a coordinated series of cognitive, behavioral, and speech interventions directed at enhancing an individual's potential. They stress that professionals should provide information regarding the operation's effectiveness, risks, social implications, and alternatives. Parents should be allowed to make their own decisions.

Recently, Smith (1999) published a review of thirteen intervention studies for children with autism conducted since 1980, and pointed to a number of methodological weaknesses such as: lack of experimental or quasi-experimental design, small sample size, and use of therapists who had insufficient training and experience. He also stressed that since autism is a biological disorder in origin, learning-based interventions, which are currently popular, should be integrated with findings from biomedical research.

Some recent studies focused on a comparison of youngsters with Down's syndrome and those with autism. Loveland and Kelley (1988) discussed adaptive behavior in adolescents and young adults with autism and Down's syndrome. These two groups matched on verbal age equivalent but did not differ in adaptive skills assessed by the Vineland Social Maturity Scale. However, findings suggest that the groups display different patterns of adaptive behavior.

With increasing age, persons with Down's syndrome appeared to acquire adaptive skills in all domains, whereas those with autism did not. The adaptive skills of subjects in the Down's syndrome group kept pace with or exceeded verbal and nonverbal mental age equivalent autistic children.

Some research focused on the emotional reactions of mothers of handicapped children. Special education literature of the 1960s identified guilt and mourning as two prevalent emotions found among mothers of handicapped children. Marz (1990) investigated ethnic and racial differences among mothers of handicapped children. The overall findings were of shock, sorrow, and thoughts of suicide. Interestingly, Hispanic mothers did not display depression or anger but, rather, appeared to be resigned and self-sacrificing.

Earlier research on learning disabilities in the United States has been related to the studies on reading disorders variously described as "word blindness" (Orton, 1937), "developmental dyslexia" (Critchley, 1964), and "dyslexia" (Myklebust & Johnson, 1962). In the 1970s, Sabatino (1973) introduced the term *auditory dyslexia* into the professional literature. Studies dealing with perceptual aspects of learning disabilities were reviewed by Hammill and Wiederholt (1973); Keogh (1973); and Mann and Goodman (1976). Mann and Goodman reported that numerous studies have seriously questioned the value of perceptual training. A historical perspective on learning disabilities, as well as a broad review of the field, has been provided by Wiederhold (1974) and by Lloyd, Hallahan, and Kauffman (1980).

Most children with learning disabilities are educated in resource programs. Wiederhold and Chamberlain (1989) identified five types of resource programs: (a) categorical: students and teachers are assigned to categorical groupings; (b) cross-categorical: teachers serve students in more than one disability area; (c) noncategorical: this model was designed to meet the needs of students with mild or moderate learning or behavioral problems, including both the handicapped and nonhandicapped; (d) specific skills resource program: organized around the training of skill areas. Teachers in specific skills programs usually are certified in remedial reading, mathematics, and speech and language, rather than special education; (e) itinerant resource program: this program can be described as "resource program on wheels." Itinerant programs are employed primarily with low incidence handicapping conditions. All resource models include assessment, teaching, and consulting services.

In a national study, Lombardi, Odell, and Novotny (1991) investigated students at-risk. Several factors were associated with being at risk. They include retention, course failure, dropping out of school, drug abuse, and sexual abuse. Included in the study were 22,018 fourth through seventh and tenth graders, 9,652 teachers, and 276 principals. As a general rule, special education students enrolled in general classes are higher functioning than students who attend special education classes. However, a greater percentage of students who had a categorical label associated with special education, but who were enrolled in general classes, did not have higher critical at-risk scores than did other students enrolled in these classes. The researchers found that in order to prevent at-risk students from failure, similar educational strategies to those associated with special education could be used. These include smaller classes, specially trained teachers, individualized instruction, and close cooperation with parents.

In their study, Kress and Elias (1993) pointed out that special education students are a high-risk group for the development of future substance abuse. Especially vulnerable in this respect are emotionally disturbed and learning-disabled students. The writers argue that a strong and urgent need exists to address the problem of substance abuse among the special education population. They recommend development of preventive programs based on empirical research. In their judgment, it is also important that significant emphasis be placed on the development of general social skills training, specific nonverbal communication ability, and problem-solving skills.

Maag and Behrens (1989) investigated depressive symptomatology among learning-disabled and emotionally disturbed adolescents. Their findings confirmed that many learning disabled and emotionally disturbed adolescents experienced moderate-to-severe levels of depressive symptomatology. Depression was found to exist among many handicapped students regardless of their classification and placement label. Teaching emotionally disturbed children to distinguish reality from fantasy on television became a focus of research by Sprafkin, Gadow, and Kant (1987–1988). This study attempted to assess the effect of television viewing skills curriculum on the television-related knowledge and attitudes of emotionally disturbed children. Children who received the curriculum made significantly more accurate reality-fantasy discriminations concerning television program content than the control group. In the opinion of the writers, the main results of this study revealed that the television curriculum can be an effective intervention for teaching emotionally disturbed children to discriminate between reality and fantasy in the television content. Kauffman, Lloyd, and McGee (1989) investigated the attitudes of teachers toward students' maladaptive behavior. In general, special education and regular classroom teachers did not differ significantly in their attitudes. Approximately 20 percent considered many behaviors unacceptable, but indicated willingness to take the responsibility for teaching youngsters who do not have critical skills. Nearly 30 percent were unwilling to accept responsibility without technical assistance. About 30 percent of the teachers considered few behaviors critical or unacceptable but were willing to take responsibility for them.

Tirosh and Conby (1993) investigated autistic children with hyperlexia. Five children with autism and hyperlexia and five children with autism but no hyperlexia were matched for sex and IQ levels. The results revealed that children with hyperlexia displayed more persistent echolalia, superior visual-motor performance, and more favorable response to vestibular stimulation. The researchers were unable to demonstrate a specific etiology or biological factor that would predispose to hyperlexia as opposed to autism. As those children mature, they tend to persist in tasks that they are able to perform adequately.

In the United States, Sindelar et al. (1988) listed thirty-five efficacy studies of special education conducted from 1932 to 1977. With the exception of two studies (Bennett, 1982; Schell, 1959), the rest had been conducted since the 1960s. In general, special class placement has proved to be no more effective than regular class placement on measures of achievement and social adjustment.

Earlier studies attempted to establish the superiority of special class or resource room instruction for mildly handicapped students. More recent research attempted to document an effective approach in educating exceptional children with mainstreamed classrooms.

A study by Marston (1987–1988) investigated the impact of regular and special education on mildly handicapped children. The weekly improvement of reading scores was assessed. This study suggested that special education can be a significant educational intervention.

It is a well-known fact that minority students are significantly overrepresented in the EMR classes. Artiles and Trent (1994) pointed out that in the 1970s the participation of African Americans in the EMR classes was 3.5 times greater than whites. The writers suggest that the field of special education has failed to develop a comprehensive historical and sociological analysis of minority students. Artiles and Trent recommend that we should examine how the belief systems, biases, prejudices, and socioeconomic inequities that have existed for centuries in American society have influenced our nation's schools.

The writers of this study (Oswald, Continko, Best, & Singh, 1999) discussed complex demographic variables as they influence the identification of minority students for special education. More specifically, the study focused on African American students classified as mildly mentally retarded or seriously emotionally disturbed. The study pointed out that African American students are nearly 2.5 times as likely to be identified as mildly mentally retarded and about 1.5 times as likely to be identified as seriously emotionally disturbed in comparison to their non-African American peers. An interesting interaction was observed between poverty and classification. As poverty increased, more African American students were classified as mildly mentally retarded. However, as poverty increased fewer students were identified as severally emotionally disturbed. A disproportionate representation of African American students classified as emotionally disturbed was highest in the wealthiest communities. Forty-eight young adults with mild mental retardation were examined to investigate the effects of learned helplessness on decision-making. "Learned helplessness" as a trait suggests feelings of lack of control over the results of one's actions. Individuals who obtained high scores on the learned helplessness test made less appropriate decisions in comparison to subjects who obtained low scores on learned helplessness. The study also suggested that competent decision-making will not occur simply by making available relevant information. Apparently the confidence in the decision one makes facilitates the decision-making process (Jenkins, 1999).

One of the arguments raised in favor of special education self-contained placement has been that small teacher-student ratios facilitate acquisition of educational skills. However, a study by Thurlow, Ysseldyke, and Wotrula (1989) found extreme variations in the state-recommended teacher-student ratios, in how those ratios are defined, and in how they are interpreted. The writers recommend development of more logical and rational policy related to student-teacher ratios in special education. Justification for differential classification of exceptional children for educational programming was investigated by Ysseldyke, O'Sullivan, Thurlow, and Christenson (1989). Their research was based on comparison of thirty LD, thirty-two ED, thirty EMR, and thirty nonhandicapped students.

Hope and Andrews (1992) attempted to validate the conduct problem construct by intercorrelating scores on three measures: Behavior Problem Checklist, Conner's Teacher Rating Scale, and the Child Behavior Checklist–Teachers' Report Form. The writers suggested three major implications of their study for research: continued efforts are needed to clarify the nature of the conduct problem construct; further efforts should be made to explore the nature of the teacher-judgment process; and there is a need for sound psychometric assessment of the research instruments. In conclusion, they also recommended that efforts be made to ensure standardized administration of teacher-rating scales and that teachers be given more training in the assessment process.

Nietupski et al. (1997) presented an extensive review of curricular research in seven disabilities covering a twenty-year period from 1976 to 1995. The data bank includes 785 articles, which appeared in twenty-one journals. This number represented 16 percent of the publications across those journals over the twenty-year period. There was a 25 percent decline in the average annual frequency of curricular research in the 1991 to 1995 period. It is of interest that fewer articles appeared that addressed skill building. The writers suggested that more work is needed in curricular areas to determine what to teach students with severe disabilities.

Mean ratings on six clusters (instructional planning, instructional presentation, student understanding, task relevance, practice, and feedback) and a total score revealed few significant differences among categories of students. No differences were found in general education, mathematics, and reading. The researchers question differential placement, in view of the fact that the qualitative nature of instruction is the same for students assigned to different categories. To facilitate better cooperation between regular and special education, Bauwens, Haureade, and Friend (1989) suggested cooperative teaching models. The model requires that general and special educators work in coordinated fashion to jointly teach academically and behaviorally heterogeneous groups of students in educationally integrated settings. Team teaching was initially advocated in the 1960s as a means to enhance the overall quality of educational programming.

With the increased application of microcomputers in special education, some researchers were interested in their effectiveness. Cosden (1988) investigated the perception of computer effectiveness by special and regular elementary school teachers. In general, both groups expressed positive attitudes toward microcomputers. However, special education teachers reported that computer instruction had its greatest impact on low achievers, while regular teachers perceived that the technology had a similar impact on all students or on high achievers in particular.

Western Europe

In Europe, research with exceptional children has been affiliated with universities, children's hospitals, and research institutes. In Austria, biological and medical research related to mental retardation has been associated with the children's hospital of the University of Vienna and with the Vienna City Hospital (Dybwad, 1971). The University of Louvain in Belgium contains a renowned center for educational research. In Denmark, research related to mental retardation has been promoted by the Danish Society for the Scientific Study of Oligophrenia (Dybwad, 1971). The universities of Marburg and Heidelberg, as well as the Max Plank Institute in Berlin, are well-known facilities in Germany where research on mental retardation is conducted. France's earlier contributions to research on exceptionalities are universally recognized. In this regard, it is sufficient to mention the names of Itard, Seguin, and Binet, as well as Lequve's discovery of the chromosomal aberration in Down's syndrome.

In the Netherlands, coordination of multidisciplinary research efforts has been carried out by the Dutch Society for the Scientific Study of Mental Deficiency (Dybwad, 1971).

One of the most famous research facilities is the Jean Piaget Institute, located in Geneva, Switzerland. The seminal work of Piaget and his coworkers in developmental psychology has enhanced tremendously our understanding of child development. Of more immediate significance to special educators are the studies of Inhelder, who has applied Piaget's theory to the field of mental retardation.

Research with handicapped children in Nordic countries was discussed earlier by Dybwad (1971), Stukat (1973, 1982), and Juul (1989).

Many research studies in Norway and Sweden have been conducted in the area of learning disorders and brain injury. In the 1960s, research institutes were established at some schools of education. Stukat (1973) reported that Scandinavian researchers maintained a liaison with American universities, such as Illinois and Yeshiva. Norway's most significant contribution to research in mental retardation was the discovery of PKU (phenylketonuria) in 1934 by Folling. Research in Norway is conducted at the Institute for Educational Research at the University of Oslo and the University of Bergen. The so-called Bergen project (Juul, 1989) is a joint longitudinal project of learning disabilities in which Denmark, Finland, Norway, and Sweden are participating. The goal of this project is to investigate the educational, social, and psychological dimensions of learning disabilities.

Switzerland has eight institutes where special education research is conducted. Three are located in Zurich, two in Firbourg, and one each in Basel, Bern, and Geneva. Of this number, five are university-based and three are separate research facilities.

Comprehensive research with children who have motor disorders was conducted in Sweden in the 1970s and early 1980s and reported by Stukat (1985). The research was conducted in cooperation between the University of Gothenberg and the Bracke regional habilitation center. Studies done in Sweden in 1975 reported that motor handicaps in children were associated in 48 percent with brain damage, 28 percent with spinal or skeletal deformities, and 24 percent with various other conditions.

Most frequently, motor disorders were associated with cerebral palsy. For example, in a group of forty children with motor handicaps, twenty-eight had cerebral palsy, seven spina bifida, and five other dysfunctions. In addition to motor disorders, most children had one or more other dysfunctions. In this group, seven had mental retardation, two were severely hearing impaired, and one had defective vision. Stukat (1985) also reported that approximately 30 percent of cerebral palsied children are found to be mentally retarded, 75 percent have speech difficulties, and 25 percent are visually impaired.

Central and Eastern Europe

In Eastern Europe, known research facilities were located in Hungary, Czechoslovakia (Bratislava), and Poland. A psychological clinic that opened in Bratislava in 1957 soon became a leading research and service facility in Czechoslovakia (Bazany, 1963).

In Poland, research with exceptional children is conducted at universities and pedagogical institutes. However, research efforts are not coordinated. Hulek (1989) recommended that a section on special education should be created within the Educational Research Institute.

Research with exceptional children in the former Soviet Union was conducted at the Institute of Defectology, the Academy of Pedagogical Sciences of the USSR, and at various universities. Defectologists and special educators publish their findings in the publications of the academy, *Defectologia* (Defectology), and *Voprosy Psikhologii* (Problems of Psychology). Within the Institute of Defectology are located twenty-one research laboratories. The institute has no teaching responsibilities. Eikeland (1975) reported that: "These laboratories are state central laboratories undertaking mainly scientific research in their own special field, and from the results of those investigations they work out educational programs to be effectuated through the whole of the Soviet Union" (p. 75).

Child development research provides a foundation for the study of exceptionalities, since our knowledge of average, normal development helps us to understand deviations from the norm, as exceptionalities are defined. Historically, since the pedology movement at the beginning of the present century (Holowinsky, 1988), the contributions of Piaget, Vygotsky, and Zaporozhets have been widely acknowledged. In the 1930s, Geneva, and Kharkiv in Ukraine SSR, became recognized as centers of research in developmental psychology.

Etiology and its interaction with the nature of handicapping conditions was discussed in Chapter 3. In this chapter, current research on etiological factors will be highlighted. The most frequently studied were those factors associated with mental retardation and dual diagnosis. There is also some interest in fetal alcohol syndrome (FAS).

Moskovina and Sagdullayev (1989) reported that alcoholism in parents of children with mental retardation varies from 14.3 to 70.5 percent. Fetal alcohol syndrome is associated with pre- or postnatal growth retardation, CNS impairment, and peculiar facial dysformity. Fetal alcohol syndrome and mental retardation in children is almost twice the incidence rate in those children whose mother or both parents were alcoholics than in those children where only the father was alcoholic.

Mastiukova (1989), writing on the same topic, reported that alcohol is most damaging during the first days and weeks of embryonic development. The incidence of FAS is approximately 1:600 within the general population. Mastiukova's research was conducted in the laboratory of clinicogenetic research of the Scientific Research Institute of Defectology of the Academy of Pedagogical Sciences. Most subjects in Mastiukova's sample were found to be mildly retarded with deficiency in verbal intelligence. Vedeneyeva (1989) investigated deafness found among mentally retarded children. She reported that the number of deaf mentally retarded children was close to 13 percent. It was established that nearly 69 percent of mentally retarded deaf children lost their hearing prior to the first year of life. Etiological factors were distributed as follows: congenital–35 percent; complications arising from treatment by antibiotics–21 percent; meningitis–16 percent; other infections–10 percent; unknown etiology–18 percent.

The importance of genetic counseling as a preventive measure has been discussed by Danielov and Utin (1987). Among forty-five patients with hereditary mental retardation, most (thirty-three) had autosomic recessive type heredity, nine had X-linked recessive heredity, and three were diagnosed with a dominant gene syndrome. In the exogenous group, mental retardation in one or both parents had no influence on the frequency of mental retardation. In endogenous groups, the frequency of mental retardation was considerably and significantly higher when there was parental mental retardation. The risk factor for siblings was highest when both parents were mentally retarded.

A risk comparison of maternal and paternal mental retardation shows that a child's risk of being mentally retarded was much higher if the mother was mentally retarded. This finding is consistent with literature in the United States. The authors are suggesting a complex interaction of hereditary, cultural, and social factors.

Kazakova and Khokhrina (1981) investigated morphological changes in the brain following intranatal asphyxia. They conducted the neurohistorical study of brains of neonates who survived from several hours to two days after birth. Ten neonates (M-6; F-4), average weight 2,950 gr., were studied. The cause of death in all cases was asphyxia. The authors reported that neonates surviving for different lengths of time disclosed characteristic features of development of anoxic encephalopathy and showed that extensive irreversible change took place in the neurons, mainly in the cerebral cortex and cerebellum. They also reported: "Comparing the results of our examination of the brain of neonates with the brain of an adult who had suffered asphyxia at birth revealed characteristics that demonstrated that the pathological process had the same genesis in both cases."

In both the neonates and in the adult many years after birth asphyxia, the irreversible hypoxic changes in neurons dominated the picture. Detection of these changes in the very first hours of life, their increasing severity the longer the neonate lived, and pronounced chronic hypoxic encephalopathy, with destructive changes in neurons as long-term sequelae, indicate that neurons are extremely sensitive to oxygen deficiency in the early postnatal period, and that the pathological process following a pathogenic event acting on the brain is progressive, as has been observed by a number of investigators in both experimental and autopsy materials. However, the fact that the subcortical sections of the brain stem were less damaged points out that different sections of the brain vary in their sensitivity to oxygen starvation (p. 59).

Lilin (1978) reviewed Bertyn's book *Twin Method in the Study of Oligophrenia in Children,* published in Moscow in 1975. The value of the findings is underscored by the extensive sample used in this research. Bertyn selected 143 pairs of twins from among 5,109 youngsters attending thirty-two special (auxiliary) schools. Fifty MZ pairs were identified (26 F; 24 M) and 93 DZ pairs (23 F, 38 M, 32 both sexes pairs). There were 154 M and 130 F among 286 individual mentally retarded youngsters. A high incidence of oligophrenia was found among parents (38% in MZ and 35% in DZ). More mothers (50.3%) than fathers (21.6%) of oligophrenics were found to be mentally retarded. It was also found that 35.5 percent of the siblings of MZ retarded twins were themselves mentally retarded and 35 percent of DZ twins had siblings who were mentally retarded.

Etiology of oligophrenia was investigated by Antropov and Grintsov (1979) in 1975 youngsters (96 M and 79 F) who were attending a boarding school for the mentally retarded. Detailed clinical studies established four etiological groups: parental alcoholism (N = 44), familial (N = 47), birth trauma (N = 41), and infection of the CNS during infancy (N = 43). It is of interest that parental alcoholism is listed in nearly 25 percent of cases, a classification that is not even mentioned separately in the AAMD classified (Grossman, 1973).

Meyerova and Sokolova (1980) reported that acromegaly is seldom seen in oligophrenics. Portnov's book, *Contemporary Problems of Oligophrenia* (1975), has been reviewed by Savchenko (1980). The book edited by Portnov contains reports of the proceedings of the Moscow Scientific Research Institute of Psychiatry. Four clinical groups of oligophrenics were identified: (a) generally arrested psychological development associated with the underdevelopment of more recent evolutionary systems; (b) oligophrenic feeblemindedness; (c) oligophrenic feeblemindedness with symptoms of dementia; and (d) oligophrenia associated with motoric and sensory disorders. It is interesting that Portnov suggested that the traditional terms *idiocy, imbecility,* and *debility* should be retained.

Blumina (1980) discussed one hundred cases of children with late-treated PKU who were attending auxiliary school. She reported that only six children were mildly retarded. Ninety-four were retarded at either the severe or moderate level. Three clinical varieties of PKU were identified: dementia-like, schizophrenia-like, and neurotic-like. In most of the oligophrenics with PKU, cognitive, affective, and communication skills were severely impaired. In 75 percent of the untreated PKU cases, speech is absent or consists of a few separate words. The incidence of PKU in the population at large varies from 1:5,000 to 1:15,000 cases.

Blumina (1984) suggested an ontogenetic approach to the diagnosis of oligophrenia. She began her discussion by pointing out that the CNS functions as a holistic, well-integrated system. Those in turn may lead to tertiary changes. Blumina based her classification on the etiological model suggested by Sakhareva, which specified that developmental pathology should be viewed in terms of three stages: embryological, letal, and peri- and postnatal. Blumina reported that in 70–90 percent of all cases of mental retardation, genetic factors can be identified. Such an assertion should be understood within the context of the Soviet terminology of mental retardation, which considers as oligophrenics only those in whom there is an evidence of organic involvement. It is clear that in a psychometrically-based classification of the mentally retarded (as in the case in the United States); one would not expect 70–90 percent of the retarded to be of genetic etiology.

Blumina's extensive study was based on a clinical investigation of 543 children between 1970 and 1982. The distribution of oligophrenia among 543 children as it related to the etiology was as follows: during the prenatal period, 405; at the time of birth, 93; early postnatal cases, 45. Among the 405 whose oligophrenia was associated with prenatal etiology, 179 cases were traced to the embryonic development and 226 to the stage of fetal development.

Mastiukova (1973) noted that among 103 cerebral-palsied children surveyed by her, 25–35 percent were of average or higher intelligence level, while 65–75 percent revealed various intellectual inadequacies. Frequently observed were memory deficit, inadequate focusing of attention, low frustration tolerance, rigidity, poor spatial and time perception, mirror writing, and other specific learning difficulties.

More recently, Trubnikova (1988) investigated thirty cerebral-palsied children, eight and nine years of age, who were attending elementary school. As a control group, thirty children were used who attended an auxiliary school (self-contained special school). Articulation disorder was noticed in more than 90 percent of children with cerebral palsy.

Moskovina, Bertyn, and Opolinsky (1979) studied etiological factors of 595 hard-of-hearing and deaf children. The most frequent etiological factors identified were prematurity and infectious illnesses during the first years of life. In every case, a combination of etiologies, rather than one clear source, was found.

Sarayev (1988) compared the intellectual development of deaf and hearing children, seven to fifteen years of age. Between seven to eight years of age, hearing youngsters manifested a better level of functioning than deaf. However, the curve for the hearing remained nearly even, while the curve for the deaf showed initial acceleration and then leveled off at approximately fifteen years of age. On the other hand, intellectual growth of youngsters with hearing continued to increase past adolescence.

Some defectological literature devoted considerable attention to the discussion of children with cerebral palsy. Studies appeared focusing on characteristics (Vasylenko, 1980), perceptual difficulties (Kalizhniuk & Sapunova, 1975), cognitive development (Mastiukova, 1973), and educational difficulties (Mamaichuk, 1976). Vasylenko noted that defects in visual-spatial perception were predominantly observed among cerebral-palsied children. The study also revealed that young cerebral-palsied children often express fears of new and unexpected situations.

Kalizhniuk and Sapunova (1975) reported that in contrast to children of average ability, who by six or seven years of age demonstrate the presence of hemispheric dominance, lack of dominance was in evidence in cerebral-palsied children.

The prevailing view of mental retardation in the former Soviet Union maintains that the condition is related to a diffused maldevelopment or defect of the cortical hemispheres, which in turn leads to a pathological inertia of the central nervous system. The concept of oligophrenia, used in the Soviet Union, is more closely comparable to our concept of moderate and severe mental deficiency. Luria (1963) suggested that the more severely deficient among the retarded have suffered damage to the brain stem and subcortical areas as well as to the cerebral cortex; the moderately retarded have suffered lesser damage to subcortical and cortical areas. Luria maintained that the mildly retarded have only superficial damage to the cerebral hemispheres. Pevzner (1961) also has been recognized as a noted researcher in the field of mental retardation. Recently, Blumina (1984) reported that approximately 75 percent of all cases of oligophrenia reveal endogenous etiology and 25 percent exogenous.

Ployvannaya et al. (1985) compared short-term memory characteristics of mentally retarded and normal school children. They reported that in children attending auxiliary school, productivity of visual and auditory short-term memory is on the average 21–38 percent below that of normally developing children. However, productivity of visual short-term memory in youngsters, retarded and nonretarded, is higher than auditory short-term memory. They also concluded that memory loss depends not only on the interval between presentation and recall, but also on the type of information presented. A review of research with mentally retarded preschoolers in the Soviet Union was published by Holowinsky (1985).

A more recent review of mental retardation research in the former Soviet Union by Holowinsky (1990) summarized the findings as follows: Families of mentally retarded children have a lower level of education, lower occupational status, and a larger number of siblings. There is a significantly higher number of males than females (2:1) among psychotic-like oligophrenics. There is lower STM productivity (auditory, verbal, visual) in mentally retarded children in comparison with the nonretarded controls. There is higher productivity with visual rather than auditory-verbal stimuli. There are higher risk factors for mental retardation in children if the mother, rather than the father, was mentally retarded. It might be of interest that these general findings are similar to the trends reported in the U.S. literature on mental retardation.

A concept similar to learning disabilities was introduced into the Soviet defectological literature in the 1960s. Such research began in 1965 at the scientific research Institute of the Soviet Academy of Pedagogical Sciences (Pevzner & Rostiagaylova, 1981). The research focused on areas of attention, memory, intellectual functioning, and educational achievement. Tsipina (1985) reported that complex clinical neuropsychological, and psychoeducational research with developmentally delayed children is currently being conducted under the leadership of Vlasova, Pevzner, Lubovsky, and Nykashena.

Podobed (1988) investigated short-term memory performance among the mentally retarded, learning disabled, and children of average intelligence. Statistically significant differences were found between these three groups. Learning-disabled children performed better than mentally retarded but less well than children of average intelligence. Memory for numbers was higher than the memory for words.

In the 1980s, Kydykbayeva (1985), Arkhip (1987), and Vavina and Kavalchuk (1986) commented on a very interesting social policy issue in a multicultural, multinational state such as the USSR, namely the status of the Russian language in schools for the mentally retarded. Arkhip expressed concern with the level of Russian language training in the auxiliary schools for the mentally retarded.

Kydykbayeva (1985) reported on the difficulties of teaching mentally retarded children from Kirghiz. The problem lay in using the Russian alphabet and applying it to the Kirghiz language, which is phonetically different.

Banhegyi (1963) reported on 1,100 juvenile delinquents studied by the Psycho-Educational Clinic in Bratislava. The overall results confirmed trends reported in the West. Characteristics predominantly associated with juvenile delinquency were as follows: (a) disrupted family, especially absence of the father, lack of supervision, alcoholism of parents, delinquency of siblings, low educational level of parents; (b) incomplete school education, significant potential-achievement discrepancy; and (c) relatively high percentage of cases with a low level of mental abilities and frequent incidence of disturbances and anomalies in personality development.

The clinic published its research in the form of a book titled *Psycho-educational Care of Children*. Of interest are studies of social policy focus involving large samples. For example, Bazany and Adamovic (1963) investigated familiarity with occupational choices by students attending the eighth and eleventh grades of schools in Bratislava. The study was based on answers to questionnaires returned by more than three thousand students. The study revealed a low level of information about occupational choices and frequent change of goals. It is obvious that for this age group, the family represented the main source of information about occupations.

Research with exceptional children in Hungary has a long history dating to the end of the nineteenth century. In 1900, the Institute of Therapeutic Pedagogy was organized in Budapest. The institute conducts research and maintains exchange programs with other countries. Research has been conducted on social-moral judgments of children and reviewed by Csapo (1987).

In Poland, interesting research on normalization and mainstreaming issues conducted by the Department of Therapeutic Pedagogy of Warsaw University has been reported by Hulek (1979a). He suggested that three major variables create a suitable climate for mainstreaming: changes in society's attitudes toward disabled persons; changes in the regular school system; and development of various social and rehabilitation services. This particular research focused on problems related to the goals of chronically disabled persons, teaching methods related to handicapped children, and the possibilities of cooperation between special schools and a school for normal children. An interesting study was conducted by Perlik (1981), who discussed early prevocational orientation of children. It is apparent that in the socialist countries, youngsters as early as elementary grade age are exposed to the idea of eventual educational planning.

In Poland, which is still to a considerable extent an agricultural society, questions of the interaction of demographic variables continue to interest educational researchers. As examples of such studies, those of Bednarczyk-Smolinska (1982) and Dutkiewicz (1983) may be mentioned.

Bednarczryk-Smolinska (1982) reported a study involving 827 youngsters attending eighth grade in elementary schools in the villages of the Warsaw district. Her results revealed that more than half of those studied (62% of girls and 49% of boys) chose specific personal models. Two conflicting trends in the choice of models became apparent. One trend, described as traditional, is related to farm work. Another trend was inspired by the contemporary influence of education and social institution. It was found that teenagers from villages strongly express the opinions of their parents.

Dutkiewicz (1981) compared the achievement, socioeconomic status, and intellectual development of urban and rural children. The sample included 602 urban and 695 rural children. Mental abilities were assessed by Raven's Progressive Matrices and the Domino Test (D48). The analysis revealed differences between urban and rural primary school graduates, with urban children surpassing rural children in achievement. Research results revealed that school does not sufficiently compensate for unfavorable environmental conditions.

Lipkowski (1978) and Ignar-Golinowska (1985) discussed problems faced by so-called difficult young people. Ignar-Galinowska's (1985) extensive study involved 3,469 students fourteen years of age (1,675 boys and 1,974 girls) living in eight urban and five rural areas. Forty-five percent of the children studied reported some educational difficulties. It was reported that girls had better school achievement than boys, especially during pubescence. In general, teenagers from rural areas had more difficulties with educational achievement than those from urban areas.

Asia and Africa

In Japan, the National Institute of Special Education (NISE) is publishing a NISE bulletin devoted to special education issues. In June 1989, the institute began publication of a newsletter, which covers special education issues in other countries of Asia and the Pacific.

In China, facilities for research on exceptionalities seem virtually nonexistent. As reported by Piao (1989), in 1980 a chair of defectology was established at the Beijing Pedagogical University. In 1987, within the Central Pedagogical Scientific Research Institute, a special section of defectology was established. Only recently the Central Institute of Education Science set up a research office under the supervision of the State Education Commission. The office employs a small number of scientists. Another center on special education was established at Beijing University (Dinzhu, 1989).

Yang and Wang (1994) report that in the late 1990s two special education research institutes were established: the Special Education Research Division of the Central China Education Research Center in Beijing and the Beijing Normal University Special Education Research Center.

An important variable in the process of education is the dynamic interaction between students' and teachers' personalities. This problem was investigated by Fisler, Kent, and Fraser (1998) using a sample of 108 teachers from eight secondary schools (grades eleven and twelve) in Tasmania, Australia. More specifically, the writers investigated the relationship between how students and teachers perceive teacher-student interpersonal behaviors. They concluded that the teacher's personality appeared to be associated with the teacher's self-perception of being "friendly, helpful, fostering students' freedom, responsibility, and opportunity for independent work in class."

Mpofu et al. (1997) reported on the results of a survey conducted in twelve east and southern Africa countries: Botswana, Eritrea, Ethiopia, Lesotho, Malawi, Namibia, Swaziland, Tanzania, Uganda, Kenya, Zambia, and Zimbabwe. The data collected can at best be considered indicative of a trend, but not a representative one, since only forty-two special education leaders responded. The writers concluded that although differences among countries were apparent, utilization of school psychology services in the twelve countries is generally low. The general conclusion of the survey was that many countries in Africa are striving to meet the general education need and lack resources to meet students' needs in these countries. School psychology services are little more than a dream belonging to a few.

Dissemination of Research Findings

The findings of special education research have been disseminated through journals, reviews, and textbooks. There are approximately fifteen journals in the United States devoted directly or indirectly to special education. Widely recognized are the following journals: *Exceptional Children, Journal of Learning Disabilities, The Journal of Special Education,* and *Remedial and Special.* The review of special education has been published in four volumes: *The First Review of Special Education,* 1973; *The Second Review of Special Education,* 1974; *The Third Review of Special Education,* 1976; *The Fourth Review of Special Education,* 1980. *The Encyclopedia of Special Education* was published in 1987.

Patton, Palloway, and Epstein (1989) reviewed the quality of special education textbooks. The review was based on questionnaire responses from "experts" in such fields as learning disabilities, mental retardation, and behavioral disorders. Some respondents viewed current texts as redundant and uninfluential. "Market needs," rather than scholarship, were considered a problem in text publication.

In the former Soviet Union, in the early 1980s, the Scientific Research Institute of Defectology conducted work in five areas: developmental diagnosis, study of visual and auditory handicaps, perceptual development in handicapped children, and research with preschool children. In that period, the institute prepared for press seventy-eight monographs, sixteen collections of research papers, and fifty-six curriculum guides. The section of psychology and developmental physiology is responsible for the journals *Defectology* and *Voprosy Psikhologii* (Bodoliou, 1986).

Special education studies in Poland are published in the *Informator Szkolnictwa Specjalnego* (Bulletin of Special Education), *Nowa Szkola* (New School), *Skzola Specejalna* (Special School), and *Edukacja* (Education, formerly *Badania Oswiatowe* Educational Research). A few highlights of current research interests will be provided. Hulek (1989) expressed concern that there is insufficient dissemination of information about research results. He also recommended publication of a quarterly journal, *Advances in Special Education,* which would publish research in the area of special education and related scholarship.

In the former Czechoslovakia, research relative to exceptional children has been published in *Psychology and Psycho-pathology of Children,* a quarterly publication devoted to research on exceptional children. Special educators in the former Yugoslavia published their studies in *Special School,* a journal that appears six times a year.

Chapter 10

POSTSCRIPT–FUTURE TRENDS

This brief chapter will attempt to summarize issues and trends which are currently in evidence. Some discussion will also focus upon trends which may become of importance in the near future.

Service delivery has been influenced and will continue to be influenced by cultural, social, economical, and political variables. In spite of the centuries of efforts on behalf of handicapped and exceptional individuals current programs reveal lack of consistency or some resemblance across cultures and regions. An impression is created that support for special education is related directly to the level of socioeconomic development and political stability. For example, countries like Afghanistan or Cambodia are primarily concerned with their survival rather than the quality or extent of special education services. It would be a stretch of the imagination to expect that such national groups as, for example, Checkens and Kurds, who are fighting for their physical existence and preservation of their languages, will find time to develop programs for exceptional learners in the new future.

In a recent article, Harkins (1998) presented a philosophical point of view in support of positive attitudes toward individuals with disabilities. He argued that our action or inaction will make a huge difference in how the individuals with disabilities will live in the next century.

The incidence of disabilities is increasing in the developing countries. There is a great need for effective rehabilitation and early intervention. Starr (1992) reported that by the year 2000, most of the world's disabled population will live in the developing countries. It is obvious that when families are poor, starving, and unemployed, education is not seen as a basic necessity. Starr pointed out that a success of early intervention at the family and community level depends upon several factors such as: the needs of individual families and children, and the willingness of families and communities to participate.

At an administrative level, the success of the intervention program depends upon government legislation, priorities and financial commitment, program accessibility, availability of trained personnel and resources.

Only a few years ago, Kumar (1984) reported that in India, 50 percent of the primary schools did not have a concrete structure, drinking water, or a playground; 40 percent were without blackboards; 70 percent did not have libraries; and 85 percent did not have lavatories. These conditions are difficult to imagine for an American educator. However, similar conditions exist in many other countries and regions.

It is obvious that needs and potentials for the program development worldwide are tremendous. It should be anticipated that with a decrease in international tension and the improvement in the standard of living, a significant increase in the number and quality of special education programs will become evident.

There are significant differences among countries with respect to the issues of normalization, integration, and mainstreaming of exceptional students. In some countries, for example, China, the question is not even debated. In others, segregation of the handicapped and exceptional is the rule.

Mainstreaming of special education students became very popular in the United States and the Scandinavian countries as a response to the philosophy of normalization. Italy experimented with total mainstreaming in the 1970s but abandoned this policy after a few years as impractical.

The popularity of mainstreaming in the United States can be judged by the number of articles on this topic in professional journals. From 1965 to 1970, only 25 articles on mainstreaming were published. From 1970 to 1975, however, 121 such articles appeared (Meisgeier, 1976).

Although normalization and mainstreaming are frequently discussed interchangeably, it should be remembered that there is a basic difference between these two concepts. It might be said that normalization is an a priori philosophical ideal, which could be reached through mainstreaming. In other words, mainstreaming is the outgrowth of the philosophy of normalization and the legal rights movement of the 1960s. As Hallahan and Kauffman (1986) tell us, professionals try to implement the normalization principle through delabeling, mainstreaming, and deinstitutionalization. Bruininks and Warfield (1978) summarized the popular notion about normalization:

> planning and managing for retarded people services that require attention to normative cultural patterns; allowing retarded people to experience normal routines of the day and normal routines of the life cycle that generally accompany increasing maturity; respective choices and desires and providing normal economic and civic privileges; providing education, training, care and residential living facilities of normal size and appearance; using generic services whenever possible rather than a separate ones. (p. 191–192)

Since the 1960s, a number of reviews of literature were published that have discussed a historical and philosophical basis for mainstreaming, for example, Madden and Slaving, 1983; Meisels, 1986; and Semmel, Gottlieb and Robinson, 1979.

There is a difference between mainstreaming simply as an administrative arrangement in which children from self-contained special education classes are returned to regular programs and real integration. Several issues related to mainstreaming are identified in the literature and include the need for continuous individualized instruction, acceptance of the mainstreamed youngsters by their peers as well as by the regular classroom teacher, and the preparation of regular classroom teachers to work with children who need specialized instruction.

It also should be kept in mind that the impetus for mainstreaming has always been directed more toward facilitating social competence than insuring academic performance. In the 1960s, Dunn (1968), in his pioneering article, focused on the need to eliminate social segregation as one of the main goals of mainstreaming. However, in spite of the two decades of efforts, it appears that the final judgment on mainstreaming cannot yet be made in terms of its long-range educational and social impact.

A recent comprehensive study by Gregory, Shanahan, and Walberg (1985), based on the survey data of thirty thousand high school sophomores, showed a number of differences between nonlearning disabled students and their mainstreamed learning- disabled peers. Learning-disabled students manifested poor academic achievement, low motivation, and poor self-perception. It is apparent that mainstreaming efforts did not eradicate group differences between learning-disabled and nonlearning disabled.

Recent trends in special education emphasize the value of mainstreaming and inclusion. This trend suggests a need for studies that would identify variables associated with success in mainstreamed elementary science classes. Scruggs and Mastropieri (1994) identified seven variables which appeared to be associated with mainstreaming success. They listed these variables as: administrative support, support from special education personnel, positive classroom atmosphere, appropriate curriculum, effective general teaching skills, peer assistance, and disability-specific teaching skills.

Zigmond (1995) described a program developed at the University of Pittsburgh. All students with learning disabilities were reassigned to full-time education classes. Special education teachers cooperated in teaching in all classes. Students with learning disabilities had the opportunity to participate in all activities in the general education classes, such as group lessons, independent practice, cooperative learning groups, holiday activities, recess, assemblies, and social events. All students in the school had opportunities to work with modified materials, modified assignments, and modified tests. Modified

grades could be also earned, so that all students in the school had the opportunity to succeed. Also, one-to-one tutoring was available on a limited basis
before and after school. Zigmond also described the so-called Kansas model
of collaborative teaching. All students with learning disabilities or those classified as educable mentally handicapped at a given grade level cooperated
with the general education classroom teacher for three to four hours per day.
An interesting aspect of the program was the utilization of other students. Students in the collaborative teaching classrooms had opportunities to participate
in all general education activities with individual help from a classmate
assigned as a "student buddy."

The educational experience of pupils with learning disabilities in an elementary school in Virginia was described by Baker (1995). The model
required that a special education teacher modify her or his role and a general education teacher be willing to participate in a cooperative teaching. School
personnel reported that the success of this model was contingent on interest
and commitment of those involved.

Zigmond (1995) pointed out that it is the least-restrictive appropriate
placement provision that has changed schooling for students with disabilities.
The movement toward integration emerged at the time when there is growing concern among educators and the general public that education in the
United States is not meeting the needs of a great number of children.

Manset and Semmel (1997) compared eight different inclusive models for
elementary students with mild disabilities. They expressed an opinion that the
answer to the question of whether inclusive programs are effective for students with mild disabilities is at best inconclusive. In their judgment, the evidence clearly indicates that a mode of inclusive programming that is superior
to more traditional special education service-delivery models does not exist at
present. Manset and Semmel (1997) concluded that the data from their review
does not support the dismantling of special education services.

Zigmond and Baker (1995), in their general comments on current and
future practices in inclusive schooling, stressed the importance of the specialized preparation of special education. They stressed that in their vision of
inclusive schooling, which includes in-class support and intensive alternative
instruction, there will continue to be a need for special educators with specialized skills.

More recently some special educators began to express reservations about
a total inclusion practice. Levin (1997) in *The New York Times,* quoted Douglas
Fuchs, a professor of special education at Vanderbilt University, as saying, "It
has not been demonstrated that regular classrooms, even fortified regular
classrooms using the best practices, can accommodate all children all the
time." A more negative and stronger opinion against total inclusion has been
expressed by Chesley and Calaluce (1997). The writers refer to inclusion as

our national obsession. In their opinion, full inclusion for all is a myth that exists in the hearts of its supporters, those who have lost sight of reality. The danger is that many students with disabilities graduate from high school without the skills required to be successful in the adult world.

In addition to mainstreaming, other issues will acquire prominence, such as: delabeling, service for transient cultural minorities, education of children and adolescents with AIDS, impact of sociopolitical changes and ecological conditions.

Delabeling

Since the emergence of the normalization movement, special educators have been concerned with the problem of identifying children in need of help by focusing upon educationally relevant classifications and avoiding etiological classifications.

Smith (1999) suggests a revolutionary view of disabilities in what he describes as a post-disciplinary approach through social construction and cultural cartography metaphor. He argues that programs developed in the past to provide care for the developmentally disabled in reality created a population labeled as dependent upon others. He points out that, "in the bureaucratic structures found within schools, special educators may become unintended gatekeepers and boundary guards to the normalized landscape of regular education" (p. 131). Smith suggests that educators should be involved in social and political change processes. They should not be satisfied only by disseminating information and knowledge.

A classification which focuses upon educational rather than etiological variables has been proposed in New Jersey. The new administrative code, when signed into law by the governor, will classify children into three groups: those eligible for related services, those eligible for a part-time special education program, and those eligible for a full-time special education program. Severely and moderately handicapped children will be eligible for full-time programs. The "selection of the appropriate full-time program will be based on matching the specific instructional characteristics of the pupil with the established program eligibility criteria" (Cooperman, 1986).

Apart from a philosophical aspect of the delabeling issue, which is acceptable to a broad range of education, there are some other substantive issues, which should be mentioned. In an abstract sense, complete delabeling is logically impossible. In the context of cognitive development, class inclusion, classification, and labeling are inherently necessary. As a matter of fact, the development of our language is based upon concept development, or in the other words, assignment of "labels" to objects and events.

The argument in the special education literature for delabeling focused on removal of negative labels and not on removal of all classifications.

Another issue to consider in the discussion of delabeling and declassification is the level of socioeconomic development. It appears that economically developing countries with few special education services available are relying on labeling as a process of identification of exceptional children. Such conditions still use traditional categories. More economically prosperous countries, with well-developed special education services, are pursuing the policy of mainstreaming and delabeling.

Transient Culture Minority Students

Services for transient cultural minority students are but one aspect of future special education programs. For the purposes of this discussion, we may identify as a transient cultural minority such groups as, for example, migrant workers in the United States or transient industrial workers with families in European countries. Here we may think of North Africans in France, or Turks, Bulgarians or Romanians in Germany. Apart from unique characteristics specific to each group, there are a number of common issues and trends.

Some of the more important issues can be identified as: different language, culture, socioeconomic variables, as lack of continuity of educational programming. Transient minority children almost always speak at home language, which is different from the one in the host country. Apart from the routine educational difficulties associated with the disrupted lifestyle, linguistic difficulties accentuate the problem of adjustment.

In terms of socioeconomic variables, migrant children usually are of low socioeconomic level. Associated uncomfortable living conditions do not provide for the acquisition of proper study habits. Owing to the frequent moving from location to location, transient learners are exposed to the negative influence of the lack of continuity of educational growth. More research is needed in order to investigate complex educational issues and characteristics of the transient populations. In the future, training of special educators and school psychologists may have to be expanded in order to focus on this special population.

Recently, there has been interest in the fields of genetics and mental retardation, how genetic disorders may affect behavior. Hodopp and Fidler (1999) suggested that such a discussion led to the studies that focused on how different genetic mental retardation disorders are related to cognitive, linguistic, emotional, and behavioral problems. They point out that: "individuals with different genetic mental retardation syndromes are predisposed to different cognitive and linguistic strengths and weaknesses, as well as to different

amounts and types of maladaptive behaviors" (p. 135). Hodapp and Fidler are
suggesting that in the future, information from genetic studies may have direct
application to the teaching methodology in special education.

Education of Children and Adolescents with AIDS

In the near future, complex problems for special education will be presented by children with AIDS (Acquired Immune Deficiency Syndrome)
(Byers, 1989). In 1989, a total of 1,054 pediatric cases had been reported and
502 of these were children below 13 years of age. For these children, the virus
seems to have a more profound effect on brain development and subsequently on the maintenance of motor, intellectual, and developmental milestones. The etiology appears to be related to the calcification of basal ganglia.
Educational complications in surviving children are obvious. Byers (1989)
points out that specific treatments for children infected with HIV (Human
Immunodeficiency Virus) require further research validation, and this should
be a challenge for the field of special education. It is anticipated that with the
passage of Public Law 99-457, which establishes programs of early intervention services to handicapped or developmentally delayed infants and toddlers
(birth through CA 2), children with AIDS will receive necessary special education services. Bartel and Meddock (1989) discussed problems presented by
AIDS in adolescents with learning disabilities. The writers stressed the value
of education in preventing infection and underscored that specific protective
responses can be learned by anyone.

Recently, very significant changes have been evident in eastern Europe
and the Soviet Union. These changes no doubt will affect special education
programs in those regions. Some of the possible anticipated changes are discussed here.

a. The shift from state-controlled to a market economy may create unemployment during the transition period. Those most affected by unemployment will be less skilled, that is, those persons handicapped physically,
intellectually, and emotionally. This situation obviously will place additional
demands on special education.

b. Hopefully, increased standards of living will enable the development of
new programs. It also should be possible to develop new technologies for
persons with a variety of physical, communication or sensory disorders.

c. Two political developments, for example, the decentralization of the
Soviet Union and the democratization of China will no doubt have important
repercussions.

The decentralization of the Soviet Union, the reestablishment of new
independent states, and the formation of the Russian federation will shift all

service-delivery efforts from the centralized control of Moscow. This change will necessitate training of teachers and auxiliary support personnel in language other than Russian. It will also become necessary to reorganize the Academy of Pedagogical Sciences and the Institute of Defectology. Such, or similar, institutions will no doubt be established in other republics.

With the anticipated democratization of China, very significant opportunities will become available for special education. With a population of more than one billion and virtually no services available for exceptional children, the potential for the development of services is almost impossible to estimate. It will take years to train researchers, administrators, and teacher trainers for millions of exceptional individuals.

Global ecological problems and potential nuclear disasters should also be kept in mind as factors contributing to the high-risk potential population. This became more evident following the Chernobyl tragedy in April 1986, which focused upon irradiation as a high-risk factor in mental retardation.

Earlier studies by Murphy (1929; 1949) established a correlation between pelvic X-rays and high-risk potential for mental retardation. The effects of nuclear bombing in Japan were summarized by Miller (1956) and Yamazaki (1966). Miller suggested that the incidence of neurological defects associated with nuclear explosions was related to three factors: the intensity of radiation, the gestational age of the fetus, and the distance of the mother from the center of the explosion. Yamazaki (1966) provided a comprehensive review of the effects of irradiation on the developing nervous system. The most critical time seems to be between the seventh and fifteenth week of gestation. The tragedy of Chernobyl occurred in April 26, 1986. Based upon Yamazaki's suggestion, those most at risk for mental retardation from Chernobyl would have been children conceived approximately January 28, 1986, and March 18, 1986. Those children began kindergarten in the fall of 1991 and the first grade in the fall of 1992. They may constitute a statistical universe for the studies on high-risk potential.

In anticipation of increased international efforts in special education, UNESCO (United Nations Educational, Scientific, and Cultural Organization) initiated in 1983 the development of a "teacher education resource pack" (Ainscow, 1990). The project was divided into three phases. During the first phase (1982–1985), a survey of fourteen countries was conducted by a research team from the University of London's Institute of Education. Two questionnaires were completed by approximately one hundred teachers in each country. In the second phase (1985–1987), a series of workshops was held to discuss implications of the report developed during the first phase. At the end of the third phase (1988–1991), dissemination of teacher education material should have completed. The material entitled "Special Needs in the Classroom" was field tested in 1990. The instructional material encompasses the following crucial features: discussion of active approaches to problem solving; involvement of participants in the negotiation of their own learning objectives, demonstration, practice and feedback, and continuous evaluation.

The future for special education in the context of past practices and issues has been elaborated recently by Kauffman (1999). He identified several past practices that will have implications for the development of special education in the future. Some of Kauffman's critical comments can be summarized as follows: many special educators are unaware and not interested in the history of the field; many are defensive and apologetic; many special educators are unprepared to focus on teaching and learning. However, "much of the research in special education today is not about teaching and learning, and many special educators do little or no direct intensive instruction using the best teaching procedures"; postmodernism and radical deconstructivist philosophy in education is indirectly hindering the development of remedial practices; focusing upon inclusion without improving methodology of teaching will not, by itself, achieve results with exceptional learners. In spite of some critical observation, Kauffman (1999) believes that special education has a future as a profession and a discipline. It has a database of reliable empirical research, clearly defined goals and objectives and the history of an important, socially relevant mission.

In conclusion, a number of observations can be made about special education from a global perspective. First of all, a global perspective about needs and goals of special education has been influenced in the past by a narrow perspective of experiences in industrialized nations such as the United States and western Europe. Socio-political and cultural realities in the twenty-first century will shift to such regions as Africa, China, and Central Asia. National and ethnic groups fighting for their survival and basic economic needs may not value special education to the extent that we do. Within the cultural context, for example, of Afghanistan, Kurdistov, or other developing nations, there may be a different interpretation of the role of industrialized nations. Nevertheless, new technologies such as microcomputers and interactive television will provide exciting opportunities for special education worldwide.

BIBLIOGRAPHY

Abramson, M. (1980). Implications of mainstreaming: A challenge for special education. In L. Mann & D. Sabatino (Eds.), *The fourth review of special education*. New York: Grune & Stratton.

Agaphanova, K.V. (1982). Psychological service in school (roundtable). *Voprosy Psikhologii, 3,* 62–93.

Ahmad, A.B.H., & Singh, S. (1989). News of special education in Malayasia. *Newsletter for Special Education in Asia and the Pacific.*

Ainscow, M. (1990). Special needs in the classroom: The development of a teacher education resource pack. *International Journal of Special Education, 1,* 13–19.

Alberto, P.A., & Troutman, A.C. (1986). *Applied behavioral analogies for teachers* (2nd ed.). Columbus, OH: Charles E. Merrill.

Aleksandrovskaya, M.M., & Boitsova, O.S. (1974). Organization of early identification and registration of mentally and physically handicapped children. *Defectologia, 6,* 3–9.

Algozzine, R.F., & Sutherland, J. (1977). Non-psycho-educational foundations of learning disabilities. *The Journal of Special Education, 1,* 91–99.

American Psychiatric Association. (1980). *Diagnostic and statistical manual of mental disorders* (3rd ed.). Washington, DC: APA.

American Psychological Association. (1984). Accredited doctoral programs in professional psychology. *American Psychologist, 39,* 1466–1472.

Andrews, R.J., & Atkinson, J.K. (1976). The training of special education in Australian Tertiary Institutions. *Exceptional Children, 23,* 175–197.

Arick, J.R., & Krup, D.A. (1993). Special education administrators in the United States: Perceptions on policy and personnel issues. *The Journal of Special Education, 3* (27), 348–364.

Arieti, S. (1974). *Interpretation of schizophrenia* (2nd ed.). New York: Basic Books.

Artiles, A., & Trent, S.C. (1994). Overrepresentation of minority students in special education: A continuing debate. *The Journal of Special Education, 4*(27), 410–438.

Ashby, S.J. (1976). The development of the ability to combine activities in problem solving. Unpublished doctoral dissertation. University of Connecticut.

Assael, D. (Ed.). (1985). Directory, 1984–85 edition: *Handicapped children's early education program.* Chapel Hill, NC: University of North Carolina, Technical Assistance Development System.

Babenkova, R.D. (1973). Training of mentally retarded children: How to breathe correctly during physical exercise. *Defectologia, 3,* 88–90.

Baine, D. (1988). *Handicapped children in developing countries.* Edmonton: University of Alberta Printing Service.

Baker, J.M. (1995). Inclusion in Virginia: Educational experience of students with learning disabilities in one elementary school. *The Journal of Special Education, 29* (2), 116–123.

Baldwin, S. (1985). Models of service delivery: An assessment of some applications and implications for people who are mentally retarded. *Mental Retardation, 1* (23), 6–13.

Ballance, K.E., & Kendall, D.C. (1969). Report on legislation and services for exceptional children in Canada. Revised edition; Council for Exceptional Children, Canadian Committee.

Banach, C. (1979). Reorganization of the system of education in Czechoslovakia. *Bandania O'swiatowe (Educational Research), 4* (16), 132–136.

Banhegyi, F. (1963). Juvenile delinquency, analysis of some factors of its incidence. In M. Bazany (Ed.), *Psychologicka vychovna strostlivost o dieta* (Psycho-educational care of children). Bratislava: Slovak Educational Publisher.

Baran, J. (1974). Preparation of teachers of special schools at the Graduate School of Education in Krakow. *Szkola Specjalna* (Special School), *3,* 257–261.

Bardon, J.I., & Bennett, V.C. (1974). *School psychology.* Englewood Cliffs, NJ: Prentice-Hall.

Baroff, G.S. (1974). *Mental retardation.* New York/London: John Wiley & Sons.

Baroff, G.S. (1999). General learning disorder: A new designation for mental retardation. *Mental Retardation, 1* (37), 68–70.

Bartel, N.R., & Maddock, T.D. (1989). AIDS and adolescents with learning disabilities: Issues for parents and educators. *Journal of Reading, Writing and Learning Disabilities International, 4,* 299–311.

Bartlett, R.H. (1977). Politics, litigation and mainstreaming: Special education demise? *Mental Retardation, 1,* 24–27.

Bateman, B. (1982). Legal and ethical dilemmas of special educators. *Exceptional Education Quarterly, 4,* 57–69.

Batting, W.F. (1975). Within individual differences in "cognitive" process. In R.L. Solso (Ed.), *Information processing and cognition* (pp. 195–228). Hillsdale, NJ: Lawrence Erlbaum Associates.

Bauer, R.A. (1952). *The new man in Soviet psychology.* Cambridge, MA: Harvard University Press.

Bauwins, J., Horeade, J.J., & Friend, M. (1989). Cooperative teaching: A model for general and special education integration. *Remedial and Special Education, 2,* 17–23.

Bazany, C., & Adamovic, K. (1963). Some problems of choice of occupation by pupils of general educational schools. In M. Bazany (Ed.), *Psychologicka vychovna strostlivost o dieta* (Psycho-educational care of children). Bratislava: Slovak Educational Publisher.

Becker, R.L. (1987). The reading-free vocational interest inventory: A topology of vocational clusters. *Mental Retardation, 5* (25), 171–179.

Becker, R.L., & Becker, E.Z. (1983). Revision of the reading-free vocational interest inventory. *Mental Retardation, 4*(21), 144–150.

Bednarczyk-Smolinska, D. (1982). Personal models of rural youth. *Badania Oswiatowe* (Educational Research), *3* (27), 87–104.

Begab, M.J. (Ed.). (1972). Classification of mental retardation. Supplement to the *American Journal of Psychiatry, 11* (128), 1–45.

Belcerek, M. (1977). Organization of special education in Poland. In A. Hulek (Ed.), *Therapeutic pedagogy.* Warsaw: State Scientific Publications.

Bender, W. (1988). The other side of placement decisions, assessment of the mainstream learning environment. *Remedial and Special Education, 5,* 28–33.

Bennett, A. (1932). A comparative study of subnormal children in the elementary grades. *Teachers College contribution to education.* New York: Columbia University Press.

Bercovici, S. (1981). Qualitative methods and cultural perspectives in the study of deinstitutionalization. In R.H. Bruininks, C.E. Meyers, B.B., Sigford, & K.C. Lakin (Eds.), *Deinstitutionalism and community adjustment of M. R. people.* Monograph of the AAMD, W.R. Washington, DC: AAMD.

Berryman, J. (1989). Attitudes of the public toward educational mainstreaming. *Remedial and Special Education, 4,* 44–50.

Bienkowski, J., & Gasiorowski, M. (1979). Main trends in reform in general education schools in the socialist countries. *Badinia Oswiatowe* (Educational Research), *2*(14), 48–56.

Bigge, J., & Sirvis, B. (1986). Physical and health impairments. In N.G. Haring & L. McCormick (Eds.), *Exceptional children and youth* (4th ed., pp. 313–354). Columbus, OH: Merrill.

Binswanger, L. (1963). *Being in the world.* New York: Basic Books.

Birnbaum, A., & Cohen, H.J. (1998). Managed care and quality health services for people with developmental disabilities: Is there a future for UAP's. *Mental Retardation, 4* (36), 325–330.

Black, R., & Langone, J. (1997). Social awareness and transition to employment for adolescents with mental retardation. *Remedial and Special Education, 4* (18), 214–222.

Black, W. (1974). The word explosion in learning disabilities: A notation of literature trends 1962–1974. *Journal of Learning Disabilities, 5,* 66–67.

Blackhurst, A.E., & Hofmeister, A.M. (1980). Technology in special education. In L. Mann & D. Sabatino (Eds.), *The fourth review of special education.* New York: Grune & Stratton.

Blue, M., & Beaty, L.L. (1974). Use of the Peabody Language Development Kits in specific language dysfunction. *The Journal of Special Education, 1,* 73–79.

Blumina, M.G. (1984). Ontogenetic approach to oligophrenia diagnosis. *Defectologia, 3,* 19–24.

Bobla, I.M. (1987). Development of special education for advanced children in the Byelorussian SSR. *Defectologia, 5,* 33–39.

Bodaliou, A.A. (1986). Contemporary status and perspectives of psychology, defectology, and developmental psychology. *Voprosy Psikhologii, 4,* 5–14.

Bodaliou, A.A., & Demidova, S.I. (1987). The psycho-educational provisions of the reform of general educational and professional school (review of the data collected by the Coordinating Board of the Presidium of the Academy of Pedagogical Sciences of the USSR). *Voprosy Psikhologii, 3,* 18–27.

Bogayavlenskaya, D.B. (1980). Psychodiagnosis and school. *Voprosy Psikhologii, 4,* 184–186.

Bogucka, J. (1994). Mentally retarded children in integrated kindergarten and school in Poland. *International Journal of Special Education, 1* (9), 65–70.

Bondar, V.I., & Sasenko, N.F. (1983). Training of defectology specialists in Kiev pedagogical institute. *Defectologia, 4,* 69–71.

Bonnet, K.A. (1989). Learning disabilities: A neurological perspective in humans. *Remedial and Special Education, 3,* 8–20.

Boorer, D.K., & Kirchia, J.B. (1987). Special education in Papua New Guinea: An overview. *International Journal of Special Education, 2,* 151–160.

Borthwick-Duffy, S.A., & Eyman, R.E. (1990). Who are the dually diagnosed? *American Journal on Mental Retardation, 6* (94), 586–595.

Bowker, L., Gross, H., & Klein, M. (1980). Female participation in delinquent gang activities. *Adolescence, 59,* 509–519.

Boyanjiu, K. (1985). Rumanian communist party policy in the sphere of peoples education and characteristics of labor education, occupational training and social involvement of exceptional children and youth. *Defectologia, 2,* 58–62.

Bozhovich, E.D. (1983). Experimental organization of psycho-pedagogical consultation in school. *Voprosy Psikhologi, 6,* 8.

Braddock, D. (1977). *Opening closed doors: The deinstitutionalization of disabled individuals.* Reston, VA: Council of Exceptional Children.

Braddock, D., Hemp, R., & Fujura, G. (1987). National study of public spending for mental retardation and developmental disabilities. *American Journal of Mental Deficiency, 2* (92), 121–133.

Braddock, D., & Heller, T. (1985). The closure of mental retardation institutions 1: Trends in the United States. *Mental Retardation, 4* (23),168–176.

Braddock, D., & Heller, T. (1985). The closure of mental retardation institutions II: Implications. *Mental Retardation, 5* (23), 222–230.

Brand, J.S. (1987). Mexico, special education in. In C. Reynolds & L. Mann (Eds.), *Encyclopedia of special education.* New York/Singapore: John Wiley & Sons.

Braswell, D. (1987). France, special education. In C.R. Reynolds & L. Mann (Eds.), *Encyclopedia of special education.* Newark/Toronto: John Wiley & Sons.

Braswell, D. (1987). Western Europe, special education. In C.R. Reynolds & L. Mann (Eds.), *Encyclopedia of special education.* Newark, NJ/Toronto: John Wiley & Sons.

Brown, D.T. (1989). Psychological service in New Zealand. In P. Saigh & T. Oakland (Eds.), *International perspective on psychology in the schools.* Hillsdale, NJ: Lawrence Erlbaum Associates.

Brown, L., & Bryant, B.R. (1984). The why and how of special norms. *Remedial and Special Education, 4,* 52–61.

Bruck, H. (1974). Perils of behavior modification in treatment of anorexia nervosa. *Journal of the American Medical Association, 230,* 1419–1422.

Bruininks, R.H., & Warfield, G. (1978). The mentally retarded. In E.L. Meyer (Ed.), *Exceptional children and youth: An introduction.* Denver, CO: Love.

Brunet, L., Lubovsky, V.I., Ibanex, M., & Wadall, R. (1983). *Terminology of special education* (rev. ed.). Paris: UNESCO.

Burli, A. (1987). Switzerland, special education. In C.R. Reynolds & L. Mann (Eds.), *Encyclopedia of special education.* Newark, NJ/Toronto: John Wiley & Sons.

Byers, J. (1989). AIDS in children: Effects or neurological development and implication for the future. *The Journal of Special Education, 1,* 5–16.

Cardon, B.W. (1975). Law, professional practice and university preparation: Where do we go from here? *Journal of School Psychology, 4,* 377–386.

Carlson, K., & Simcoe, A. (1999). Personal communication.

Carlson, L. (1980). Special education in Saskatchewan. In M. Csapo & L. Goguen (Eds.), *Special education across Canada*. Vancouver, BC: Centre for Human Development and Research.

Caro, I., & Miralles, M. (1989). School psychology in Spain. In P. Saigh & T. Oakland (Eds.), *International perspectives on psychology in the schools*. Hillsdale, NJ: Lawrence Erlbaum Associates.

Cartwright, G.P., & Hall, K.A. (1974). A review of computer uses in special education. In L. Mann & D. Sabatino (Eds.), *The second review of special education*. Philadelphia: Journal of Special Education Press.

Cates, D. (1994). Preparing teachers of children with multiple disabilities for the 21st century. *International Journal of Special Education, 2* (9), 101–106.

Cegelka, P.T., & Prehm, H.J. (1982). *Mental retardation*. Columbus, OH: Charles E. Merrill.

Cegelka, W.J. (1982). The competencies needed by persons responsible for classifying children with learning disabilities. *The Journal of Special Education, 1* (16), 65–73.

Chalfont, J.C., & Psych, M.V. (1984). Teacher assistant teams (workshop material). Tucson, AZ: University of Arizona.

Chalfont, J.C., & Van Duser Pysh, M. (1989). Teacher assistance teams: Five descriptive studies on 96 teams. *Remedial and Special Education, 6,* 49–58.

Chamberlain, J. (1989). School psychology services in Ireland. In P. Saign & T. Oakland (Eds.), *International perspectives on psychology in the schools*. Hillsdale, NJ: Lawrence Erlbaum Associates.

Chang, M.K. (1992). Training of special educators for underdeveloped countries: A conceptual model. *International Journal of Special Education, 1* (7), 82–88.

Chase, J.B. (1975). Developmental assessment of handicapped infants and young children with special attention to visually impaired. *The New Outlook for the Blind,* 341–364.

Chepelev, V.O. (1970). *Public education in the Ukrainian SSR*. Kiev: Radyanska Shkola Publishing House.

Chesley, G.M., & Caluluce, P.D. (1997). The deception of inclusion. *Mental Retardation, 6* (35), 488–490.

Chikombah, C.E.M. (1988). *Education issues in Zimbabwe since independence*. Stockholm University, Institute of International Education.

Cimera, R.E. (1998). Are individuals with severe mental retardation and multiple disabilities cost efficient to serve via supported employment program? *Mental Retardation, 4* (36), 280–293.

Church, E.G. (1980). Special education in Alberta, past accomplishments, present issues and future prospects. In M. Csapo & L. Goguen (Eds.), *Special education across Canada*. Vancouver, BC: Centre for Human Development and Research.

Clausen, J. (1966). *Ability structure and subgroups in mental retardation*. Washington, DC/London: Spartan Books.

Cole, M. (1984). The world beyond our borders: What might our students need to know about it. *American Psychologist, 39,* 998–1006.

Coleman, J.M., Pullis, M.E., & Minnett, A.M. (1987). Studying mildly handicapped children's adjustment to mainstreaming: A systematic approach. *Remedial and Special Education, 6* (8), 19–31.

Commission of the European Communities. (1986). Progress with regard to the implementation of the policy of integrating handicapped children into ordinary schools. Brussels.

Condon, M. (1993). Rehabilitation and special education in Kunming, Peoples Republic of China. *International Journal of Special Education, 2* (81), 134–146.

Cooperman, S. (1986). *A plan to revise special education in New Jersey.* Trenton, NJ: State Department of Education.

Cosdew, M.A. (1988). Microcomputer instruction and perception of effectiveness by special and regular education elementary school teachers. *The Journal of Special Education, 2,* 242–253.

Csapo. M. (1988). Development of education and special education in the kingdom of Swaziland. *International Journal of Special Education, 2,* 125–140.

Csapo, M. (1987). Comparison of socio-moral judgments of Hungarian regular and special school students in grade two. *International Journal of Special Education, 2,* 161–183.

Csapo, M. (1984). Special education in the USSR: Trends and accomplishments. *Remedial and Special Education, 5,* 5–15.

Csapo, M., & Gogner, L. (Eds.). (1980). *Special education across Canada.* Vancouver, BC: Centre for Human Development and Research.

Cutts, N.E. (Ed.). (1955). *School psychologist at mid-century.* Washington, DC: American Psychological Association.

Danford, J.S., Barkley, R.A., & Stokes, T.F. (1991). Observations of parent-child interactions with hyperactive children: Research and clinical implications. *Clinical Psychology Review, 6* (11), 703–729.

Danielov, M.B., & Utin, A.V. (1987). Medico-genetic counseling of families of the mentally retarded empirical risk data. *Soviet Neurology and Psychiatry, 1* (20), 46–53.

Danielson, L.C., & Bauer, J.N. (1978). A formula-based classification of learning disabled children: Examination of the issue. *Journal of Learning Disabilities, 11,* 163–176.

Davis, W.E. (1989). The regular education initiative debate: Its promises and problems. *Exceptional Children, 2,* 440–446.

de la Meuse, N.M. (1989). School psychology in Chile. In P. Saigh & T. Oakland (Eds.), *International perspective on psychology in the schools.* Hillsdale, NJ: Lawrence Erlbaum Associates.

Demidov, A.Y. (1973). An inborn heart disease under Down's syndrome. *Defectologia, 2,* 15–17.

Demontyeva, N.D., Poperechnaya, L.N., & Tabunova, E.V. (1988). The problem of needs in severely mentally retarded adolescents. *Defectologia, 6,* 23–28.

DeMyer, M.K. (1976). The nature of the neuropsychological disability in autistic children. In E. Schopher & R. Reichler (Eds.), *Psychopathology and child development.* New York/London: Plenum Press.

Denckla, M. (1972). Clinical syndromes in learning disabilities: The case of splitting vs. lumping. *Journal of Learning Disabilities, 7,* 26–72.

Depaepe, M. (1985). Science, technology and paedology: The concept of science at the Faculte Internationale de Pedologic in Brussels (1912–1914). *Science Paedagogica Experimentalis, 1,* 14–28.

Desforges, M.F. (1995). Assessment of special educational needs in bilingual pupils: Changing practice? *School Psychology International, 1* (16), 5–19.

Detterman, D.K., & Thompson, L.A. (1997). What is so special about special education? *American Psychologist, 10* (52), 1082–1090.

Diagnostic and Statistical Manual of Mental Disorders (3rd ed. rev.). (1987). Washington, DC: American Psychiatric Associates.

Diamond, G.W. (1989). Developmental problems in children with HIV infection. *Mental Retardation, 4,* 213–217.

Diedzic, S. (1986). Educational care of the severely retarded. *Szkola Specjalna, 3,* 206–222.

Dinzhu, L. (1989). Special education in China. *Newsletter for Special Education in Asia and the Pacific, 1,* 3.

Documentation. (1989). Publication De-Deutschen Demokratisahen Republic, Ministerion fur Volksbildung.

Dolek, N., Inceoglu, D., & Ozdemir, N. (1989). School psychology in Turkey. In P. Saign & T. Oakland (Eds.), *International perspective on psychology in the schools.* Hillsdale, NJ: Lawrence Erlbaum Associates.

Doll, E.A. (1974). Feeble–mindedness versus intellectual retardation. *American Journal of Mental Deficiency, 51,* 456–459.

Donald, D., & Csapo, M. (1989). School psychology in South Africa. In P. Saigh & T. Oakland (Eds.), *International perspective on psychology in the schools.* Hillsdale, NJ: Lawrence Erlbaum Associates.

Doren, B., & Benz, M.R. (1998). Employment inequality revisited: Predictors of better employment outcomes for young women with disabilities in transition. *The Journal of Special Education, 4* (36), 425–443.

Drash, Ph.W., Raven, S.A., & Murrin, M.R. (1987). Total habilitation as a major goal of intervention in mental retardation. *Mental Retardation, 2* (25), 67–69.

Dubrovyna, I.V., & Prykhozhan, A.M. (1982). Psychological service in school (roundtable). *Voprosy Psikhologii, 3,* 62–93.

Ducey, Ch., & Simon, B. (1975). Ancient Greece and Rome. In J.G. Howells (Ed.), *World history of psychiatry.* New York: Brunner/Mazel.

Dumont, F., & Karer-Fine, E. (1989). School psychology in Canada: A selective service of recent research trends. *Professional School Psychology, 4* (3), 209–217.

DuPaul, G.J., Guevremont, D.C., & Barkley, R.A. (1991). Attention deficit hyperactivity disorder in adolescence: Critical assessment parameters. *Clinical Psychology Review, 3* (11), 231–247.

Dunn, L.M. (1968). Special education for the mildly retarded–Is much of it justifiable? *Exceptional Children, 34,* 5–22.

Dutkiewicz, K. (1983). Influence of social variables on mental abilities of primary school graduates in urban rural areas. *Badania Oswiatowe, 1* (1), 71–86.

Dziedzic, J. (1976). Problems of education of physical education teachers for ten year special schools. *Szkola Specjalna, 2*, 54–63.

Dziedzic, S. (1977). History of the development of special education in Poland. In A. Hulek (Ed.), *Therapeutic education.* Warsaw: State Scientific Publishers.

Dziedzic, S. (1969). Pseudo-oligophrenia. *Szkola Specjalna, 4* (31), 359–366.

Egel, A.L., Koegel, R.L., & Schreibman, L. (1980). Review of educational-treatment procedures for autistic children. In L. Mann & D. Sabatino (Eds.), *The fourth review of special education.* New York: Grune & Stratton.

Eikeland, T. (1973). A short visit to Moscow and The Institute of Defectology, and some late-reflections on pre-school language training. *Scandinavian Audiology, 2* (2), 75–81.

Eisenberg, B.I. (1981). Study of suggestibility in oligophrenics. *Defectologia, 1,* 28–33.

Elder, P.S., & Bergman, J.S. (1978). Visual symbol communication instruction with non-verbal multiply handicapped individuals. *Mental Retardation, 2,* 109–112.

Eldridge, M. (1968). *A history of the treatment of speech disorders.* Edinburgh & London: Ea. S. Livingstone, Ltd.

Elliott, S.N. (1991). Authentic assessment: An introduction to a neobehavioral approach to classroom assessment. *School Psychology Quarterly, 4* (6), 273–278.

Ek, V.V. (1985). Mathematics class in preliminary course for the mentally retarded. *Defectologia, 4,* 415–450.

Elska, V. (1985). Organization of vocational training of abnormal children in special schools in Polish Peoples Republic. *Defectologia, 1,* 62.

Em, E.B. (1974). Pedagogical study of elementary grade pupils of an auxiliary school. *Defectologia, 1,* 33–40.

Emanulsson, I. (1985). Integration of handicapped pupils in Sweden: Concepts, research experience, present practices. National Swedish Board of Education, Information Section S-10642, Stockholm.

Epeni, Y. (1981). The development of schools for special education in Japan. *NISE Bulletin, 1,* 10–16.

Evans, R.A. (1964). Word recall and associative clustering in mental retardation. *American Journal of Mental Deficiency, 69,* 413–418.

Ewalt, J.R. (1972). Differing concepts of diagnosis as a problem in classification. In M.J. Begab (Ed.), *Classification of mental retardation.* Supplement to the *American Journal of Psychiatry, 11* (125), 1–45.

Eyman, R., Meyers, E., & Tarjan, P. (Eds.). (1973). *Socio-behavioral studies in mental retardation.* Los Angeles, CA: University of Southern California. (AAMD Monographs, N. 1).

Ezello, B.N. (1989). School psychology in Nigeria. In P. Saigh & T. Oakland (Eds.), *International perspective on psychology in the schools.* Hillsdale, NJ: Lawrence Erlbaum Associates.

Farnham-Diggory, S. (1972). *Information processing in children.* New York: Academic Press.

Federal Register. (1977, August 23). Volume 24, No. 163. Washington, DC: U.S. Government Printing Office.

Feniak, C. (1988). Labeling in special education: A problematic issue in England and Wales. *International Journal of Special Education, 2,* 117–124.

Fex, Britt-Inger. (1987). Sweden, special education. In C.R. Reynolds, & L. Mann (Eds.), *Encyclopedia of special education.* Newark, NJ/Toronto: John Wiley & Sons.

Figueroa, R.A. (1983). Test bias and Hispanic children. *The Journal of Special Education, 4,* 431–452.

Filkina, L.M. (1977). Actual extent of social pre-school upbringing of atypical children and several problems of its further development. *Defectologia, 1,* 3–11.

Finn, C.E. Jr., Manno, B.V., Birleim, L.A., & Vanourek, G. (1997). *Charter schools in action: Final report.* Washington, DC: Hudson Institute.

Fish, M.C., & Vorwald, R.V. (1989). School psychology inEl Salvador. In P. Saigh & T. Oakland (Eds.), *International perspective on psychology in schools.* Hillsdale, NJ: Lawrence Erlbaum Associates.

Fisher, D., Kent, H., & Fraser, B. (1998). Relationships between teacher-student interpersonal behavior and teacher personality. *School Psychology International, 2* (19), 99–121.

Fishman, M.N., & Malinauskene, V.A. (1979). An EEG study of emotionally disturbed oligophrenic adolescents. *Defectologia, 1,* 19–24.

Formakova, A.I. (1974). Individual upbringing and training of children with complicated form of oligophrenia. *Defectologia, 2,* 55–59.

Foster-Gaitskell, D., & Pratt, C. (1989). Comparison of parent and teacher ratings of adaptive behavior of children with mental retardation. *American Journal on Mental Retardation, 2,* 177–182.

Fuchs, D. (1997). (As quoted in *The New York Times,* December 28, 1997.)

Fuchs, D., Fuchs, L., & Fernstrom, P. (1993). A conservative approach to special education reform: Mainstreaming through transenvironmental programming and curriculum based measurement. *American Educational Research Journal, 1* (30), 149–179.

Fuchs, D., Fuchs, L., Power, M.H., & Dailey, A.M. (1985). Bias in the assessment of handicapped children. *American Educational Research Journal, 2,* 185–199.

Fuchs, L.S., & Fuchs, D. (1986). Curriculum-based assessment of progress toward long-term and short-term goals. *The Journal of Special Education, 1,* 69–83.

Fuchs, L.S., & Fuchs, D. (1984). Criterion-referenced assessment without measurement: How accurate for special education? *Remedial and Special Education, 4,* 29–33.

Gaiduk, F.M., Slepovitch, E.S., & Asanova, N.K. (1984). Practice of organizing service for developmentally backward children in Byelorussian SSR. *Defectologia, 2,* 32–35.

Garvan-Pinhas, A., & Schmelkin, L.P. (1989). Administrators' and teachers' attitudes toward mainstreaming. *Remedial and Special Education, 4,* 38–44.

Gavor, I.I. (1976). Work of auxiliary boarding school with parents of students. *Defectologia, 3,* 72–78.

Gazova, A.P. (1985). Labor training of deaf students. *Defectologia, 4,* 29–32.

Gearheart, B.R., Weisbahn, M.W., & Gearheart, C.J. (1988). *The exceptional student in the regular classroom* (4th ed.). Columbus, Toronto: Charles E. Merrill.

Gerner, M. (1990). Living and working overseas: School psychologists in American international schools. *School Psychology Quarterly, 1* (5), 21–32.

Gibasiewicz, J. (1976). Work of self-instruction team of special nursery school teachers. *Szkola Specjalna, 4,* 43–47.

Gittins, J.A. (1980). Special education in British Columbia. In M. Csapo & L. Goguen (Eds.), *Special education across Canada*. Vancouver, BC: Centre for Human Development and Research.

Glueck, S., & Glueck, E.T. (1934). *One thousand juvenile delinquents*. Cambridge, MA: Harvard University Press.

Goetzinger, C.P., & Proud, G. (1975). The impact of hearing impairment upon the psychological development of children. *American Journal of Auditory Research, 1,* 1–16.

Goguen, L.J. (1980). Right to education for exceptional children in Canada: A growing national concern. In M. Csapo & L. Goguen (Eds.), *Special education across Canada*. Vancouver, BC: Centre for Human Development and Research.

Goldhamer, H., & Marshall, A. (1953). *Psychosis and civilization*. Glencoe, IL: The Free Press.

Good, H.G. (1956). *A history of American education*. New York: Macmillan.

Gordienko, E.A. (1985). Status of education of abnormal children in Uzbek SSR. *Defectologia, 1,* 34–39.

Gordienko, E.A., & Zapriagayev, G.G. (1984). Prevention of delinquency among mentally retarded teenagers. *Defectologia, 3,* 45–49.

Gottlieb, J., Alter, M., Gotlieb, B.W., & Wishman, J. (1994). Special education in urban America: It is not justifiable for many. *The Journal of Special Education, 4* (27), 453–466.

Greenham, F.M., MacMillan, D.L., & Siperstein, G.N. (1995). Critical analysis of the 1992 AAMR definition: Implications for school psychology. *School Psychology Quarterly, 1* (10), 1–20.

Gregory, J.F., Shanahan, T., & Walberg, H. (1985). Learning disabled 10th graders in mainstreamed settings: A descriptive analysis. *Remedial and Special Education*.

Grey, M. (1978). *Neuroses*. New York: Van Nostrand Reinhold.

Grigonis, A.V. (1987). Recall of visual material in mentally retarded children. *Defectologia, 4,* 3–6.

Grigoryeva, L.P., Konulratyeva, S.I., & Stashevsky, S.V. (1988). Perception of color drawings by school children with normal and impaired vision. *Defectologia, 5,* 20–29.

Grimes, S.K., & Vitello, S.J. (1990). A follow-up study of family attitudes toward deinstitutionalization: Five to seven years later. *Mental Retardation, 29,* 219–223.

Grossman, H.J. (1983). *Classification in mental retardation*. Washington, DC: American Association on Mental Deficiency.

Grossman, H. (Ed.). (1973). *Manual of terminology and classification in mental retardation*. Washington, DC: American Association on Mental Retardation.

Grossman, H.J. (Ed.). (1983). *Classification in mental retardation*. Washington, DC: American Association on Mental Deficiency.

Guglielnis, P.S., & Tatrow, K. (1998). Occupational stress, burnout and health in teachers: A methodological and theoretical analysis. *Review of Educational Research, 1*(68), 61–91.

Guillemard, J.C. (1989). School psychology in France. In P. Saigh & T. Oakland (Eds.), *International perspectives on psychology in the schools*. Hillsdale, NJ: Lawrence Erlbaum Associates.

Gumpel, T. (1996). Special education law in Israel. *The Journal of Special Education, 4* (29), 457–468.

Haiduk, F.M., Slepovitch, E.S., & Asanova, N.K. (1984). Practice of organizing service for developmentally backward children in Byelorussian SSR. *Defectologia, 2*, 32–35.

Hakola, S. (1992). Legal rights of students with attention deficit disorders. *School Psychology Quarterly, 4* (2), 285–298.

Hallahan, D., & Kauffman, J. (1978). *Exceptional children: An introduction to special education*. Englewood Cliffs, NJ: Prentice-Hall.

Halleck, S.L. (1972). Delinquency. In B.B. Wolman (Ed.), *Manual of child psychopathology*. New York: McGraw-Hill.

Hamdi, N., & Hamdi, N. (1989). School psychology in Jordan. In P. Saigh & T. Oakland (Eds.), *International perspective on psychology in the schools*. Hillsdale, NJ: Lawrence Erlbaum Associates.

Hammill, D.D., & Wiederholt, J.L. (1973). Review of Frostig Visual Perception Test and related training program. In L. Mann & D. Sabatino (Eds.), *The first review of special education*. Philadelphia: Journal of Special Education Press.

Hand, J. (1982). Special education in Australia. *Exceptional Child, 29*, 137–148.

Handicapped Students in the Danish Educational System. (1986). A survey prepared for the IX international school psychology colloquium. Ministry of Education.

Hanneman, R., & Blacher, J. (1998). Predicting placement in families who have children with severe handicaps: A longitudinal analysis. *American Journal of Mental Retardation, 4* (102), 392–408.

Harding, V.B. (1982). Designing continuing education programs for special educators. *Exceptional Education Quarterly, 4* (2), 77–86.

Hardman, M.L., Drew, C.J., & Egan, M.W. (1996). *Human exceptionality, society, school and family* (5th ed.). Boston/Toronto: Allyn and Bacon.

Harkins, D. (1998). Hope, opportunity and possibility: Supporting people with developmental disabilities at the end of the 20th century. *Mental Retardation, 2* (36), 163–165.

Harris, J.R. (1974). A participant observer study: The everyday life of a group of delinquent boys. *Adolescence, 33*, 31–48.

Hartman, A.C. (1979). The directive teaching instructional management system: How it can help teachers. *The Directive Teacher, 4*, 3–5.

Hasselbring, T.S. (1984). Computer-based assessment of special-needs students. In R.E. Bennett & C.A. Maher (Eds.), *Microcomputers and exceptional children*. New York: The Haworth Press.

Hatlen, Ph.H., Hall, A.P., & Tuttle, D. (1980). Education of visually handicapped: An overview and update. In L. Mann & D. Sabatino (Eds.), *The fourth review of special education*. New York: Grune & Stratton.

Haywood, H.C. (1977). Alternative to normative assessment. In P. Mitler (Ed.), *Research to practice in mental retardation* (Vol. 11). Baltimore: University Park Press.

Heber, R.F. (1961). A manual on terminology and classification in mental retardation. *American Journal of Mental Deficiency, 64.* Monograph supplement (2nd ed.).

Heifitz, L.J. (1987). Integrating religious and secular perspectives in the design and delivery of disability services. *Mental Retardation, 3* (25), 127–133.

Helge, D. (1987). Strategies for improving rural special education program evaluation. *Remedial and Special Education, 4,* 53–60.

Heller, T. (1930). Uben dementia infantilis. *Zeitshrift Kinderforsheng, 37,* 661–667. (Hulse, U.C. translation. About dementia infantilis.) *Journal of Nervous Mental Disorders,* 1954, *119,* 471–477.

Henderson, R. (1989). Delivery of special education in Australia, New Zealand and the United States, similarities and differences. *International Journal of Special Education, 1,* 25–32.

Herries, J. (1968). The elements of speech in 1773. In R.C. Alston (Ed.), *English 1500–1800 linguistic.* Menston: The Scholar Press Limited.

Hessler, G.L. (1986). The issue of intellectual ability in severe discrepancy analysis for the determination of learning disabilities. *Remedial and Special Education, 7* (40), 58–60.

Hewett, F.M., & Forness, S.R. (1977). *Education of exceptional learners* (2nd ed.). Boston: Allyn & Bacon.

Hickson, J., & Skvy, M. (1990). Creativity and cognitive modificability in gifted disadvantaged pupils: A promising alliance. *School Psychology International, 4* (11), 295–303.

Hill, B.K., & Lakin, K.C. (1986). Classification of residential facilities for individuals with mental retardation. *Mental Retardation, 2* (24), 107–115.

Hill, M., & Wehman, P. (1983). Cost benefit analysis of placing moderately and severely handicapped individuals into competitive employment. *Journal of the Association for the Severely Handicapped, 8* (1), 30–38.

Hobson, R.P., Ouston, J., & Lee, A. (1989). Recognition of emotion by mentally retarded adolescents and young adults. *American Journal on Mental Retardation, 4,* 434–444.

Holland, K. (Ed.). (1960). *Report of the 11E seminar on Education in the Soviet Union.* November 19–20, 1959. New York: Institute of International Education.

Holmes, B. (Ed.). (1980). *International yearbook of education* (Volume 32). Paris: UNESCO.

Holmes Group. (1986). *Tomorrow's teachers: A report of the Holmes Group.* East Lansing, MI: The Holmes Group.

Holowinsky, I.Z. (1980). Qualitative assessment of cognitive skills. *Journal of Special Education, 14,* 155–163.

Holowinsky, I.Z. (1980). Special education in Poland and the Soviet Union: Current developments. In L. Mann & D. Sabatino (Eds.), *The fourth review of special education.* New York: Grune & Stratton.

Holowinsky, I.Z. (1982). Current mental retardation research in the Soviet Union. *The Journal of Special Education, 3,* 369–378.

Holowinsky, I.Z. (1983). *Psychology and education of exceptional children and adolescents.* Princeton, NJ: Princeton Book Company Publishers.

Holowinsky, I.Z. (1983). Research on developmentally delayed children in the Soviet Union. *The Journal of Special Education, 3* (17), 365–369.

Holowinsky, I.Z. (1984). Assessment of cognitive skills in the USSR: Historical trends and current developments. *The Journal of Special Education, 4* (18), 541–545.

Holowinsky, I.Z. (1984). Terminology, classification and educational services for the mentally retarded in the USSR. In J.M. Berg (Ed.), *Perspective and programs in mental retardation.* V. 1, Social, Psychological and Educational Aspects. Baltimore: University Park Press, International Association for the Scientific Study of Mental Deficiency.

Holowinsky, I.Z. (1985). Task for improvement of teaching mathematics in special schools in light of main trends of the reform of comprehensive and professional school. *Defectologia, 2,* 36–39.

Holowinsky, I.Z. (1986). An international perspective on terminology, prevalence, and classification of cognitive disabilities. *The Journal of Special Education, 3,* 385–391.

Holowinsky, I.Z. (1986). School psychology in the USA and USSR. *School Psychology International, 7,* 35–39.

Holowinsky, I.Z. (1988). Vygotsky and the history of pedology. *School Psychology International.*

Holowinsky, I.Z. (1993). Chornobyl nuclear catastrophe and the high risk potential for mental retardation. *Mental Retardation, 1* (31), 35–40.

Holowinsky, I.Z. (1996). Chornobyl children: Psycho-educational development ten years after the catastrophe. *The Ukrainian Quarterly, 1* (52), 5–13.

Holtzman, W.H. (1989). School psychology in Mexico. In P. Saigh & T. Oakland (Eds.), *International perspective in schools.* Hillsdale, NJ: Lawrence Erlbaum Associates.

Hope, R.D., & Andrews, D.A. (1992). Assessing conduct problems in the classroom. *Clinical Psychology Review, 1* (12), 1–21.

Howells, J.G. (1975). *World history of psychiatry.* New York: Brunner/Mazel.

Hroza, T.A. (1985). History of education of visually impaired children in Ukrainian SSR. *Defectologia, 2,* 69–76.

Hu, S., Oakland, T., & Salili, F. (1988). School psychology in Hong Kong. *School Psychology International, 1,* 21–28.

Huebner, E.S. (1991). Bias in special education decisions: The contribution of analogue research. *School Psychology Quarterly, 1* (6), 50–66.

Hulek, A. (1978). Personnel preparation: International comparison. Paper presented at the First World Congress on Future Special Education. Sterling, Scotland, June.

Hulek, A. (1979). Basic assumptions in mainstreaming exceptional children and youth. *Badamna Oswiatowe* (Educational Research), *3* (15), 99–112.

Hulek, A. (1979). Foundations of the integration training and education system of handicapped children and youth. *Badania Oswiatowe, 3* (15), 99–114.

Hulek, A. (1989). *Current status and direction of restarting of special education in Poland.* Warsaw-Moscow: State Scholarly Publishers.

Hulek, A. (1986). Personnel in special education. *Paideia, 13,* 261–270.

Iano, R.P. (1986). The study and development of teaching: With implications for the advancement of special education. *Remedial and Special Education, 5* (7), 50–61.

Idol, L. (1989). The resource consulting teacher: An integrated model of service delivery. *Remedial and Special Education, 6,* 38–49.

Ignar-Golinowska, B. (1985). School failures of fourteen-year-old students with different progress in adolescence. *Badania Oswiatowe, 3* (11), 89–104.

Ingram, C.P. (1960). *Education of the slow-learning child* (3rd ed.). New York: Ronald.

Intapliata, J., Crosby, N., & Neider, L. (1981). Foster family care for mentally retarded people: A qualitative review. In R.H. Bruininks (Ed.), *Deinstitutionalization and community adjustment of the mostly retarded people.* Washington, D.C.

Ippolitova, M.V. (1985). Task for improvement of teaching mathematics in special schools in light of main trends of the reform of comprehensive and professional school. *Defectologia, 2,* 36–39.

Irvin, P. (1977). Pedro de Ponce de Leon (1520–1584): A biographical sketch. *The Journal of Special Education, 4,* 347.

Irwin, P. (1974). Valentin Hay (1745–1822). A biographical sketch. *The Journal of Special Education, 1* (8), 4.

Irwin, P. (1977). Samuel Heinicke (1727–1790): A biographical sketch. *The Journal of Special Education, 1,* 2.

Ivannykov, V.A. (1982). Psychological service in school (roundtable). *Voprosy Psikhologii, 4,* 75–103.

Jacob, E. (1987). Qualitative research traditions: A review. *Review of Educational Research, 1* (57), 1–50.

Jacob, E. (1988). Classifying qualitative research: A focus on tradition. *Educational Research, 1,* 16–25.

Jarosz, F. (1979). Actual status and anticipated development of special education in Peoples Poland. *Studia Pedagogiczne, 40,* 77–90.

Johnson, D., & Myklebust, H.R. (1967). *Learning disabilities.* New York/London: Grune & Stratton.

Johnson, G.O. (1963). *Education for slow learners.* Englewood Cliffs, NJ: Prentice-Hall.

Johnson, R., & Carter, M. (1980). Flight of the young: Why children run away from their homes. *Adolescence, 58,* 483–489.

Jordan, R., Libby, S., & Powell, M.S. (1995). Theories of autism: Why do they matter? *School Psychology International, 3* (16), 291–303.

Juul, K.D. (1989). Some common and unique features of special education in the Nordic countries. *The fourth review of special education.* New York/London: Grune & Stratton.

Juul, K.D. (1980). Special education in Western Europe and Scandinavia. In L. Mann & D.A. Sabatino (Eds.), *The fourth review of special education.* New York/London: Grune & Stratton.

Juul, K.D. (1978). European approaches and innovations in serving the handicapped. *Exceptional Children, 44,* 322–330.

Kabele, F. (1978). *Czechoslovakia in economic aspects of special education.* Paris: UNESCO.

Kabzems, V.L. (1959). Teacher training in special education in Zimbabwe. Paper presented at the International Conference on Special Education, University of British Columbia, Vancouver, BC, May 17–20, 1989.

Kahn, J.V. (1977). A comparison of manual and oral language training with mute retarded children. *Mental Retardation, 3,* 21–23.

Kairov, L.A. (1963). The new CPSU program and the tasks of pedagogical science. *Soviet Pedagogy, 3,* 3–16.

Kairov, I.A., Makarenko, H.S., & Medynsky, E.N. (1950). *A.S. Makarenko's collected works.* Moskow: Academy of Pedagogical Sciences of R.S.F.S.R.

Kalizhniuk, E.A., & Sapunova, Y.V. (1975). Disturbance of visual-spatial perception of C.P. pre-school children and several methods of its remediation. *Defectologia, 6,* 17–24.

Kamin, L.J. (1976). Heredity, intelligence, politics and psychology. In N.J. Block & P. Dworkin (Eds.), *The IQ controversy.* New York: Pantheon Press.

Kanner, L. (1960). Itard, Seguin, Howe: Three pioneers in the education of retarded children. *American Journal of Mental Deficiency, 65,* 2–10.

Kanner, L. (1976). Historical perspective on developmental deviation. In E. Schopler & R. Riechler (Eds.), *Psycho-pathology and child development.* New York: Plenum Press.

Kanner, L. (1949). Problems of nosology and psycholodynamics of early infantile autism. *American Journal of Orthopsychiatry, 19,* 416–426.

Kanner, L. (1943). Autistic disturbances of affective content. *Nervous Child, 2,* 217–250.

Karpova, A.N., Kerpov, B.A., & Isayev, D.N. (1977). Investigation of eye movements in the process of reading in oligophrenic children. *Defectologia, 5,* 25–33.

Karpukhina, P.P. (1980). Differential approach to studying children during the onset of stuttering. *Defectologia, 1,* 66–70.

Karrer, R. (Ed.). (1976). *Developmental psychophysiology of mental retardation: Concepts and studies.* Springfield, IL: Charles C Thomas.

Karvialis, V., Budriavichi, A., Rushkus, Y., Dzekunskene, D., Slavitskas, B., Shatavichus, V., & Skatinaite, E. (1986). Problems of organization of labor training in school for mentally retarded in Lithuanian-SSR. *Defectologia, 2,* 27–32.

Kasanin, J., & Kaufman, M.R. (1929). A study of the functional psychoses in children. *American Journal of Psychiatry, 86,* 307–384.

Kauffman, J.M., Lloyd, J.W., & McGee, K.A. (1989). Adaptive and maladaptive behavior: Teachers' attitudes and their technical assistance needs. *The Journal of Special Education, 2,* 185–200.

Kauffman, J.M., Strang, H.R., & Loper, A.B. (1985). Using micro-computers to train teachers of the handicapped. *Remedial and Special Education, 5* (6), 13–17.

Kaufman, J.M. (1985). *Characteristics of children's behavior disorders* (3rd ed.). Columbus, OH: Charles E. Merrill.

Kavale, K.A. (1982). Metaanalysis of the relationship between visual perceptual skills and reading achievement. *Journal of Learning Disabilities, 15,* 42–51.

Kavale, K.A., & Foremen, S.R. (1987). History, politics and the general education initiative: Sleeters reinterpretation of learning disabilities as a case study. *Remedial and Special Education, 5,* 6–12.

Karvelis, V.J. (1979). Progress of special education in Lithuania. *Defectologia, 1,* 33–38.

Katz, S., & Kravetz, S. (1989). Plastic surgery for persons with Down syndrome: From evaluation to recommendations. *American Journal on Mental Retardation, 2,* 119–121.

Kauffman, J.M. (1999). Commentary: Today's special education and its message for tomorrow. *The Journal of Special Education, 4* (32), 244–254.

Kaufman, J.M., & Pullen, P.L. (1989). REI movement throwing baby out with the both? *Virginia Journal of Education, 82* (8), 16–19, 27.

Kazakova, P.B., & Khokhrina, N.T. (1981). Morphological changes in the brain following intranatal asphyxia (the pathogenesis of mental retardation). *Soviet Neurology and Psychiatry, 3* (14), 49–63.

Kazdin, A. (1992). Child and adolescent dysfunction and paths toward maladjustments: Targets for intervention. *Clinical Psychology Review, 8* (12), 795–819.

Kearney, C.A., & Silverman, W.K. (1992). Let's not push the "panic" button: A critical analysis of panic and panic disorders in adolescents. *Clinical Psychology Review, 3* (12), 293–307.

Keeton, A. (1980). Policies and practices in Ontario special education: A time for change. In M. Csapo & L. Goguen (Eds.), *Special education across Canada.* Vancouver, BC: Centre for Human Development and Research.

Kendall, C.N. (1918). Foreword. In State of New Jersey Department of Public Instruction. *The teaching of children mentally three years or more below the norm.* Trenton, NJ: State Gazette.

Kennedy, S., Scheirer, J., & Rogers, A. (1984). The price of success: Our monocultural science. American Psychologist, 39, 996–998.

Kirejczyk, K. (1975). Half-century of activity of The Special Education Section of The Polish Teacher's Association. *Szkola Specjalna, 1,* 7–18.

Kirk, S.A. (1981). Foreword to the first edition. In D.F. Moores *Educating the deaf: Psychology, principles and practices* (2nd ed.). Boston: Houghton Mifflin.

Kirk, S., & Bateman, B. (1962). Diagnosis and remediation of learning disabilities. *Exceptional Children, 29,* 73–78.

Kirk, S., McCarthy, J., & Kirk, W. (1968). *The Illinois test of psycholinguistic abilities.* Urbana, IL: University of Illinois Press.

Klar-Stefanska, R. (1980). Problems of training teachers in psychology viewed in the light of studies on naive psychological knowledge. *Psychologia Wychowawcza* (Educational Psychology), *1,* 21–36.

Kolaska, J. (1968). *Education in Soviet Ukraine.* Toronto: Peter Martin.

Kononova, I.M. (1968). Vocal reactions in children during the first year of life and their relationship to various patterns of behavior. *Voprosy Psikhologii, 5,* 119–127.

Korchin, Sh. J. (1976). *Modern clinical psychology.* New York: Basic Books.

Korea Overseas Information Service. (1988). *Facts about Korea.* Seoul: Korea Information Service Printing Company.

Korgesaar, J.L. (1988). On the development of special and remedial education in the Soviet Union. *International Journal of Special Education, 3* (1), 1–21.

Korlap, K.K., & Vitismann, M.Y. (1987). Development and the present state of defectology in Estonia. *Defectologia, 5,* 65–69.

Kose, L. (1987). Learning disabilities: Definition or specification? Response to Kavale and Forness. *Remedial and Special Education, 8* (1), 36–42.

Kostiuk, H.S. (1970). The development of Lenin's ideas in Soviet psychology of personality. *Voprosy Psikhologii, 3,* 3–24.

Kostiuk, H.S. (1972). The development of educational psychology in Ukrainian SSR. *Voprosy Psikhologii, 5,* 10–23.

Kostiuk, H.S. (1983). *Na magistraloyakh doby* (In the mainstreams of an era). Baltimore: Smolosky Publishers.

Kostrzewski, J. (1971). Life and scholarship of Docent Dr. Hab. Marii Grzywak-Kaczynskicz *Annales de Philosophie, 4* (19), 5–22.

Kozakov, A.A. (1975). Application of a photo-electrical instrument presenting color information to the blind. *Defectologia, 1,* 71–75.

Kozhevnikov, E.M. (1973). The socialist state and communist education of the younger generation. *Soviet Pedagogy, 1,* 3–13.

Kozulin, A. (1986). The concept of activity in Soviet psychology: Vygotsky, his disciples and critics. *American Psychologist, 3,* 264–275.

Kram, C. (1963). Epilepsy in children and youth. In W.M. Cruickshank (Ed.), *Psychology of exceptional children and youth* (2nd ed.). Englewood Cliffs, NJ: Prentice Hall.

Krasnobrodsky, R. (1973). Vykhovannia lubovi do ridnoho kraju zasobamy muzyky. *Doshkilne Vykhovannia, 9,* 23–25.

Krasovetsky, H. (1995). The problems of child collective in the context of school humanization. *Ridna Shkola, 2* (3), 8–15.

Kress, J.S., & Elias, M.J. (1993). Substance abuse prevention in special education population: Review and recommendations. *The Journal of Special Education, 1* (27), 35–52.

Kreusler, A. (1976). *Contemporary education and moral upbringing in the Soviet Union.* Milwaukee, WI: University of Wisconsin, University Microfilms International.

Kubijovych, V. (1971). *Ukraine* (A concise encyclopedia) (Vol. 2). Toronto: University of Toronto Press.

Kubiszyn, T. (1997). The 1997 amendments to the individuals with Disabilities Education Act. *The School Psychologist, 3* (51), 88–90, 96.

Kuman, K. (1984). Breaking away. *Future, 11,* 12. Paris: UNESCO.

Kuzmina, V.K. (1978). Specific traits of educational approach to oligophrenic adolescents with neurotic and psychotic manifestations. *Defectologia, 3,* 60–68.

Kuzmitskaya, M.I. (1977). Preparation of trainable retardates to practical life (home and social adaptation). *Defectologia, 5,* 89–91.

Kydykbayeva, S.B. (1985). Characteristics of acquisition of skills of phonetically correct writing in Kirghiz mentally retarded school children. *Defectologia, 3,* 32–36.

Laaksonen, P. (1989). Developmental phases in school psychological work? Reflections on the work of psychologists in Finland. *School Psychology International, 1,* 3–9.

Lakin, K.C., Bruininks, R.H., & Sigford, B.B. (1981). Deinstitutionalization and community adjustment: A summary of research and issues. In R.H. Bruininks, C.D. Meyers, B.B. Sigford & K.C. Lakin (Eds.), *Deinstitutionalization and community adjustment of mentally retarded people.* Washington, DC: Monograph of the American Association on Mental Deficiency, N4.

Lambert, N., Windmiles, M., Tharinger, D. & Cole, L. (1981). *AAMD-ABS school edition.* Washington, DC: American Association on Mental Deficiency.

Lapskin, V., & Zhivina, A. (1981). Sixty years of higher defectological education in the USSR and the role of defectological department of the Lenin Pedagogical College of Moscow in training in diplomate defectologists. *Defectologia, 6,* 78–87.

Las, H. (1978). Attempts to acquaint students of special education with the problems of community consolidated school. *Szkola Speczalna, 2,* 116–125.

La Vole, J.C. (1989). School psychology in the Peoples Republic of China. In P. Saigh & T. Oakland (Eds.), *International perspectives on psychology in the schools.* Hillsdale, NJ: Lawrence Erlbaum Associates.

Lebedinsky, V. (1985). A new book on methods of psychological diagnostics and correction. *Defectologia, 1,* 92–93.

Lerner, J.W. (1984). *Learning disabilities: Theories, diagnosis, and teaching strategies* (4th ed.). Boston: Houghton Mifflin.

Lestinen, L. (1988). *Higher education and research in Finland.* Helsinki: Yliopistopain.

Lew, A. (1987). Netherlands, special education in. In C.R. Reynolds & L. Mann (Eds.), *Encyclopedia of special education.* Newark, NJ/Toronto: John Wiley & Sons.

Lilin, Ye. (1978). Twins and oligophrenia. *Defectologia, 2,* 74–76.

Lindsay, G. (1989). Educational psychology in the schools of England and Wales. In Ph. Saigh & T. Oakland (Eds.), *International perspectives on psychology in the schools.* Hillsdale, NJ: Lawrence Erlbaum Associates.

Lindsay, G.A. (1988). The identification of special education needs. *School Psychology International, 1,* 61–68.

Lipkowski, O. (1977). Tenth anniversary of the death of Marie Grzegorzewska. *Szkola Specjalna, 2,* 83–86.

Lipkowski, O. (1978). The lack of social adaptation of youth as viewed by social opinion. *Badania Oswiatowe, 3* (11), 48–64.

Lipkowski, O. (1971). Special education within a system of public education. *Nowa Szvola, 6,* 8–15.

Lipkowski, O. (1968). Current status and developmental tendencies of special education in Europe. *Szkola Specjalna, 3,* 223–238.

Little, D.M. (1980). The Canadian dilemma in teacher education: Self preservation or self renewal? In M. Csapo & L. Goguen (Eds.), *Special education across Canada.* Vancouver, BC: Centre for Human Development and Research.

Litvak, A.G., Ushakova, I.P., & Pivovarova, N.P. (1987). Training of defectologists: Ways of reconstruction. *Defectologia, 5,* 63–65.

Lloyd, J., Hallahan, D.P., & Kauffman, J.M. (1980). Learning disabilities: A review of selected topics. In L. Mann & D. Sabatino (Eds.), *The fourth review of special education.* New York: Grune & Stratton.

Loboda, S., & Kusenko, V. (1974). Vehymo lubyty ridnu batkivshchynec. *Doshkilne Vykhovannia, 4,* 16–26.

Lombardi, T.R., Odell, K.S., & Novotny, D.E. (1991). Special education and students at-risk: Findings from a national study. *Remedial and Special Education, 1* (12), 56–63.

Loveland, K.A., & Kelly, M.L. (1988). Development of adaptive behavior in adolescents and young adults with autism and Down-syndrome. *American Journal on Mental Deficiency, 1,* 84–93.

Lozbiakova, M.I. (1973). Pronunciation of speech sounds in five-year-olds. *Defectologia, 1,* 69–76.

Lubovsky, V. (1987). Some urgent problems of the Soviet. *Defectologia, 5,* 3–12.

Lukasiewic, J. (1972). The ignorance explosion: A contribution to the study of confrontation of man with the complexity of science based society and environment. *Transaction of the New York Academy of Sciences, 5* (34), 373–392.

Luria, A.R. (1963). *The mentally retarded child.* New York: Pergamon Press.

Luria, A.R. (1966). *Higher cortical functions in man.* New York: Basic Books.

Luria, A.R. (Ed.). (1983). *The mentally retarded child.* New York: Pergamon Press.

Lutskina, R.K., & Grushevskaya, M.G. (1985). Third republican science-practical conference on Kazakhstan defectologists. *Defectologia, 4,* 91–92.

Maag, J.W., & Behrens, J.T. (1989). Depression and cognitive self-statements of learning disabled and seriously emotionally disabled adolescents. *The Journal of Special Education, 1,* 17–27.

Machikhina, V.Ph. (1977). Development of special education in the Kazakh SSR. *Defectologia, 4,* 4–9.

Machikhina, V.F. (1975). The experience of the ministry of education in the Lithuanian SSR in managing special schools. *Defectologia, 6,* 3–8.

MacMillan, D., Gresham, F.M., Siperstin, G.N., & Bocian, K.M. (1996). The labyrinth of IDEA: School decisions on referred students with subaverage general intelligence. *American Journal on Mental Retardation, 2* (101), 161–175.

Madden, N.A., & Slavin, R.E. (1983). Mainstreaming students with mild handicaps: Academic and social outcomes. *Review of Educational Research, 53,* 519–569.

Magerotte, G. (1987). Belguium, special education. In C.R. Reynolds & L. Mann (Eds.), *Encyclopedia of special education.* Newark, NJ/Toronto: John Wiley & Sons.

Magne, O. (1988). Hearing impaired children in Swedish education. *International Journal of Special Education, 1,* 81–87.

Maksymenko, S.D. (1978). New constitution of the USSR and the possibilities of the development of psychological science. *Radianska Shkola, 6,* 37–47.

Malapka, S.W.G. (1992). Educational planning and special education in developing countries: A match or mismatch? *International Journal of Special Education, 2* (7), 188–192.

Malkova, Z. (1987). *The Soviet Union today and tomorrow: Education.* Moscow: Novasti Press.

Mamaichuk, I.I. (1976). The dynamics of cognitive activities of C.P. preschool children. *Defectologia, 3,* 29–35.

Mann, L., & Goodman, L. (1976). Perceptual training: A critical retrospect. In E. Schopler & R.J. Reichler (Eds.), *Psychopathology and child development.* New York/London: Plenum Press.

Manset, G., & Semmel, M.I. (1997). Are inclusive programs for students with mild disabilities effective? A comparative review of model programs. *The Journal of Special Education, 31* (2).

Markova, A.K. (1982). Psychological service in school (roundtable). *Voprosy Psikhologii, 3,* 62–93.

Markovskaya, I.F. (1977). Neuropsychological analysis of clinical types in developmentally delayed children. *Defectologia, 6,* 3–11.

Martini, L., & MacTurk, R.H. (1985). Issues in the enumeration of handicapping conditions in the United States. *Mental Retardation, 4* (23), 182–185.

Martyiv, M. (1996). Shadows of state controlled schools. *Universum, 9* (10), 34–35.

Mary, N.L. (1990). Reactions of Black, Hispanic and White mothers to having a child with handicaps. *Mental Retardation, 1* (28), 1–7.

Masland, R.L., Sarason, S.B., & Gladwin, T. (1958). *Mental subnormality.* New York: Basic Books.

Maslow, A. (1954). *Motivation and personality.* New York: Harper & Row.

Mastiukova, E.M. (1989). Visual and intellectual disorders in fetal alcohol syndrome. *Defectologia, 6,* 9–13.

Mastiukova, Y.M. (1973). On the development of cognitive activity in C.P. children. *Defectologia, 6,* 24–30.

Mastripieri, M., & Scruggs, T. (1992). Science for students with disabilities. *Review of Educational Research, 4* (62), 377–411.

Matasov, Y.T. (1989). Some characteristics of thinking of the mentally retarded school children. *Defectologia, 5,* 15–21.

Mathison, S. (1988). Why triangulate? *Educational Research, 2,* 13–18.

Matiushkyn, A.M. (1982). Psychological service in school (roundtable). *Voprosy Psikhologii, 3,* 62–93.

McDonnell, J.M., Hardman, M.L., McDonnell, A.P.,& Kiefer-O'Donnell, R. (1995). *Introduction to persons with severe disabilities.* Boston: Allyn and Bacon.

McLaughlin, M.J., & Henderson, K. (1998). Charter schools in Colorado and their response to the education of students with disabilities. *The Journal of Special Education, 2* (32), 99–107.

May, D.C. (1988). Plastic surgery for children with down-syndrome: Normalization or extremism. *Mental Retardation, 1,* 17–19.

McLeish, P. (1975). *Soviet psychology: History, theory, content.* London: Mathuen.

Medinsky, Y.N. (1954). *Public education in the USSR.* Moscow: Foreign Language Publishing House.

Meichenenbaum, D. (1983). Teaching thinking: A cognitive behavioral approach. In *Interdisciplinary voices in learning disabilities and remedial education.* Austin, TX: Pro-ed.

Meisals, J. (Ed.). (1986). *Mainstreaming: Past and future issues.* Hillsdale, NJ: Lawrence Erlbaum Associates.

Meisgeier, C. (1976). A review of critical issues underlying mainstreaming. In L. Mann & D. Sabatina (Eds.), *The third review of special education.* New York/London: Grune & Stratton.

Menolascino, F.L. (1977). *Challenges in mental retardation: Progressive ideology and sources.* New York: Human Services Press.

Mercer, C., & Payne, J. (1975). Programs and services. In J. Kauffman & J. Payne (Eds.), *Mental retardation, introduction and personal perspective.* Columbus, OH: Charles E. Merrill.

Merrill, M.A. (1948). *Problems of child delinquency.* London: Harrap.

Meyerova, R.A., & Sokolaeva, R.V. (1980). Importance of dysplasia in visual diagnosis of several nosological forms of oligophrenia. *Defectologia, 1,* 9–12.

Michael, E. (1989). Special education in Israel. *International Journal of Special Education, 1,* 59–65.

Miles, M. (1989). Disability policies in Pakistan: Is anyone winning? *International Journal of Special Education, 1,* 1–15.

Miles, M. (1988). Special education in Pakistan: Development issues. *International Journal of Special Education, 1,* 39–50.

Minasian, A.M. (1970). Education of handicapped children in the Armenian Soviet Socialist Republic. *Defectologia, 1,* 25–34.

Missiuse, C., & Samuels, M.T. (1989). Dynamic assessment of preschool children with special needs: Comparison of mediation and instruction. *Remedial and Special Education, 2.*

Moe, M.T., & Gay, R.K. (1997). *The emerging investment opportunity in education.* San Francisco: Montgomery Securities.

Molchanovskaya, I.V. (1981). Study of reading skills in the mentally retarded students with profound visual disability. *Defectologia, 5,* 21–26.

Moore, D.F. (1976). A review of education of the deaf. In L. Mann & D. Sabatino (Eds.), *The third review of special education.* New York: Grune & Stratton.

Moores, D.F. (1987). *Educating the deaf: Psychology, principles, and practices* (3rd ed.). Boston: Houghton Mifflin.

Moores, D.F. (1985). Educational programs and services for hearing impaired children: Issues and options. In F. Powell, T. Finitzo-Hickes, S., Friel-Patts, & D. Henderson (Eds.), *Education of the hearing impaired child* (pp. 3–20). San Diego, CA: College-Hill.

Mora, G. (1975). Haley. In J.G. Howells (Ed.), *World history of psychiatry.* New York: Brunner/Mazel.

Morgulis, I.S. (1959). Some problems of the theory of special education. *Defectologia, 5,* 3–6.

Morningstar, M.E. (1997). Critical issues in career development and employment preparation for adolescents with disabilities. *Remedial and Special Education, 5* (18), 307–320.

Morston, D. (1987–1988). The effectiveness of special education: A time series analysis of reading performance in regular and special education settings. *The Journal of Special Education, 4,* 13–26.

Moskovina, A.G., Bertyn, G.P., & Opolinsky, E.S. (1979). The problems of the origin of hearing disorders in children. *Defectologia, 2,* 6–12.

Moskovina, A.G., & Sagdullayev, A.A. (1989). The role of biological and social factors in the origin of mental retardation in children of alcoholic parents. *Defectologia.*

Mpofu, E., Zindi, E., Oakland, T., & Paresuh, M. (1997). School psychology practices in east and southern Africa: Special educators perspective. *The Journal of Special Education, 3* (31), 387–402.

Muminova, L.R. (1989). Advancement in education of defectologists in the condition of higher and general school reform. *Defectologia, 6,* 74–78.

Murphy, D.M. (1986). The prevalence of handicapping conditions among juvenile delinquents. *Remedial and Special Education, 3,* 7–17.

Murray-Seegert, C. (1992). Integration in Germany: Mainstreaming or swimming upstream? *Remedial and Special Education, 1* (13), 34–44.

Myers, B.A. (1989). Misleading cues in the diagnosis of mental retardation and infantile autism in the preschool children. *Mental Retardation, 2,* 85–90.

Myers, C.D., Sigford, B.B., & Lakin, K.C. (Eds.). (1981). De institutionalization and community adjustment of mentally retarded people. Washington, DC: Monograph of the American Association for Mental Deficiency, N4.

N.N. (1983). New curricula, an important factor of defectologists training advancement in pedagogical institutes. *Defectologia, 5,* 3–6.

Nagelschmitz, H. (1985). The special school system of the Federal Republic of Germany. *Buildung und Wissenschaft,* 9–10.

Napier, G. (1972). The visually disabled. In B.R. Gearheart (Ed.), *Education of the exceptional child.* Scranton, PA: International Educational Publishers.

National Advisory Committee for the Handicapped. (1976). *The unfinished revolution: Education for the handicapped, 1976 annual report.* Washington, DC: U.S. Government Printing Office.

National Advisory Committee on Handicapped Children, *Special Education for Handicapped Children* (First annual report). (1968). Washington, DC: Department of Health, Education, and Welfare.

Nazarova, N.M. (1985). Vocational orientation for defectology department applicants. *Defectologia, 5,* 62–67.

Nelson, R.O., Peoples, A., Hay, L.R., Johnson, T., & Hay, W. (1976). The effectiveness of special training techniques based on operant conditioning: A comparison of the methods. *Mental Retardation, 3,* 34–38.

Nesbit, W.C. (1987). Special education strivings in India: Recent impressions. *International Journal of Special Education, 2,* 195–205.

Newfield, G.R. (1979). Deinstitutionalization procedures. In R. Wiegerin & J.W. Pelosi (Eds.), *Developmental disabilities: The DD movement* (pp. 115–126). Baltimore: Brookes.

Nietupski, J., Hamre-Nietupski, S., Curtin, S., & Shrikanth, K. (1997). A review of curricular research in severe disabilities from 1976 to 1995 in six selected journals. *The Journal of Special Education, 1* (31), 36–56.

Nirje, B. (1969). The normalization principle and its human management implications. In R.B. Kugel & W. Wolfensberger (Eds.), *Changing patterns for residential services for the mentally retarded.* Washington, DC: President's Committee on Mental Retardation.

Nisi, A., O'Oro, L., Vivian, D., & Meazzini, P. (1989). School psychology in Italy. In Ph. Saigh & T. Oakland (Eds.), *International perspective on psychology in the schools.* Hillsdale, NJ: Lawrence Erlbaum Associates.

Nkabinda, Z. (1993). The role of special education in changing South Africa. *The Journal of Special Education, 1* (21), 107–115.

Noskova, L.P., & Kuznyetsova, G.V. (1980). Diagnosis of developmental disorders and the state of preschool upbringing of abnormal children in the socialist countries. *Defectologia, 3,* 83–88.

Noskova, L.V., & Mironova, S.A. (1980). Social system of preschool upbringing of abnormal children in Kazakh SSR. *Defectologia, 6,* 58–62.

Notification of the Ministry of Education, Science and Culture, Elementary, and Secondary Education. (1978). Bureau Director-General, N. 309, October 6.

Novick, J. (1987). *A study of potential achievement discrepancy, I.Q. constancy, and scatter of scores in a matched sample of educable mentally retarded and learning disabled students.* An unpublished doctoral dissertation, Rutgers University.

Oakland, T., & Cunningham, J. (1997). International school psychology associates definition of school psychology. *School Psychology International, 3* (18), 195–201.

Ogamo, H. (1978). The impact of Japanese culture on special education programming. In A.H. Fink (Ed.), *International perspectives on future special education.* Reston, VA: CEC.

Ogilvy, C.M. (1994). What is the diagnostic significance of specific learning difficulties. *School Psychology International, 1* (15), 55–68.

Ogland, V.S. (1972). Language behavior of EMR children. *Mental Retardation, 2,* 30–32.

Oinzhu, L. (1989). Special education in China. *Newsletter for special education in Asia and the Pacific, 1,* 3.

Orlando, C.P. (1983). Review of reading research in special education. In L. Mann & D. Sabatino (Eds.), *The first review of special education.* Philadelphia: Journal of Special Education Press.

Orlov, A.B. (1988). Possibilities of humanizing education. *Voprosy Psikhologii, 6,* 142–146.

Orlov, A.B. (1988). Problems of the restarting of psycho-educational training of teachers. *Voprosy Psikhologii, 1,* 16–26.

Orlova, L.M. (1979). K.N. Kornilov's struggle for marxism in psychology. *Voprosy Psikhologii, 1,* 62–74.

Orton, S.T. (1937). *Reading, writing and spelling problems in children.* New York: Norton.

O'Sullivan, P.J., Martson, D., & Magmusson, D. (1987). Categorical special education teacher certification: Does it affect instruction of mildly handicapped pupils? *Remedial and Special Education, 5* (8), 13–19.

Pambookian, H.P., & Holowinsky, I.Z. (1987). School psychology in the USSR. *Journal of School Psychology, 25,* 209–221.

Panckhurst, F., Panckhurst, J., & Elkins, J. (1987). *Special education in New Zealand.* Wellington, New Zealand: Council for Educational Research.

Parette, H.P., & Hourcad, J.J. (1986). Management strategies for orthopedically handicapped students. *Teaching Gifted Children, 18* (4), 282–286.

Parmenten, T.R. (1993). International perspective of vocational options for people with mental retardation: The promise and the reality. *Mental Retardation, 6* (31), 359–368.

Parnicky, J., Kahn, H., & Burdett, A. (1971). Standardization of the VISA (Vocational Interest and Sophistication Assessment Technique). *American Journal of Mental Deficiency, 4,* 442–449.

Patton, J.H., & Braithwaite, R. (1990). Special education certification/recertification for regular educators. *The Journal of Special Education, 1* (24), 117–124.

Patton, J.R., Polloway, E.A., & Epstein, M.H. (1989). Are there seminal works in special education? *Remedial and Special Education, 3,* 54–59.

Pavlova, N. (1978). Silver jubilee of the first auxiliary school of Moldavia. *Defectologia, 2,* 87–88.

Pawlik, E. (Ed.). (1985). *International directory of psychologists* (4th ed.). Amsterdam/New York: Elsevier Science Publishers B.V.

Pawula, F. (1981). Education and training of teachers in socialist states and in selected capitalist countries. *Badania Oswiatowe* (Educational Research), *1* (21), 68–83.

Pelicier, I. (1975). France. In J.G. Howells (Ed.), *World history of psychiatry.* New York: Brunner/Mazel.

Penova, M.N., & Zabramnaya, S.D. (1984). Contents, structure and methods of organizing medical-educational practicum activity for students in mental retardation. *Defectologia, 2,* 73–78.

Perkins, W.H. (1977). *Speech pathology, an applied behavioral science* (2nd ed.). St. Louis, MO: C.V. Mosby.

Perlik, M. (1981). Conditions connected with the choice of profession by pupils of elementary schools. *Badania Oswiatowe, 3* (23), 91–98.

Peterson, D.R., Quay, H.C., & Tiffany, T.L. (1963). Personality factors related to juvenile delinquency. In R.E. Grinder (Ed.), *Studies in adolescence.* New York: Macmillan.

Petrova, V.G., Noskova, L.P., & Turik, G.G. (1987). International seminar: Teachers of the mentally retarded. *Defectologia, 4,* 89–92.

Petrova, V.G. (1986). Verbal memory study in mentally retarded schoolchildren. *Defectologia, 5,* 3–8.

Pevzner, M.S. (1961). *Oligophrenia: Mental deficiency in children.* New York: Consultants Bureau.

Pevzner, M.S. (1966). *Children with developmental deviations.* Moscow: Education Publishing Co.

Pevzner, M.S. (1970). Etiopathogenesis and classification of oligophrenia. (Translated by G. Malasko.) *Special School, 4,* 289–293.

Pevzner, S. (Ed.). (1973). *Clinical genetic research of oligophrenia.* Moscow: Pedagogy Publishing.

Pevzner, M.S., Bertyn, G.P., & Donskaya, N.Yv. (1979). Clinical psycho-educational study of mentally retarded hard of hearing schoolchildren. *Defectologia, 3,* 3–11.

Pevzner, M.S., Bertyn, G.P., & Mareyeva, R.A. (1980). Clinical-psychological-educational study of mentally retarded children with profound visual and hearing disorders. *Defectologia, 4,* 9–16.

Pevzner, M.S., & Rostiagaylova, L.I. (1981). Clinical-psychological characteristics of developmental backwardness under compensated hydrocephalus. *Defectology, 5,* 10–17.

Phelps, L.A., & Hanley-Maxwell, C. (1997). School to work transition for youth with disabilities: A review of outcome and practices. *Review of Educational Research, 2* (67), 197–277.

Piao, Y. (1989). Education of abnormal children and development of special training in China. *Defectologia, 3,* 54–59.

Pinsky, B.I., & Boganovskaya, N.D. (1985). Practical exercises at the lessons of mathematics as a means of cognitive remediation in mentally retarded school children. *Defectologia, 2,* 39–42.

Platt, J.S. (1986). Vocational education in connection with a piece of a bigger pic. *Remedial and Special Education, 3* (7), 48–56.

Plotnick, I.E. (1987). Psychology in the Latrian Soviet socialist republic. *Voprosy Psikhologii, 6,* 10–16.

Podobed, V.L. (1988). Characteristics of verbal memory of developmentally backward fourth graders. *Defectologia, 6,* 3–9.

Poindexter, A. (1989). Psychotropic drug patterns in a large ICF/MR facility: A ten year experience. *American Journal on Mental Retardation, 6,* 624–627.

Pologrove, L., & McNeil, M. (1989). The consultation process: Research and practice. *Remedial and Special Education, 1,* 6–14.

Polyvannaya, M.F., Cheretyanko, E.O., Lypetskaya, A.N., Rytykova, L.S., & Sirmon, A.V. (1985). Comparison of short term memory characteristics in mentally retarded and normal school children. *Defectologia, 5,* 7–14.

Ponariadova, G.M. (1979). The dynamics of attention organization in developmentally backward and mentally retarded schoolchildren. *Defectologia, 4,* 16–21.

Popova, M.I. (1968). Some features of speech manifestation in children of the first half-year of the second year of life. *Voprosy Psikhologii, 4,* 116–122.

Prater, M., Serna, L.A., Sileo, T.W., & Katz, A.R. (1995). HIV disease: Implications for special educators. *Remedial and Special Education, 2* (16), 68–79.

President's Commission on Higher Education. (1947).

Proskura, O.V. (1969). The role of teaching in the formation of seriation actions in preschool children. *Voprosy Psikhologii, 15,* 37–45.

Proskura, O.V. (1975). Egocentrism phenomena in the comprehension of spatial relations by preschool children. *Voprosy Psikhologii, 4,* 44–51.

Provotorov, V.P. (1975). Another evidence of Party's care for children and adolescents with mental and physical impairments. *Defectologia, 3,* 3–7.

Putnam, R.W. (1979). Special education: Some cross-national comparisons. *Comparative Education, 1* (15), 83–91.

Raku, A.I. (1981). Parental responsibilities in the upbringing of mentally retarded students. *Defectologia, 3,* 83–86.

Raimy, V.C. (1950). *Training in clinical psychology.* Englewood Cliffs, NJ: Prentice-Hall.

Raku, A.I. (1977). Status of the mentally retarded child in the family. *Defectologia, 4,* 55–58.

Ramcy, S.L., Krauss, M.W., & Simeonnow, R.J. (1989). Research on families: Current assessment and future opportunities. *American Journal on Mental Retardation, 3,* 11–14.

Rampaul, W.E., Freeze, D.R., & Bock, J. (1992). A model for international special education service delivery in developing countries. *International Journal of Special Education, 2* (7), 101–108.

Raviv, A. (1989). School psychology in Israel. In P. Saigh & T. Oakland (Eds.), *International perspective on psychology in the schools*. Hillsdale, NJ: Lawrence Erlbaum Associates.

Reagan, T. (1985). The deaf or a linguistic minority: Educational consideration. *Harvard Educational Review, 55,* 265–277.

Reid, R., & Katsiyannis, A. (1995). Attention deficit hyperactivity disorders and section 504. *Remedial and Special Education, 1* (16), 44–53.

Reid, R., Maag, J.W., Vasa, S.F., & Wright, G. (1994). Who are the children with attention deficit hyperactivity disorder? A school based survey. *The Journal of Special Education, 2* (28), 117–138.

Reynolds, C.R., & Stowe, M. (1985). *Severe discrepancy analysis.* Philadelphia: TRAIN.

Reynolds, M.C. (Ed.). (1980). *A common body of practice for teachers: The challenge of public law 94-142 for teacher education.* Washington, DC: U.S. Office of Education BEH.

Reynolds, M.C., Wang, M.C., & Walberg, H.J. (1987). The necessary restarting of special and regular education. *Exceptional Children, 2,* 391–398.

Richardson, S.A. (1977). Mental retardation in the community: The transition from childhood to adulthood. In P. Mittler (Ed.), *Research to practice in mental retardation* (Vol. 1, Care and Intervention). Baltimore: University Park Press.

Rikhye, C.A. (1987). Japan–Special education in. In C.R. Reynolds & L. Mann (Eds.), *Encyclopedia of special education.* New York: John Wiley & Sons.

Ritchie, M.H. (1989). School psychological service down under: An Australian perspective. In P. Saigh & T. Oakland (Eds.), *International perspective on psychology in the schools.* Hillsdale, NJ: Lawrence Erlbaum Associates.

Ritchie, M.H. (1989). School psychology research in Australia. *Professional School Psychology, 2,* 129–135.

Roszkiewicz, I. (1976). Psychological and educational aspects of mental dullness. *Szkola Specjalna, 2,* 33–38.

Roy, B.N. (1989). Report on the status of special education in India. *Newsletter for Special Education in Asia and the Pacific, 1,* 2–3.

Rozanova, T.V. (1974). Problems of special education in Yugoslavia. *Defectologia, 3,* 49–57.

Rozhdestvenskaya, M. (1979). Psychological diagnosis of intelligence and personality. *Defectologia, 5,* 89–90.

Rudman, H. (1977). The standardized test flap. *Kappan, 3* (59), 179–185.

Russell, R.W. (1984). Psychology in its world context. *American Psychologist, 39,* 1017–1026.

Rutter, M., & Yule, W. (1973). Specific reading retardation. In L. Mann & D. Sabatino (Eds.), *The first review of special education.* Philadelphia: Journal of Special Education Press.

Safran, S.P. (1989). Special education in Australia and the United States: A cross-cultural analysis. *The Journal of Special Education, 3* (23), 330–341.

Sapor-Shevin, M. (1978). Another look at mainstreaming: Exceptionality, normality and the nature of difference. *Phi Delta Kappan, 60,* 119–121.

Sarayev, S.Y. (1988). A study of the intellectual function in the deaf school children as assessed by the Wechsler scale. *Defectologia, 6,* 17–23.

Savchenko, V. (1980). New studies in the problem of oligo-phrenia. *Defectologia, 1,* 87–95.

Savelle, J.M., Twohip, P.T., & Rachford, D.L. (1986). Empirical status of Feuerstein's "Instrumental Enrichment" (FIE) technique as a method of teaching thinking skills. *Review of Educational Research, 4* (56), 381–409.

Savchenko, V. (1980). New studies in the area of oligophrenia. (Review of research 1974–1979). *Defectologia, 1,* 87.

Schalock, R.L. (1985). Comprehensive community services: A plea for interagency collaboration. In R.H. Bruinicks & K.C. Lakin (Eds.), *Living and learning in the least restrictive environment.* Baltimore: Brookes.

Schalock, R.L., Stark, J.A., Snell, M.E., Coulter, D.L., Polloway, E.A., Luckasson, R., Reiss, S., & Spitalnik, D.H. (1994). The changing conception of mental retardation: Implications for the field. *Mental Retardation, 3* (32),181–193.

Scheerenberger, R.C. (1981). Deinstitutionalization: Trends and difficulties. In R.H. Bruininks, C.D. Meyers, B.B. Sigford, & K.C. Lakin (Eds.), *Deinstitutionalization and community adjustment of mentally retarded people.* Washington, DC: Monograph of the American Associate on Mental Deficiency, N. 4.

Scheerenberger, R.C. (1976). A survey of public residential facilities. *Mental Retardation, 1,* 32–36.

Schell, J.S. (1959). Some differences between mentally retarded children in special and in regular classes in the schools of Mercer County: *Dissertation Abstract International, 20,* 607–608.

Schmidt, L.R., & Baltes, P.B. (1971). German theory and research on mental retardation. In N.L. Ellis (Ed.), *International review of research in mental retardation* (Vol. 5). New York/London: Academic Press.

Schnil, G. (1987). Education and upbringing of physically handicapped children in the German Democratic Republic. *Defectologia, 1,* 57–64.

Schofer, R.C., & Lilly, M.S. (1980). Personnel preparation in special education. In L. Mann & D. Sabatino (Eds.), *The fourth review of special education.* New York: Grune & Stratton.

Scruggs, T.E., & Mastropieri, M.A. (1994). Successful mainstreaming in elementary science classes: A qualitative study of three reputational cases. *American Education Research Journal, 4* (31), 785–813.

Scruggs, T.E., Mastropieri, M.A., Forness, S.R., & Kavale, K.A. (1988). Early language intervention: A quantitative synthesis of single-subject research. *The Journal of Special Education, 3,* 259–283.

Sekowska, Z. (1983). Preparation of teachers to work with exceptional youngsters attending general public school with special consideration of higher grades. *Studia Pedagogiczne, 45,* 73–79.

Selikhova, O.L. (1973). Experience of treatment of profoundly retarded adolescents in an auxiliary school. *Defectologia, 3,* 55–58.

Semmel, M.I., Gottlieb, J., & Robinson, N.M. (1979). Mainstreaming: Perspectives in educating handicapped children in the public school. In D.C. Berliner (Ed.), *Review of research in education* (Vol. 7, pp. 223–279). Washington, DC: American Educational Research Association.

Sereda, H.K., & Snopyk, B.I. (1970). Unity of short-term and long-term memory mechanisms. *Voprosy Psikhologii, 6,* 60–75.

Seyfarth, J., Hill, J.W., Orlove, F., McMillan, J., & Wehman, P. (1987). Factors influencing parents vocational aspirations for their children with mental retardation. *Mental Retardation, 6* (25), 357–362.

Shake, M.C., Allington, R., Gaskins, R., & Marr, M.B. (1989). How remedial teachers teach vocabulary. *Remedial and Special Education, 5,* 51–58.

Shakhlovskaya, S.N., Rechitskaya, E.G., & Zabramnaya, S.D. (1989). The All Union Scientific conference of college students in defectology. *Defectologia, 1,* 77–83.

Shinkarenko, V. (1984). A new research in education of the mentally retarded. *Defectologia, 4,* 84–86.

Shirapowa, F., Kodema, M., & Manita, A. (1989). School psychology in Japan. In P. Saigh & T. Oakland (Eds.), *International perspectives on psychology in the schools.* Hillsdale, NJ: Lawrence Erlbaum Associates.

Shore, M. (1947). *Soviet education: Its psychology and philosophy.* New York: Philosophical Library.

Short, J.F. (1966). Juvenile delinquency: The socio-cultural context. In L.D. Hoffman and M.L. Hoffman (Eds.), *Child development research* (Volume 2). New York: Russell Sage Foundation.

Shown, D. (1987). Africa, special education in. In C. Raynolds & L. Mann (Eds.), *Encyclopedia of special education.* New York/Singapore: John Wiley & Sons.

Simpson, R.L., Whelan, R.J., & Zabel, R.H. (1993). Special eduction personnel preparation in the 21st century: Issues and strategies. *Remedial and Special Education, 2* (14), 7–22.

Sindelar, P.T., Allman, C., Monda, L., Vail, C.O., Wilson, C.L., & Schloss, P.J. (1988). The power of hypothesis testing in special education efficacy research. *The Journal of Special Education, 3,* 284–296.

Sindelar, P.T., & Schloss, P.J. (1986). The reputation of doctoral training programs in special education. *The Journal of Special Education, 1* (20), 49–61.

Sirvis, B. (1982). The physically disabled. In E.L. Meyen (Ed.), *Exceptional children and youth: An introduction* (2nd ed.). Denver, CO: Love.

Sitko, M.C., & Semmel, M.I. (1973). Language and language behavior of the mentally retarded. In L. Mann & D. Sabatino (Eds.), *The first review of special education.* Philadelphia, PA: Journal of Special Education Press.

Skaarbrevik, D.J., & Gottlieb, J. (1973). Historical trend and present status of education for the retarded in Norway. *Education and Training of the Mentally Retarded, 8,* 3–9.

Skuy, M., & Shmiklin, D. (1987). Effectiveness of the learning potential assessment device with Indian and Coloured adolescents in South Africa. *International Journal of Special Education, 2,* 131–151.

Sleeter, C.E. (1986). Learning disabilities: The social construction of a special education category. *Exceptional Children, 53* (1), 46–64.

Sloan, W., & Stevens, H.A. (1976). *A century of concern: A history of the American Association on Mental Deficiency.* Washington, DC: American Association on Mental Deficiency.

Smith, S.E. (1993). Cognitive deficits associated with fragile X syndrome. *Mental Retardation, 5* (31), 279–284.

Smith, S.M. (1989). Congenital syndromes and mildly handicapped students: Implications for special education. *Remedial and Special Education, 3,* 20–31.

Snell, M.E. (Ed.). (1987). *Systematic instruction of persons with severe handicaps* (3rd ed.). Columbus, OH: Charles E. Merrill.

Solntseva, L.I. (1979). Creation of multi-sensory bases for compensation of blindness of early childhood. *Defectologia, 5,* 61–68.

Sommander, K., Emanuelsson, I., & Kelban, L. (1993). Pupils with mild mental retardation in regular Swedish schools, prevalence, objective characteristics and subjective evaluators. *American Journal on Mental Retardation, 6* (97), 692–702.

Soodak, L.C., Podell, D.M., & Helman, L.R. (1998). Teacher, student, and school attributes as predictors of teacher's responses to inclusion. *The Journal of Special Education, 4* (31), 480–498.

Spitz, R. (1951). The psychogenic diseases in infancy: An attempt at their etiological classification. *Psychoanalytical Study of the Child, 6,* 225–275.

Sprafkin, J., Gadow, K.G., & Kant, G. (1987–1988). Teaching emotionally disturbed children to discriminate reality from fantasy on television. *The Journal of Special Education, 4,* 99–107.

Stadnenko, N.M. (1984). Development of thinking in mentally retarded children in the educational process. *Defectologia, 5,* 25–30.

Stainback, S., & Stainback, W. (1985). *Integration of students with severe handicaps into regular schools.* Reston, VA: Council for Exceptional Children.

Stancliffe, R.J., & Lakin, K.C. (1998). Analysis of expenditures and outcomes of residential alternatives for persons with developmental disabilities. *American Journal on Mental Retardation, 6* (102), 552–569.

Starr, E. (1992). Early intervention in developing countries: Implementation issues and dilemmas. *International Journal of Special Education, 1* (7), 17–26.

Staud, V., & Misiak, H. (1984). American psychologists and psychology abroad. *American Psychologist, 39,* 1026–1032.

Stevens, H.A., & Heber, R. (1984). *Mental retardation: A review of research.* Chicago: University of Chicago Press.

Strauss, A.A., & Lehtinen, L.E. (1947). *Psychopathology and education of brain-injured children.* New York: Grune & Stratton.

Strelkova, T.A. (1981). Peculiarities of classification operation in developmentally backward preschool children. *Defectologia, 5,* 61–70.

Strupczenska, B., & Doroszewicz, K. (1980). Professional development in teachers and the instructional system at the Institute of Teacher's Training. *Psychologia Wychowaweza* (Educational Psychology), *1,* 62–69.

Sukhova, V.B. (1985). On deaf children preparedness for studying mathematics in school. *Defectologia, 3,* 43–49.

Summers, E.G. (1986). The information flood in learning disabilities: A bibliometric analysis of journal literature. *Remedial and Special Education, 7* (1).

Sutherland, E.H., & Cressey, D.R. (1970). *Criminology* (8th ed.). Philadelphia: J.B. Lippincott.

Swanson, H.L. (1993). An information processing analysis of learning disabled children's problem solving. *American Educational Research Journal, 4* (30), 861–895.

Swanson, H.L., & Alford, L. (1987). An analysis of the current status of special education research and journal outlets. *Remedial and Special Education, 6* (8), 8–18.

Takahashi, A. (1973). Japanese literature and developments. In J. Wortis (Ed.), *Mental retardation and developmental disabilities* (Vol. 5). New York/London: Brunner/Mazel.

Tarjan, G. (1964). The next decade: Expectations from the biological sciences. *Mental retardation: A handbook for the primary physician.* A report of the American Medical Association Conference on Mental Retardation, April 9–11, pp. 123–133.

Terman, L.M. (1925). *Genetic studies of genius* (vol. 1). Mental and physical traits of a thousand gifted children. Palo Alto, CA: Stanford University Press.

Thurlow, M.J., Ysseldyke, J.E., & Wotruba, J.W. (1989). State recommended student-teacher ratios for mildly handicapped children. *Remedial and Special Education, 2,* 37–43.

Tirosh, E., & Comby, J. (1993). Autism with hyperlexia: A distinct syndrome? *American Journal of Mental Retardation, 1* (98), 84–93.

Tobyshakov, K. (1987). Vocational education and orientation in rural school for the mentally retarded. *Defectologia, 4,* 19–22.

Tomiak, J.J. (1972). *The Soviet Union.* Hamden, CT: Archon Books.

Tomasik, E., & Zolczynska, E. (1975). Graduates of State Institute of Special Education in Warsaw and their status. *Szkola Specizalna, 4,* 28–38.

Tredgold, R.F., & Soddy, K. (1956). *A textbook of mental deficiency* (9th ed.). London: Tindall & Cox.

Triandia, H.C., & Brislin, R.W. (1984). Cross-cultural psychology. *American Psychologist, 39,* 1006–1017.

Trubnikova, N.M. (1988). Impairment of articulation and its correction in young children with cerebral palsy and mental retardation. *Defectologia, 6,* 37–42.

Tsartsidze, M.G. (1987). Characteristics of intentional behavior development in children with oligophrenia. *Defectologia, 1,* 17–22.

Tsipina, N. (1985). Science-practice conference on problems of education and upbringing of developmentally backward children. *Defectologia, 2,* 87–88.

Tsvetkova, L.S. (1972). Basic principles of a theory of reeducation of brain-injured patients. *The Journal of Special Education, 2,* 135–146.

Tsymbaliuk, A.N. (1973). Comprehension of topic pictures by developmentally backward children under experimental training. *Defectologia, 3,* 25–32.

Tsybenova, N.Ch. (1982). Psychological service in school (roundtable). *Voprosy Psikhologii, 3,* 62–93.

Tucker, J., Stevens, L., & Ysseldyke, J. (1983). Learning disabilities: The experts speak out. *Journal of Learning Disabilities, 16,* 6–13.

Turnbull, A. (1978). A parent-professional interaction. In M. Snell (Ed.), *Moderately and severely handicapped.* Columbus, OH: Charles E. Merrill.

Turnbull, A.P., Turnbull, H.R., Summers, J.A., Brotherson, M.J., & Benson, H.A. (1986). *Families, professionals and exceptionality: A special partnership.* Columbus, OH: Charles E. Merrill.

Tuunainen, K. (1988). Future trends in Scandinavian special education. *International Journal of Special Education, 1,* 81–87.

Tyszka, H. (1993). The origin, development and current status of special education in France. *International Journal of Special Education, 1* (8), 15–26.

U.K. Department of Education and Science Curricula. (1989). N 22/89, 29.

Ukrainske Radianska Entsylkopedia, Vol. 4. (1964). Kiev: Academy of Sciences of Ukrainian SSR.

Underwood, B.J. (1975). Individual differences as a crucible in theory construction. *American Psychologist, 30,* 128–134.

Usanova, D., & Shakhovskaya, S. (1976). Need to accomplish preparation of teacher defectologists. *Defectologia, 2,* 86–90.

Valcante, G. (1987). Australia, special education in. In M. Reynolds & L. Mann (Eds.), *Encyclopedia of Special Education.* New York/Singapore: John Wiley & Sons.

Vance, H.B., & Ashwal, A.E. (1987). Middle East special education. In C. Reynolds & L. Mann (Eds.), *Encyclopedia of special education.* New York/Singapore: John Wiley & Sons.

Vankuba-Rao, A. (1975). India. In J.G. Hawks (Ed.), *World history of psychiatry.* New York: Brunner/Mazel.

Vasylenko, N.A. (1980). Psychopathological characteristics of cerebral-palsied school children. *Defectologia, 1,* 12–14.

Vavina, L.S., & Kovalchuk, A.V. (1986). Characteristics of dialogic communication of mentally retarded schoolchildren in the situation of Ukrainian-Russian bilingualism. *Defectologia, 4,* 9–14.

Vedeneyeva, T.E. (1989). A study of auditory function in mentally retarded deaf school children. *Defectologia, 2,* 23–28.

Vencovsky, E. (1975). Czechoslovakia. In J.G. Howells (Ed.), *World history of psychiatry.* New York: Brunner/Mazel.

Venger, L.A. (1974). Qualitative approach to the diagnosis of child's mental development. *Voprosy Psikhologii, 1,* 116–125.

Venzhyk, L. (1974). Status and goal of education with pre-schoolers. *Doshkilne Vykhovannia, 1,* 1–10.

Vernon, Ph.A. (1983). Recent findings on the nature of "g." *The Journal of Special Education, 4,* 389–400.

Verzichnis der Sonderschulin. (1985). Wicn Bundesministrerium fur Unterricht, Kurst and Sport.

Vespi, L., & Yewchuk, C. (1991). Social-emotional characteristics of gifted learning disabled children. *International Journal of Special Education, 1* (6), 87–99.

Vitello, S.J. (1991). Integration of handicapped students in the United States and Italy: A comparison. *International Journal of Special Education, 6,* 213–222.

Vitello, S. (1988). Handicapped students and competency testing. *Remedial and Special Education, 5,* 22–28.

Vitello, S.J. (1976). The institutionalization and deinstitutionalization of the mentally retarded in the United States. In L. Ilana & J. Sabatino (Eds.), *The third review of special education.* New York/London: Grune & Stratton.

Vlasova, T.A. (1971). Toward the new achievements of Soviet defectology. *Defectologia, 3,* 3–12.

Vormland, O. (1998). Inclusion, implementation and practices in Scandinavia. In S.J. Vitello & D.E. Mithaug (Eds.), *Inclusive schooling: National and international perspectives.* Mahwah, London: Lawrence Erlbaum Associates.

Voytko, & Hubko. (1975). Institute of psychology of the Ukrainian SSR is 30 years old. *Voprosy Psikhologii, 6,* 164–177.

Wald, B., & Rhodes, L.E. (1984). *Developing model vocational programs in rural settings for adults with severe retardation: The mobile crew model.* Paper presented at the meeting of the Association for Persons with Severe Handicaps, Chicago, IL.

Wald, I. (1971). Etiology of mental retardation. *Nowa Szkola, 6,* 32–36.

Wang, M.C., & Walberg, H.J. (1988). Four fallacies of segregationism. *Exceptional Children, 55,* 128–137.

Watters, B. (1980). Special education in the Northwest territories. In M. Csapo & L. Goguen (Eds.), *Special education across Canada.* Vancouver, BC: Centre for Human Development and Research.

Webster, J. (1989). Making a statement assessment of special educational needs in Great Britain. *International Journal of Special Education, 1,* 65–73.

Wechsler, S., & Gomes, D.C. (1989). School psychology in Brazil. In P. Saigh & T. Oakland (Eds.), *International perspective on psychology in the schools.* Hillsdale, NJ: Lawrence Erlbaum Associates.

Westling, D. (1986). *Introduction to mental retardation.* Englewood Cliffs, NJ: Prentice-Hall.

White, M.A., & Harris, M.W. (1961). *The school psychologist.* New York: Harper & Brothers.

White, R.W. (1964). *The abnormal personality* (3rd ed.). New York: Ronald Press.

Whitehead, C.W. (1986). The sheltered workshop dilemma: Reference or replacement. *Remedial and Special Education, 6* (7), 18–25.

Wideen, M., Mayer-Smith, J., & Moon, B. (1998). A critical analysis of the research on learning to teach: Making the case for an ecological perspective on inquiry. *Review of Educational Research, 2* (68), 130–179.

Wiederholt, J.L. (1974). Historical perspective on education of the learning disabled. In L. Mann & D. Sabatino (Eds.), *The second review of special education.* Philadelphia: Journal of Special Education Press.

Wiederholt, J.L., & Chamberlain, S.F. (1989). A critical analysis of resource programs. *Remedial and Special Education, 6,* 15–38.

Wilgosh, L. (1991). Underachievement and related issues for culturally different gifted children. *International Journal of Special Education, 1* (6), 82–87.

Wilkinson, L.C., et al. (1987). *A casebook of graduate level teacher education programs*. New Brunswick, NJ: Graduate School of Education, Rutgers, The State University of New Jersey.

Willer, B., Intagliata, J., & Wicks, N. (Eds.). (1981). Return of retarded adults to natural families: Issues and results. In R.H. Bruininks, C.E. Meyers, B.B., Sigford, & K.C. Lakin (Eds.), *Deinstitutionalism and community adjustment of M.R. people*. Monograph of the AAMD, W.R. Washington, DC: AAMD.

Wilson, C.P., Gutkin, T.B., Hagen, K.N., & Oats, R.G. (1998). General education teacher's knowledge and self-reported use of classroom intervention for working with difficult to teach children. *School Psychology Quarterly, 1* (13), 45–63.

Wilson, P.G., & Mazzoco, M.M. (1993). Awareness and knowledge of fragile X syndrome among special educators. *Mental Retardation, 4* (31), 221–228.

Winzer, M.H. (1998). Inclusion practices in Canada: Social, political and educational influences. In S.J. Vitello & D.E. Mithaug (Eds.), *Inclusive schooling: National and international perspectives*. Mahway, London: Lawrence Erlbaum Associates.

Wold, D. (1973). Family structure in three cases of anorexia nervosa: The role of the father. *American Journal of Psychiatry, 130,* 1394–1397.

Wolfensberger, W. (1972). *The principle of normalization in human services*. Toronto: National Institute on Mental Retardation.

Wolfensberger, W. (1964). Some observations on European programs for the mentally retarded. *Mental Retardation, 2,* 280–285.

Wolman, B.B. (Ed.). (1972). *Manual of child psychopathology*. New York: McGraw-Hill.

Wood, U.M., & Hurly, O.L. (1977). Curriculum and instruction. In J.B. Jordan, A.H. Hayden, M.B. Karnes & M.M. Woods (Eds.), *Early childhood education for exceptional children. A handbook of ideas and exemplary practices*. Reston, VA: Council for Exceptional Children.

Wycke, K.F. (1987). Argentina special education. In C. Reynolds & L. Mann (Eds.), *Encyclopedia of special education*. New York/Singapore: John Wiley & Sons.

Wycke, K.F. (1987). Nigeria special education. In. In C. Reynolds & L. Mann (Eds.), *Encyclopedia of special education*. New York/Singapore: John Wiley & Sons.

Xu, Y. (1992). Current status of special education in China. *International Journal of Special Education, 2* (71), 115–122.

Xu-Ry-Yuen. (1989). Shanghai N = Z school for deaf-mute. *Newsletter for Special Education in Asia and the Pacific, 1,* 8.

Yang, H., & Wang, H. (1994). Special education in China. *The Journal of Special Education, 1* (28), 93–106.

Yarmachenko, N.D. (1968). Upbringing and education of deaf children in Ukrainian SSR. *Radianska Shkola,* 6–8.

Yassman, L. (1976). Peculiarities of grammatical usage in developmentally delayed children. *Defectologia, 3,* 35–44.

Yassman, L. (1975). New developments in psychodiagnostic methods. *Defectologia, 2,* 89–94.

Yavkin, V.M. (1980). Psychotic disorders in oligophrenic adolescents. *Defectologia, 4,* 3–9.

Yavkin, V.M. (1973). Developmental backwardness of specific etiology. *Defectologia, 2,* 18–23.

Yeremenko, I.H. (1984). Defectology: Theory and practice in Ukrainian SSR. *Defectologia, 1,* 8–13.

Yeremenko, I.H. (1977). Conditions and perspectives of scientific research in the field of defectology in Ukrainian SSR. *Defectologia, 5,* 12–20.

Yeremenko, I.H. (1976). On differential instruction in auxiliary schools. *Defectologia, 4,* 56–63.

Yin, Chun-ming. (1989). The 10th anniversary of Chinese special education for the mentally retarded. *Newsletter for Special Education in Asia and the Pacific, 1.*

Young, T.K., Lombaradino, L.J., Rothman, H., & Vinson, B. (1989). Effects of symbolic play intervention with children who have mental retardation. *Mental Retardation, 3,* 159–165.

Youodraitis, A. (1980). Recall of incidentally learned verbal material in mentally retarded schoolchildren. *Defectologia, 5,* 20–25.

Yousef, J.M.S. (1993). Education of children with mental retardation in the Arab countries. *Mental Retardation, 2* (31), 117–121.

Ysseldyke, J.E., & Algozzine, B. (1990). *Introduction to special education* (2nd ed.). Boston: Houghton Mifflin.

Ysseldyke, J.E., & Algozzine, B. (1982). *Critical issues in special and remedial education.* Boston: Houghton Mifflin.

Ysseldyke, J.E., O'Sullivan, P.J., Thurlow, M., & Christenson, S.L. (1989). Qualitative differences in reading and math instruction received by handicapped students. *Remedial and Special Education, 1,* 14–21.

Ysseldyke et al. (Eds.). (1984). *School psychology: A blueprint for training and practice.* Minneapolis, MN: National School Psychology Inservice Training Network.

Yudilevich, Y.G. (1981). Remedial education of trainable mentally retarded with regard to their individual characteristics. *Defectologia, 3,* 51–57.

Zaika, E.V., & Kuznetsow, M.A. (1989). Short-term memory and mastering of practical skills. *Voprosky Psikhologii, 2,* 120–124.

Zamsky, W.S. (1974). *History of the education of the mentally retarded.* Moscow: Education Publishers.

Zamsky, C., & Shakhovskaya, S. (1980). With Hungarian defectologists. *Defectologia, 3,* 88–93.

Zaporozhets, O.V., Markova, T.A., & Radina, E.I. (1968). Fifty years of Soviet preschool pedagogy. *Soviet Pedagogy, 4,* 3–14.

Zharenkova, G.I. (1981). Psycho-educational study of developmentally backward students in special school. *Defectologia, 2,* 3–8.

Zhivina, A.I. (1974). Major stages of development of special education teacher training in the USSR. *Defectologia, 2,* 68–75.

Zigler, E., Balla, D., & Hodapp, R. (1984). On the definition and classification of mental retardation. *American Journal of Mental Deficiency, 3* (89), 215–230.

Zigler, E., & Trickett, P.K. (1978). IQ social competence, and evaluation of early childhood intervention programs. *American Psychologist, 9,* 789–799.

Zigmond, N. (1995). An exploration of the meaning and practice for special education in the context of full inclusion of students with learning disabilities. *The Journal of Special Education, 29* (2), 109–116.

Zigmond, N. (1995). Inclusion in Pennsylvania: Educational experience of students with learning disabilities in one elementary school. *The Journal of Special Education, 29* (2), 124–132.

Zigmond, N. (1995). Inclusion in Kansas: Educational experiences of students with learning disabilities in one elementary school. *The Journal of Special Education, 2* (29), 144–254.

Zigmond, N., & Baker, J.M. (1995). Concluding comments: Current and future practices in inclusive schooling. *The Journal of Special Education, 29* (2), 245–250.

Zimin, P.V. (1977). The Soviet school system. In N. Kuzin & M. Kondakov (Eds.), *Education in the USSR* (pp. 40–80). Moscow: Progress Publishers.

Zirpoli, T., Hallahan, D.P., & Kneedler, D. (1988). The Indonesia project: Correlates of student performance of special education teacher training program. *International Journal of Special Education, 1,* 73–79.

Zolotnycka, R. (1977). A.M. Schcherbyna, educator of the blind. *Defectologia, 2,* 90–92.

NAME INDEX

SUBJECT INDEX